Michael Wachter

Knowledge Compilation Map

Michael Wachter

Knowledge Compilation Map

Theory and Application

Südwestdeutscher Verlag für Hochschulschriften

Impressum/Imprint (nur für Deutschland/ only for Germany)
Bibliografische Information der Deutschen Nationalbibliothek: Die Deutsche Nationalbibliothek verzeichnet diese Publikation in der Deutschen Nationalbibliografie; detaillierte bibliografische Daten sind im Internet über http://dnb.d-nb.de abrufbar.

Alle in diesem Buch genannten Marken und Produktnamen unterliegen warenzeichen-, marken- oder patentrechtlichem Schutz bzw. sind Warenzeichen oder eingetragene Warenzeichen der jeweiligen Inhaber. Die Wiedergabe von Marken, Produktnamen, Gebrauchsnamen, Handelsnamen, Warenbezeichnungen u.s.w. in diesem Werk berechtigt auch ohne besondere Kennzeichnung nicht zu der Annahme, dass solche Namen im Sinne der Warenzeichen- und Markenschutzgesetzgebung als frei zu betrachten wären und daher von jedermann benutzt werden dürften.

Verlag: Südwestdeutscher Verlag für Hochschulschriften Aktiengesellschaft & Co. KG
Dudweiler Landstr. 99, 66123 Saarbrücken, Deutschland
Telefon +49 681 37 20 271-1, Telefax +49 681 37 20 271-0
Email: info@svh-verlag.de
Zugl.: Bern, Universität Bern, Universität, Dissertation, 2008

Herstellung in Deutschland:
Schaltungsdienst Lange o.H.G., Berlin
Books on Demand GmbH, Norderstedt
Reha GmbH, Saarbrücken
Amazon Distribution GmbH, Leipzig
ISBN: 978-3-8381-1444-6

Imprint (only for USA, GB)
Bibliographic information published by the Deutsche Nationalbibliothek: The Deutsche Nationalbibliothek lists this publication in the Deutsche Nationalbibliografie; detailed bibliographic data are available in the Internet at http://dnb.d-nb.de.

Any brand names and product names mentioned in this book are subject to trademark, brand or patent protection and are trademarks or registered trademarks of their respective holders. The use of brand names, product names, common names, trade names, product descriptions etc. even without a particular marking in this works is in no way to be construed to mean that such names may be regarded as unrestricted in respect of trademark and brand protection legislation and could thus be used by anyone.

Publisher: Südwestdeutscher Verlag für Hochschulschriften Aktiengesellschaft & Co. KG
Dudweiler Landstr. 99, 66123 Saarbrücken, Germany
Phone +49 681 37 20 271-1, Fax +49 681 37 20 271-0
Email: info@svh-verlag.de

Printed in the U.S.A.
Printed in the U.K. by (see last page)
ISBN: 978-3-8381-1444-6

Copyright © 2010 by the author and Südwestdeutscher Verlag für Hochschulschriften Aktiengesellschaft & Co. KG and licensors
All rights reserved. Saarbrücken 2010

Acknowledgements

First of all, I would like to thank Prof. Rolf Haenni, the supervisor of this dissertation. He inspired my scientific curiosity through many motivating and constructive discussions. His competent guidance led to a very good working atmosphere which finally resulted in the work at hand. I am also very grateful that Prof. Torsten Schaub accepted to be the co-referee of this dissertation. Thanks for his useful comments and remarks during his visits in Bern.

Many thanks go to my collaborators at various departments and university. Above all, I would like to thank Jacek Jonczy and Reto Kohlas for the splendid time we had together both inside and outside of the office. Thanks to the members of the research group for Theoretical Computer Science and Logic, led by Prof. Gerhard Jäger, and the members of the Software Composition Group, led by Prof. Oscar Nierstrasz. Both groups are situated at the University of Bern. Parts of the research presented in this dissertation were done with Marc Pouly from the group of Theoretical Computer Science, led by Prof. Jürg Kohlas, at the University of Fribourg. I would like to thank him and the whole group for the excellent team work and the inspiring seminars and meetings.

On a more private note, I thank my friends for their moral support during the writing of the dissertation and for their understanding that my first priority in the last time was to finish this work.

Last but not least, I express my deepest gratitude towards my family, especially my sister Julia and my brother Matthias, as well as my parents Verena and Karl-Heinz. Thanks for their strong support and for giving me both roots and wings.

This research is supported by the Swiss National Science Foundation, Project No. PP002-102652/1.

Bern, March 2010 (originally December 2008)

Michael Wachter

There are two things children should get from their parents:
roots and wings.

Roots to give them bearing and a sense of belonging,
and wings that relieve the one from constraints and prejudices
and give the other the opportunity to travel (or rather, fly) new ways.

Credited to Johann Wolfgang von Goethe

Abstract

Boolean functions play a crucial role in many areas of computer science and mathematics, most notably in artificial intelligence, digital system design, formal verification, mathematical logic, reliability theory, and combinatorial optimization. They are fundamental whenever knowledge is represented by constraints on Boolean variables, i.e. through a set of possible states in the corresponding multi-dimensional Boolean space.

In practice, working with Boolean functions presupposes efficient ways to represent them. Many research groups from different areas work on this subject, producing different types of representations of Boolean functions. Two basic qualities characterize these representations:

(i) their succinctness and

(ii) their set of queries and transformations supported in time polynomial in the size of the representation.

Among these types of representations are classical languages such as conjunctive and disjunctive normal forms, the well-known and widely used family of binary decision diagrams, as well as the family of the more recently proposed negational normal forms. Darwiche and Marquis provide a knowledge compilation map by opposing the characteristics of different types of representations. This map is instructive for placing new approaches in relation to existing ones, and it helps to identify the most appropriate representation for a given application.

The main contribution of this dissertation is a more comprehensive knowledge compilation map. For this, we extend the map of Darwiche and Marquis in four dimensions:

(i) new representations,

(ii) more transformations and queries,

(iii) the transition from Boolean functions to Boolean-valued ones, and

(iv) the representation of more general functions.

Furthermore, the dissertation contains a survey of several applications of the knowledge compilation map. These applications concern the generic framework of semiring valuation algebras, Bayesian networks, modular systems, (probabilistic) model verification, and solution configurations in semiring valuation algebras. Finally, we contribute to a Java-based implementation of the new knowledge compilation map. This implementation provides a common framework for the different existing and future representations of Boolean and Boolean-valued functions.

Contents

- 1 **Introduction** — 1
  - 1.1 Contribution — 3
  - 1.2 Mathematical Preliminaries — 4
    - 1.2.1 Algebra — 4
    - 1.2.2 Logic — 11
    - 1.2.3 Probability Theory — 13
    - 1.2.4 Graph Theory — 16
  - 1.3 Outline — 17

I Knowledge Compilation Map — 19

- 2 **Representing Boolean Functions** — 21
  - 2.1 Explicit Languages — 22
  - 2.2 Textual Languages — 23
  - 2.3 Graph-based Languages — 25
    - 2.3.1 Propositional DAGs — 31
    - 2.3.2 Negation Normal Forms — 34
    - 2.3.3 Classic Languages — 36
    - 2.3.4 Binary Decision Diagrams — 38
    - 2.3.5 Further Languages — 43
    - 2.3.6 Structural Reduction Rules for Graph-based Languages — 44
  - 2.4 Recapitulation: Representing Boolean Functions — 47
- 3 **Knowledge Compilation Map for Boolean Functions** — 49
  - 3.1 Succinctness — 50
  - 3.2 Queries — 54
    - 3.2.1 Predicates — 56
    - 3.2.2 Complex Queries — 56
  - 3.3 Transformations — 61
  - 3.4 Recapitulation: Knowledge Compilation Map for Boolean Functions — 66

Contents

	4	**Extending the Knowledge Compilation Map**	69
		4.1 Boolean-Valued Functions	70
		4.2 Generalizations of Boolean-valued Functions	74
		4.2.1 Functions with Codomain $\mathbb{B}^s$	76
		4.2.2 Functions with arbitrary Codomain C	76
		4.2.3 Alternative Representation	77
		4.3 Example	78
		4.4 Recapitulation: Extending the Knowledge Compilation Map	80
II		**Applying the Knowledge Compilation Map**	**81**
	5	**Semiring Valuation Algebras**	83
		5.1 Semiring Valuations	84
		5.2 Local Computation	85
		5.3 Representing Semiring Valuations	87
		5.3.1 Approach A	87
		5.3.2 Approach B	89
		5.4 Recapitulation: Semiring Valuation Algebras	90
	6	**Bayesian Networks**	93
		6.1 Logical Representation	94
		6.2 Computing Posterior Probabilities	95
		6.3 Beyond Context Specific Independence	96
		6.4 Recapitulation: Bayesian Networks	97
	7	**Reliability and Diagnostic of Modular Systems**	99
		7.1 Reliability	103
		7.2 Diagnostics	105
		7.3 Recapitulation: Modular Systems	107
	8	**Further Applications**	109
		8.1 (Probabilistic) Model Verification	109
		8.2 Solution Configurations in Semiring Valuation Algebras	113
III		**Implementation**	**119**
	9	**Framework**	121
		9.1 The `model` Package	122
		9.2 The `language` Package	125
		9.2.1 Fields and general Methods	125

		9.2.2 Methods for Queries and Transformations	127
	9.3	The Remaining Packages	129
	9.4	Recapitulation: Framework	131
10	**Algorithms**		**133**
	10.1	Inconsistency and Consistency	133
	10.2	(Counter) Model Selection and Enumeration	134
	10.3	(Counter) Model Counting and related Queries	137
	10.4	Minmal Cardinality, Maximum, and Arguments of Maximum	139
	10.5	Existential Forgetting and Term Conditioning	142
	10.6	Recapitulation: Algorithms	144

IV Conclusion   147

| 11 | **Summary** | 149 |
| 12 | **Open Problems** | 153 |

Appendix   155

A	**Proofs**		**157**
	A.1	Succinctness	157
	A.2	Queries	162
	A.3	Transformations	165
	A.4	MDAG	166
	A.5	Bayesian Networks	167
	A.6	(Probabilistic) Model Verification	168
B	**Detailed UML Diagrams of selected Classes and Interfaces**		**171**

Chapter 1

Introduction

Knowledge representation is a feature of everyday life, and most of the time we are not even aware of it. To illustrate this, let's take a closer look at how we handle emails on a daily basis. Our email is plagued with irrelevant, inappropriate messages, so-called *spam*, and we want a means to filter out these messages so we can efficiently focus on the relevant ones. Such a means is a spam filter which decides according to the content of an email, if it is spam or not. For this, a simple filter uses a set of statements identifying an email as not spam, e.g. «sender is in address book» and a set of statements identifying an email as spam, e.g. «domain of sender contains a number» like `ab3de.com`. The filter considers an email as spam, if it does not satisfy any statement of the first set, but it satisfies at least one statement of the second set. For example, an email from `mail@ab3de.com` is identified and treated as spam unless `mail@ab3de.com` is included in the address book. Of course, the spam filter should not slow us down, i.e. it has to determine quickly if an email is spam or not.

This rudimentary example already illustrates some of the main aspects of representing knowledge as pointed out by Davis et al. [1993]: A *knowledge representation*

(i) is a surrogate which is used to determine consequences by reasoning rather than taking action;

(ii) includes a set of decisions about how and what to see in the world;

(iii) incorporates how people reason intelligently, or what it means to reason intelligently in general;

(iv) is a medium for efficient computation;

Chapter 1 Introduction

(v) is a means of human expression and communication in which we tell others about the world.

Now that we have a vague idea *what* a knowledge representation is, the question is *how* to represent knowledge.

Obviously, the spam filter from above is a knowledge representation, but how do we represent it? At first, we introduce an attribute of an email for each statement in the two sets. Next, we replace the two sets by functions which determine if an email is spam or not based on the attributes of the email. The first set corresponds to a function that returns 1 as soon as one attribute holds that corresponds to a statement of the first set, and the second set corresponds to a function that returns 1 as soon as one attribute holds that corresponds to a statement of the second set. Now, the filter considers an email as spam if the first function returns 0 and the second function returns 1. From this point of view, the two functions are a kind of knowledge representation.

As mentioned before, a knowledge representation is a medium for efficient computation. To meet this stipulation, we have to choose an adequate representation of the functions. This representation is often a logical formalism. According to Cadoli and Donini [1997], a knowledge representation is based on the idea that knowledge is stored in a *knowledge base*. Knowledge bases come in various forms ranging from single formula over sets of formulae to sets of valuations. To extract information which is implicitly stored in the knowledge base, specific algorithms are applied to the base itself. Unfortunately, extracting information is sometimes very demanding from a computational point of view. One of the techniques addressing this problem is *knowledge compilation*.

Knowledge compilation is split into two parts: obtaining an adequate knowledge base and extracting information. Typically, a knowledge base is not modified very often, and the same knowledge base is used to extract information. Due to this, the idea is to proceed in two phases.

(i) *off-line reasoning*: Preprocess the knowledge base to obtain an adequate representation of the knowledge base.

(ii) *on-line reasoning*: Extract the information based on the output of the first phase.

The goal of off-line reasoning is to make on-line reasoning computationally easier with respect to reasoning without any preprocessing at all. The effort of off-line reasoning pays off when its computational cost is amortized over many (facilitated) extractions of information. For example, the spam filter may preprocess its knowledge base while we are writing an email. The obtained adequate representation enables the filter to quickly identify if an email is spam or not. Note that the filter may use this representation until we change the knowledge base.

Darwiche and Marquis [2002] introduce a *knowledge compilation map* for *Boolean functions* based on this concept. The idea of this map is to analyze and compare the different ways of knowledge compilation according to two dimensions: the *succinctness* of the representation and the algorithms for extracting information which can be applied in time polynomial in the size of the representation. The algorithms are separated into two groups:

(i) *queries*, which return some information about one or more representations without modifying them, and

(ii) *transformations*, which return a new representation based on one or more representations.

This separation is very useful for the goal of the knowledge compilation map: to provide a guide for choosing the "best" representation in order to solve a given problem. Darwiche and Marquis [2002] analyze and compare a large number of existing knowledge compilation approaches.

1.1 Contribution

Our main contribution is the extension of the map of Darwiche and Marquis in four ways:

(i) new representations,

(ii) more transformations and queries,

(iii) the transition from Boolean functions to *Boolean-valued* ones, and

(iv) the representation of more general functions.

In addition, we also show how to apply the knowledge compilation map within several applications areas. Our third contribution is a Java-based framework for the new knowledge compilation map.

Chapter 1 Introduction

1.2 Mathematical Preliminaries

The dissertation at hand relies on various mathematical concepts. In the following, we review these concepts shortly and introduce a basic notation along the way. The first section concerns *algebra*, the branch of mathematics concerning the study of structure and relation. It is based on Fischer [1997]. The second section deals with *logic*, the study of the principles of valid inference and demonstration. The corresponding parts of Russell and Norvig [2003] are the background of this survey. The section on *probability theory*, the branch of mathematics concerned with analysis of random events and uncertainty, is guided by the script of stochastics by Michael Kohlmann. Finally, the introduction to *graph theory* leans on a handout by Dorothea Wagner and Annegret Liebers. Feel free to go directly to Section 1.3, if you are familiar with these concepts.

1.2.1 Algebra

Algebra is one of the main branches of mathematics. It covers the study of structure, relation and quantity. A collection of (unique) values is a *set*. The most simple set is the set which contains no values at all, the *empty set*, denoted by $\emptyset$ (or $\{\}$). The *size* of a set X, denoted by $|X|$, is the number of values in X. Let X be an arbitrary set, and let x be an arbitrary value. Then, $x \in X$ denotes that x is an *element* of X, while $x \notin X$ denotes that x is no element of X. A set Y is a *subset* of X, denoted by $Y \subseteq X$, if and only if all elements x of Y are also elements of X. The other way around, Y is no subset of X, denoted by $Y \not\subseteq X$, if and only if there is an element x of Y that is no element of X. We use these subset definitions to explain two important quantifiers: the existential one $\exists$ (read 'there is') and the universal one $\forall$ (read 'for all'). Furthermore, $\Leftrightarrow$ denotes *if and only if* and $\Rightarrow$ denotes *implies*. The definitions of subset may now be written down as

$$Y \subseteq X \Leftrightarrow \forall x \in Y : x \in X \quad \text{and} \quad Y \not\subseteq X \Leftrightarrow \exists x \in Y : x \notin X.$$

Read ':' as 'we have' after $\forall$ and as 'such that' after $\exists$. Furthermore, Y is a *proper subset* of X, denoted by $Y \subset X$, if and only if $Y \subseteq X$ and $X \not\subseteq Y$. In addition, we may select a subset of values from a X based on a certain property, e.g. the set of elements in X which are not in Y is denoted by $\{x \in X \mid x \notin Y\}$. This notation is very useful to construct new sets.

Within this dissertation, we rely on two well-known sets: the *natural numbers* $\mathbb{N} = \{1, 2, \ldots\}$

1.2 Mathematical Preliminaries

and the *real numbers* $\mathbb{R}$. The natural numbers together with 0 are denoted by $\mathbb{N}_0$. For $a, b \in \mathbb{R}$, $a < b$ means that a is smaller than b and $a \leq b$ means that a is smaller than or equal to b. *Intervals* are defined for $a, b \in \mathbb{R}$ by

$$[a, b] = \{x \in \mathbb{R} \mid a \leq x \leq b\}, \qquad (a, b] = \{x \in \mathbb{R} \mid a < x \leq b\},$$
$$[a, b) = \{x \in \mathbb{R} \mid a \leq x < b\}, \text{ and} \qquad (a, b) = \{x \in \mathbb{R} \mid a < x < b\}.$$

The *power set* of an arbitrary set X is the set of all subsets of X, and it is denoted by $\mathcal{P}(X) = \{Y \mid Y \subseteq X\}$. Let X and Y be two arbitrary sets. X and Y are *disjoint*, if each element of one set is no element of the other set, i.e. $\forall x \in X : x \notin Y$ and $\forall y \in Y : y \notin X$.

Definition 1. Let X be an arbitrary set, then $\mathcal{P} \subseteq \mathcal{P}(X)$ is a *partition*, if and only if:

(i) $\forall P \in \mathcal{P} : P \neq \emptyset$;

(ii) $\forall P_1, P_2 \in \mathcal{P} : P_1$ and P_2 are disjoint;

(iii) $\forall x \in X \, \exists P_i \in \mathcal{P} : x \in P_i$.

An element $P \in \mathcal{P}$ of a partition $\mathcal{P}$ is a *block*.

The Cartesian product of X and Y is defined and denoted by

$$X \times Y = \{(x, y) \mid x \in X \text{ and } y \in Y\}.$$

Each subset of the Cartesian product $X \times Y$ is a *relation* from X to Y, and, in particular, a subset of $X \times X$ is a *relation* on X. A relation R on X, i.e. $R \subseteq X \times X$, is

reflexive $\Leftrightarrow$	$\forall x \in X : (x, x) \in R$;
symmetric $\Leftrightarrow$	$\forall x, y \in X : (x, y) \in R \Rightarrow (y, x) \in R$;
antisymmetric $\Leftrightarrow$	$\forall x, y \in X : (x, y), (y, x) \in R \Rightarrow x = y$;
transitive $\Leftrightarrow$	$\forall x, y, z \in X : (x, y), (y, z) \in R \Rightarrow (x, z) \in R$;
and *comparable* $\Leftrightarrow$	$\forall x, y \in X : (x, y) \in R \text{ or } (y, x) \in R$.

Chapter 1 Introduction

Furthermore, a relation R on X is

$$\begin{aligned}\text{an } \textit{equivalence relation} &\Leftrightarrow R \text{ is reflexive, symmetric, and transitive;}\\ \text{a } \textit{partial order} &\Leftrightarrow R \text{ is reflexive, antisymmetric, and transitive;}\\ \text{and a } \textit{total order} &\Leftrightarrow R \text{ is comparable and a partial order.}\end{aligned}$$

For such a relation R, we often use aRb instead of $(a,b) \in R$. For example, we already used the total order $\leq$ in this way within the definition of intervals. Note that $a < b$ is an abbreviation for $a \leq b$ and $b \not\leq a$.

The concept of relation allows us to define a *function* as a special kind of relation.

Definition 2. A relation f between X and Y is a *function*, if

(i) for each $x \in X$ there is a $y \in Y$ such that $(x,y) \in f$, and

(ii) $(x,y) \in f$ and $(x,z) \in f$ always implies $y = z$.

Because of (ii) it is common to denote $(x,y) \in f$ by $f(x) = y$. Often, we denote f by:

$$f : X \to Y$$
$$x \mapsto f(x) = y.$$

The set X is the *domain* of f and the set Y is its *codomain*. The so-called *range* of f is the set $f(X) = \{f(x) \mid x \in X\}$. The *inverse relation* of f is $f^{-1} = \{(y,x) \mid (x,y) \in f\} \subseteq Y \times X$. In general, the relation f^{-1} does not satisfy the requirements (i) and (ii) of a function. The *preimage* of a subset B of Y is the subset of X defined by $f^{-1}(B) = \{x \in X \mid f(x) \in B\}$, and the *preimage* of an element $y \in Y$ is defined by $f^{-1}(y) = f^{-1}(\{y\}) = \{x \in X \mid f(x) = y\}$.

Definition 3 (Permutation). A function π with

$$\pi : X \to X$$
$$x \mapsto \pi(x) = y$$

is called *permutation* of G, if for all $x_1, x_2 \in X$ with $\pi(x_1) = \pi(x_2)$ it holds that $x_1 = x_2$ (i.e. π is *injective*) and $\pi^{-1}(X) = X$ (i.e. π is *surjective*).

For each set X with k elements, there are

$$k! = k \cdot (k-1) \cdot (k-2) \cdots 2 \cdot 1$$

1.2 Mathematical Preliminaries

permutations ($\times$ denotes the common multiplication). We denote the set of all permutations of X by $\Pi(X)$. In case of $X = \{1, \ldots, r\}$, we also use $\Pi(1, \ldots, r)$ instead of $\Pi(\{1, \ldots, r\})$.

Definition 4 (Boolean Function). Let $\mathbb{B}$ be the set $\{0, 1\}$. A function f with

$$f : \mathbb{B}^r = \underbrace{\mathbb{B} \times \cdots \times \mathbb{B}}_{r} \to \mathbb{B}$$

$$(v_1, \ldots, v_r) \mapsto f(v_1, \ldots, v_r)$$

is called a *r-ary Boolean function*.

The set of all r-ary Boolean functions is denoted by $\mathbb{B}_r$. There are 2^{2^r} r-ary Boolean functions. A Boolean function is *finitary*, if $r < \infty$. In the following, we assume $r < \infty$, i.e. we only consider finitary Boolean functions.

In the following, let G be a set on which a *binary operation* is defined. A binary operation $\circ$ on G is a function with domain $G \times G$ and codomain G, i.e.

$$\circ : G \times G \to G$$

$$(x, y) \mapsto x \circ y.$$

A binary operation $\circ$ is

idempotent	$\Leftrightarrow$	$\forall x \in G : x \circ x = x$;
associative	$\Leftrightarrow$	$\forall x, y, z \in G : (x \circ y) \circ z = x \circ (y \circ z) = x \circ y \circ z$;
and *commutative*	$\Leftrightarrow$	$\forall x, y \in G : x \circ y = y \circ x$.

Furthermore, G might have special elements with respect to $\circ$. An element $e \in G$ is an *identity*, if $e \circ x = x \circ e = x$ for all $x \in G$. If G has an identity element e, then it is unique. Let G have such an unique identity element $e \in G$. Then, an element $y \in G$ is an *inverse* of $x \in G$, if $y \circ x = x \circ y = e$. An inverse of x is often denoted by $-x$ (additive style) or x^{-1} (multiplicative style). If $x \in G$ has an inverse element $y \in G$ and $\circ$ is associative, then y is unique.

Let $(G, \circ)$ be a set G together with an binary operation $\circ$ on G. The set G is *closed* w.r.t. $\circ$, if $a \circ b \in G$ for all $a, b \in G$. In the following, we assume that G is closed w.r.t. $\circ$. Then, $(G, \circ)$ is a *semigroup*, if $\circ$ is associative. A semigroup $(G, \circ)$ is a *group*, if G has an identity element

Chapter 1 Introduction

$e \in G$ and each $x \in G$ has an inverse element $y \in G$ (i.e. $\forall x \in G : \exists y \in G : y \circ x = x \circ y = e$). Furthermore, a semigroup or group $(G, \circ)$ is *commutative*, if $\circ$ is commutative.

Definition 5 (Union, Intersection, and Set Difference). Consider an arbitrary set X. Let $G = \mathcal{P}(X)$ be the power set of X. With $X_1, X_2 \in G$, i.e. $X_1, X_2 \subseteq X$, we define three binary operations on G:

(i) the *union* $\cup$: $(X_1, X_2) \mapsto X_1 \cup X_2 = \{x \mid x \in X_1 \text{ or } x \in X_2\}$,

(ii) the *intersection* $\cap$: $(X_1, X_2) \mapsto X_1 \cap X_2 = \{x \mid x \in X_1 \text{ and } x \in X_2\}$, and

(iii) the *set difference* $\setminus$: $(X_1, X_2) \mapsto X_1 \setminus X_2 = \{x \mid x \in X_1 \text{ and } x \notin X_2\}$.

The operations $\cup$ and $\cap$ are idempotent, associative, and commutative. The identity element of $\cup$ is $\emptyset$, and the one of $\cap$ is X. Note that $\emptyset$ is also its inverse with respect to $\cup$, while X is also its inverse with respect to $\cap$. No other element of G has an inverse with respect to $\cup$ or $\cap$. Hence, $(G, \cup)$ and $(G, \cap)$ are commutative semigroups with identity element. On the other side, $\setminus$ is neither idempotent, associative, nor commutative. There is no identity element, and, hence, no inverse elements. However, for each $Y \in G$, there is a *complement* $\overline{Y} = X \setminus Y$ with respect to X.

Definition 6 (Disjunction, Conjunction, and Negation). Consider the set $\mathbb{B} = \{0, 1\}$. We define two binary operations on $\mathbb{B}$:

(i) the *disjunction* $\vee : (b_1, b_2) \mapsto b_1 \vee b_2 = \max(b_1, b_2)$;

(ii) the *conjunction* $\wedge : (b_1, b_2) \mapsto b_1 \vee b_2 = \min(b_1, b_2)$.

In addition, we also define the *negation* $\neg$, a unary operation on $\mathbb{B}$, by

$$\neg : \mathbb{B} \to \mathbb{B}$$
$$b \mapsto \neg b = 1 - b.$$

Obviously, $\vee$ and $\wedge$ are idempotent, associative, and commutative. The identity element of $\vee$ is 0, and the one of $\wedge$ is 1. Note that 0 is its inverse with respect to $\vee$ while it does not have an inverse with respect to $\wedge$. For 1 the result slightly different, 1 is its inverse with respect to $\wedge$ while it does not have an inverse with respect to $\vee$. Hence, $(\mathbb{B}, \vee)$ and $(\mathbb{B}, \wedge)$ are commutative semigroups with identity element. Since $\neg$ is a unary operation, there are no things like inverse and identity. However, $\neg$ can be regarded as the complement with respect to 1.

1.2 Mathematical Preliminaries

Disjunction, conjunction, and negation may also be applied to Boolean functions. For this, they are defined as follows:

$$\begin{aligned}
\vee: \mathbf{B}_r \times \mathbf{B}_r &\to \mathbf{B}_r \\
(f_1, f_2) &\mapsto f_1 \vee f_2 = \max(f_1, f_2); \\
\wedge: \mathbf{B}_r \times \mathbf{B}_r &\to \mathbf{B}_r \\
(f_1, f_2) &\mapsto f_1 \wedge f_2 = \min(f_1, f_2); \\
\neg: \mathbf{B}_r &\to \mathbf{B}_r \\
f &\mapsto \neg f = 1 - f.
\end{aligned}$$

For $\mathbf{x} \in \mathbb{B}^r$, we get

$$\begin{aligned}
(f_1 \vee f_2)(\mathbf{x}) &= \max(f_1(\mathbf{x}), f_2(\mathbf{x})); \\
(f_1 \wedge f_2)(\mathbf{x}) &= \min(f_1(\mathbf{x}), f_2(\mathbf{x})); \\
(\neg f)(\mathbf{x}) &= 1 - f(\mathbf{x}).
\end{aligned}$$

Since $\vee$ and $\wedge$ are defined through $\max$ and $\min$, they may also be generalized to

$$\begin{aligned}
\vee: \mathbf{B}_r^s &\to \mathbf{B}_r \\
(f_1, \ldots, f_s) &\mapsto \bigvee_{i=1}^s f_i = f_1 \vee \cdots \vee f_s = \max(f_1, \ldots, f_s); \\
\wedge: \mathbf{B}_r^s &\to \mathbf{B}_r \\
(f_1, \ldots, f_s) &\mapsto \bigwedge_{i=1}^s f_i = f_1 \wedge \cdots \wedge f_s = \min(f_1, \ldots, f_s).
\end{aligned}$$

The same holds for the domain $\mathbb{B}^s$ instead of $\mathbf{B}_r^s$ and the codomain $\mathbb{B}$ instead of $\mathbf{B}_r$.

In the following, $+$ and $\times$ are binary operations on a set G. The operation $\times$ is *left distributive* over $+$, if and only if

$$\forall x, y, z \in G : x \times (y + z) = (x \times y) + (x \times z),$$

and it is *right distributive* over $+$, if and only if

$$\forall x, y, z \in G : (y + z) \times x = (y \times x) + (z \times x).$$

In case that $\times$ is commutative, left distributivity implies right distributivity and vice versa, and we say $\times$ *distributes* over $+$ or $\times$ is *distributive*. In the following, $(G, +, \times)$ is a set G with two binary operations $+, \times$ on G, and G is closed w.r.t. both operations.

Chapter 1 Introduction

Definition 7. $(G, +, \times)$ is a *semiring*, if

(i) $(G, +)$ is a commutative semigroup, i.e. $+$ is both associative and commutative;

(ii) $(G, \times)$ is a semigroup, i.e. $\times$ is associative; and

(iii) $\times$ is both left and right distributive over $+$.

The semiring $(G, +, \times)$ is a *ring*, if $(G, +)$ is a commutative group. A semiring or ring $(G, +, \times)$ is

- *commutative*, if $\times$ is commutative;
- *idempotent*, if $+$ is idempotent; and
- *totally ordered*, if there is a total order on G.

According to this definition, it is obvious that $(G, \cup, \cap)$ with $G = \mathcal{P}(X)$ is a semiring with identity elements for each arbitrary set X. In addition, this semiring satisfies the *absorption law*

$$\forall X_1, X_2 \in G : X_1 \cup (X_1 \cap X_2) = X_1 \cap (X_1 \cup X_2) = X_1,$$

and it is *complemented*, i.e. $\forall Y \in G : Y \cup \overline{Y} = X$ and $Y \cap \overline{Y} = \emptyset$. The absorption law gives rise to a new definition for a set G and binary operations $\circ$, $+$, and $\times$ on it.

Definition 8. $(G, \circ)$ is a *semilattice*, if $\circ$ is associative, commutative, and idempotent. $(G, +, \times)$ is a *lattice*, if the absorption law holds and the binary operations $+$ and $\times$ are both associative and commutative. A lattice $(G, +, \times)$ is

- *distributive*, if $\times$ distributes over $+$;
- *bounded*, if it is has a *least* and a *greatest* element, often denoted by 0 and 1; and
- *complemented*, if it is bounded and each element $x \in G$ has a complement $y \in G$ such that $x + y = 1$ and $x \times y = 0$.

A distributive complemented lattice is a *Boolean algebra*.

By definition, a commutative semiring satisfying the absorption law is a distributive lattice and vice versa. Note that the absorption law implies idempotency of $+$ and $\times$, i.e. a lattice $(G, +, \times)$ implies that $(G, +)$ and $(G, \times)$ are semilattices. In addition, the absorption law implies a partial order $\leq$: $x \leq y \Leftrightarrow x = x \times y$ or, equivalently, $x \leq y \Leftrightarrow y = x + y$.

1.2 Mathematical Preliminaries

Altogether, for an arbitrary set X and $G = \mathcal{P}(X)$, $(G, \cup, \cap)$ is a Boolean algebra where the least element is $\emptyset$ and the greatest element is X. Obviously, $(\mathbb{B}, \vee, \wedge)$ and $(\mathbf{B}_r, \vee, \wedge)$ are also Boolean algebras.

1.2.2 Logic

In general, logic studies the principles of valid inference and demonstration. A logic consists of two parts: the *syntax* which defines the allowable *formulae* and the *semantics* defining the meaning of the formulae. A very simple logic is *propositional logic* which consists of *propositional formulae*. Its syntax is split into two parts: *atomic* and *complex* (propositional) formulae.

(i) An atomic formula is the constant *contradiction* $\bot$, the constant *tautology* $\top$, or a single *propositional symbol*, e.g. V.

(ii) Complex formulae are constructed form simpler ones by using *logical connectives*. It is sufficient to consider the binary connectives *or* (disjunction), denoted by $\vee$ and *and* (conjunction), denoted by $\wedge$, together with the unary connective *not*, denoted by $\neg$[1]. For example, let φ and ψ be propositional formulae, then $\varphi \vee \psi$, $\varphi \wedge \psi$, and $\neg \varphi$ are also propositional formulae.

To avoid parentheses, we introduce an order for these connectives (from highest to lowest): $\neg$, $\wedge$, and $\vee$. Hence, the formula $\neg P \vee \neg Q \wedge R$ is another form of $(\neg P) \vee ((\neg Q) \wedge R)$ where P, Q, and R are propositional symbols. In addition, the negation $\neg V$ of a propositional symbol V is often denoted by $\overline{V}$, i.e. $\overline{P} \vee \overline{Q} \wedge R$ is a short form of $\neg P \vee \neg Q \wedge R$.

To introduce the semantics of propositional logic, let φ be the formula $\neg P \vee \neg Q \wedge R$. The value of φ depends on the values assigned to the propositional symbols P, Q, and R. To each symbol, we may assign the value 0 or 1. An *assignment* a fixes the value of at least one symbol of a formula, e.g. $(P = 0)$. An assignment is a *complete* one, if it fixes all symbols of a formula. With respect to φ, the assignment $(P = 1)$ is not complete, but the assignment $(P = 0, Q = 1, R = 1)$ is complete. We employ the Boolean algebra $(\mathbb{B}, \vee, \wedge)$ with $\neg$ from above to recursively compute the *truth value* of φ. The truth value of $\bot$ is 0 while the truth value of $\top$ is 1 for any assignment. Furthermore, the truth value of a complete assignment w.r.t. a formula results from replacing the symbols with the assigned

---
[1] Here, $\vee$, $\wedge$, and $\neg$ are symbols of the language not binary operations as defined before.

Chapter 1 Introduction

value and applying the corresponding operations for $\vee$, $\wedge$, and $\neg$. Let t_1 and t_2 be the truth values of the propositional formulae ψ_1 and ψ_2 w.r.t. the complete assignment a. For complex formulae consisting of ψ_1 and ψ_2, we obtain the following truth values w.r.t. a: $t_1 \vee t_2$ for $\psi_1 \vee \psi_2$, $t_1 \wedge t_2$ for $\psi_1 \wedge \psi_2$, and $\neg t_1$ for $\neg \psi_1$. For example, the truth value of φ w.r.t. $(P = 0, Q = 1, R = 1)$ is $\neg 0 \vee \neg 1 \wedge 1 = 1$, while the value of φ is $\neg 1 \vee \neg 1 \wedge 0 = 0$ given the assignment $(P = 1, Q = 1, R = 0)$. In general, a complete assignment m of a formula φ is a *model* of φ, if the truth value of φ given m is 1. Otherwise, m is a *counter-model* of φ. The *satisfying set* of φ, denoted by $[\![\varphi]\!] = \{a \mid a \text{ is a model of } \varphi\}$, is the set of all models of φ.

From an algebraic point of view a propositional formula φ with propositional symbols $V_1, \ldots, V_r$ represents the Boolean function

$$f_\varphi : \underbrace{\mathbb{B} \times \cdots \times \mathbb{B}}_{r} \to \mathbb{B}$$

$$(v_1, \ldots, v_r) \mapsto f_\varphi(v_1, \ldots, v_r) \text{ where}$$

$$f_\varphi(v_1, \ldots, v_r) = \begin{cases} 1, & \text{if } (V_1 = v_1, \ldots, V_r = v_r) \text{ is a model of } \varphi, \\ 0, & \text{if } (V_1 = v_1, \ldots, V_r = v_r) \text{ is a counter-model of } \varphi. \end{cases}$$

Note that $[\![\varphi]\!] = f_\varphi^{-1}(1)$. In the following, we assume an order of the symbols and denote $(V_1 = v_1, \ldots, V_r = v_r)$ by $(v_1, \ldots, v_r)$.

Having a notion of truth, it is time to talk about *logical reasoning*. Let φ and ψ be two arbitrary propositional formulae over the symbols **V**. φ *entails* ψ, denoted by $\varphi \models \psi$, if and only if every model of φ is also a model of ψ. This is equivalent to $[\![\varphi]\!] \subseteq [\![\psi]\!]$, and to $f_\varphi(a) \leq f_\psi(a)$ for all complete assignments a. Form this point of view, φ and ψ are *equivalent*, denoted by $\varphi \equiv \psi$, if and only if $\varphi \models \psi$ and $\psi \models \varphi$. Again, there are two equivalent conditions: $[\![\varphi]\!] = [\![\psi]\!]$ and $f_\varphi(a) = f_\psi(a)$ for all complete assignments a respectively. In the following, let λ_i denote propositional symbols or negations thereof. Furthermore, let each propositional symbol appear in at most one λ_i. Then, *term conditioning* φ on $\lambda_1, \ldots, \lambda_s$, denoted by $\varphi|\lambda_1, \ldots, \lambda_s$ and $\varphi|\lambda_1 \wedge \cdots \wedge \lambda_s$. It is defined by $\psi \wedge \varphi|\lambda_1, \ldots, \lambda_s \equiv \psi \wedge \varphi$, where the symbols of $\lambda_1, \ldots, \lambda_s$ do not occur any longer in $\varphi|\lambda_1, \ldots, \lambda_s$. Note that conditioning φ on a all symbols or their negation returns either $\bot$ or $\top$.

Up to now, we only considered propositional symbols, e.g. V. However, it is also possible to consider an assignment instead of a symbol and to allow more than two values, e.g. $V = 3$. Our prerequisites are that there is only a finite number of possible values for each symbol and that these values are both *mutually exclusive*, i.e. at most one value is the correct value, and *exhaustive* meaning that one of the values is the correct value. For each symbol V, we denote the set of possible values by Ω_V which is called the *frame* of V. In propositional logic, the frame of each symbol is $\{0, 1\}$. To obtain a logic based on assignments instead of symbols, we adapt the syntax and the semantics of propositional logic. For the syntax, we replace a propositional symbol, like V, by an assignment of V, e.g. $(V = v)$ with $v \in \Omega_V$. Additionally, an assignment might also consist of a variable V and a set $\Omega \subseteq \Omega_V$, e.g. (V, Ω). For $v \in \Omega_V$, $(V, \{v\})$ is equivalent to $(V = v)$ For the semantic, to compute the truth value of a formula with respect to a complete assignment, the assignments within a formula are replaced by 1 and 0 according to the complete assignment. For example, consider the the formula $\neg(P = 0) \vee \neg(Q = 1) \wedge (R = 1)$ with $\Omega_P = \Omega_Q = \Omega_R = \{0, 1, 2\}$. Then, the truth value of the complete assignment $(P = 1, Q = 0, R = 2)$ is 1 while the truth value of the complete assignment $(P = 0, Q = 1, R = 2)$ is 0. Note that the notions of model, counter-model, and satisfying set are carried forward. The same holds for entailment and equivalence. This new logic is a first step towards *predicate logic*.

From an algebraic point of view, a formulae φ over the symbols $\mathbf{V} = \{V_1, \ldots, V_r\}$ of this new logic corresponds to a function

$$f_\varphi : \Omega_{V_1} \times \cdots \times \Omega_{V_r} \to \mathbb{B}$$
$$(v_1, \ldots, v_r) \mapsto f_\varphi(v_1, \ldots, v_r) \text{ where}$$

$$f_\varphi(v_1, \ldots, v_r) = \begin{cases} 1, & \text{if } (V_1 = v_1, \ldots, V_r = v_r) \text{ is a model of } \varphi, \\ 0, & \text{if } (V_1 = v_1, \ldots, V_r = v_r) \text{ is a counter-model of } \varphi. \end{cases}$$

In general, a function like f_φ is called a r-ary Boolean-valued function. A Boolean-valued function f is also called *indicator* or *characteristic function* of $f^{-1}(1)$. As for Boolean functions, the operations $\vee$, $\wedge$, and $\neg$ may be applied to Boolean-valued functions.

1.2.3 Probability Theory

Briefly, *probability theory* is the branch of mathematics concerned with analysis of random events and epistemic uncertainty. A fundamental part of it is the set of possible outcomes, often denoted by Ω, e.g. $\Omega = \{1, 2, 3, 4, 5, 6\}$ for a (six-sided) dice. Since we are not only interested in the elements of Ω but also subsets of it, it is useful to postulate some conditions on the space which we are finally working with.

Chapter 1 Introduction

Definition 9. $\mathcal{A} \subseteq \mathcal{P}(\Omega)$ is a σ-algebra, if

(i) $\Omega \in \mathcal{A}$

(ii) $\forall A \in \mathcal{A} : \overline{A} = \Omega \setminus A \in \mathcal{A}$

(iii) $A_i \in \mathcal{A} : \bigcup_{i=1}^{\infty} A_i \in \mathcal{A}$

For $\Omega \neq \emptyset$ and σ-algebra $\mathcal{A} \subseteq \mathcal{P}(\Omega)$, $(\Omega, \mathcal{A})$ is called a *measurable space* and $A \in \mathcal{A}$ is called *event*.

Obviously, $(\Omega, \mathcal{P}(\Omega))$ is a measurable space. Returning to the 6-sided dice, i.e. $\Omega = \{1, 2, 3, 4, 5, 6\}$. We want to know how probable it is that the outcome of throwing the dice is 1.

Definition 10. Let $(\Omega, \mathcal{A})$ be a measurable space. A function $\mathbf{P} : \mathcal{A} \to [0, 1]$ is a *probability measure*, if is satisfies the *Kolmogorov axioms*:

(i) $\mathbf{P}(A) \geq 0$ for all $A \in \mathcal{A}$;

(ii) $\mathbf{P}(\Omega) = 1$;

(iii) $\mathbf{P}(\bigcup_{i=1}^{\infty} A_i) = \sum_{i=1}^{\infty} \mathbf{P}(A_i)$ for all pairwise disjoint events $A_i \in \mathcal{A}$.

For a probability measure $\mathbf{P}$, the triple $(\Omega, \mathcal{A}, \mathbf{P})$ is called a *probability space*.

For singletons, i.e. $A = \{\omega\}$, we use $\mathbf{P}(\omega)$ instead of $\mathbf{P}(\{\omega\})$. For a *fair* dice, we expect $\mathbf{P}(\omega) = \frac{1}{6}$ for all $\omega \in \{1, 2, 3, 4, 5, 6\}$. $\mathbf{P}(A)$ is called the *probability* of $A \in \mathcal{A}$. Two important consequences for $A, B \in \mathcal{A}$ with $A \subset B$ are

$$\mathbf{P}(A) < \mathbf{P}(B) \quad \text{and}$$
$$\mathbf{P}(B \setminus A) = \mathbf{P}(B) - \mathbf{P}(A).$$

For $B \in \mathcal{A}$, the set $\mathcal{A}_B = \{A \cap B \mid A \in \mathcal{A}\}$ is also a σ-algebra and $\mathcal{A}_B \subseteq \mathcal{A}$. We define a probability measure $\mathbf{P}_B$ on $(B, \mathcal{A}_B)$ by

$$\mathbf{P}_B(A_B) = \frac{\mathbf{P}(A_B \cap B)}{\mathbf{P}(B)} \text{ for } A_B \in \mathcal{A}_B \text{ and } \mathbf{P}(B) > 0.$$

This is used within the following definition.

1.2 Mathematical Preliminaries

Definition 11. For $B \in \mathcal{A}$ with $\mathbf{P}(B) > 0$, the function $\mathbf{P}(.\mid B)$ defined by

$$\mathbf{P}(.\mid B) : \mathcal{A} \to [0,1]$$
$$A \mapsto \mathbf{P}(A \mid B) = \frac{\mathbf{P}(A \cap B)}{\mathbf{P}(B)}$$

is the *conditional probability measure* given B.

Note that $\mathbf{P}(A \mid B)$ is the *conditional* or *posterior probability* of A given B, while $\mathbf{P}(A)$ is the *prior probability* of A. An important consequence of the conditional probability measure is the *Bayes' theorem*:

$$\mathbf{P}(A \mid B) = \mathbf{P}(B \mid A) \frac{\mathbf{P}(A)}{\mathbf{P}(B)} \text{ for } \mathbf{P}(B) > 0.$$

Furthermore, $A, B \in \mathcal{A}$ are *independent*, if $\mathbf{P}(A \cap B) = \mathbf{P}(A)\mathbf{P}(B)$. In this case, we have $\mathbf{P}(A \mid B) = \mathbf{P}(A)$ and $\mathbf{P}(B \mid A) = \mathbf{P}(B)$. Two σ-algebras $\mathcal{A}_1, \mathcal{A}_2 \subseteq \mathcal{A}$ are *independent*, if A_1 and A_2 are independent for all $A_1 \in \mathcal{A}_1$ and $A_2 \in \mathcal{A}_2$.

Consider again the six-sided dice with $\Omega = \{1,2,3,4,5,6\}$ and $\mathbf{P}(i) = \frac{1}{6}$ for $i = 1,\ldots,6$. Being solely interested if the number is odd or even we obtain

i	1	2	3	4	5	6
$X(i)$	0	1	0	1	0	1

where $X(i) = 0$ means that the dice has an odd number on top, while $X(i) = 1$ means that the dice has an even number on top. Now, consider the σ-algebra which contains only the relevant states, i.e. $\mathcal{A} = \{\emptyset, \{1,3,5\}, \{2,4,6\}, \Omega\}$ with $\mathbf{P}_{\mathcal{A}}(A) = \frac{1}{2}$ for $A = \{1,3,5\}$ or $A = \{2,4,6\}$. Then, we have

$$X^{-1}(B) = \{i \mid X(i) \in B\} \in \mathcal{A}$$

for $B \in \mathcal{B} = \{\emptyset, \{0\}, \{1\}, \{0,1\}\}$. Since this is a special case, we define:

Definition 12. A function $X : (\Omega, \mathcal{A}) \to (\mathbb{R}, \mathcal{B})$ is a *random variable*, if $X^{-1}(\mathcal{B}) \subseteq \mathcal{A}$, i.e. $\forall B \in \mathcal{B} : X^{-1}(B) \in \mathcal{A}$.

The probability measure $\mathbf{P}_X$ defined by $\mathbf{P}_X(B) = \mathbf{P}(\omega \in B)$ is called the *probability distribution* of X.

Chapter 1 Introduction

For more consistency, we denote $X(i)$ also by $X = i$ for a (random) variable X with $i \in \Omega$.

Of course, it is also possible to link several events, e.g. a single dice might be rolled several times or several dice might be rolled at the same time. For this, we assume that the events are independent.

Theorem 1. *Let $(\Omega_i, \mathcal{A}_i, \mathbf{P}_i)$, $i \in [1, r]$, be probability spaces. Then, there is exactly one probability measure $\mathbf{P}$ on $\Omega = \Omega_1 \times \ldots \times \Omega_r$, such that*

$$\mathbf{P}(A) = \mathbf{P}_1(A_1) \cdots \mathbf{P}_r(A_r)$$

for all $A = A_1 \times \cdots \times A_r$ with $A_i \in \mathcal{A}_i$.

The probability measure $\mathbf{P}$ is called the *joint probability distribution* of the corresponding random variables X_i.

1.2.4 Graph Theory

A (finite) *graph* consists of a finite set of *nodes* or vertices V and a finite number of *edges* E between these nodes. We denote a graph by $G = (V, E)$. An edge $e \in E$ between the nodes v_1 and v_2 may be directed, denoted by (v_1, v_2), or *undirected*, denoted by $\{v_1, v_2\}$. Let $e = (v_1, v_2)$ be an directed edge. Then, v_1 is the *start node* of e, v_2 is the *end node* of e. The edge e itself is an *outgoing* edge of v_1 and an *incoming* one of v_2. In addition, v_2 is a *child* of v_1 and v_1 is a *parent* of v_2. In case of $e = \{v_1, v_2\}$ both v_1 and v_2 are *end nodes*. An edge (v, v) or $\{v, v\}$ is called a *loop*. The *size* of a graph G, denoted by $|G|$, corresponds to the number of its edges. A graph $H = (V_H, E_H)$ is a *subgraph* of $G = (V, E)$ if $V_H \subseteq V$ and $E_H \subseteq E$.

A sequence $W = (v_0, v_1, \ldots, v_l)$ of (not necessary different) nodes $v_i \in V$ with $l \geq 1$, such that $(v_i, v_{i+1}) \in E$ or $\{v_i, v_{i+1}\} \in E$ for $i = 0, \ldots, l-1$, is called a *walk*. The length of W is l. v_0 is the *start node* of W, v_l the *end node* of W, and the remaining nodes v_i, $0 < i < l$ are *internal nodes*. A walk W is a *path*, if all nodes are pairwise different. A *u-v-path* is a path with start node u and end node v. The *distance* between two nodes u, v, denoted by $dist(u, v)$, is the length of the shortest u-v-path or ∞ if there is no u-v-path. A walk $W = (v_0, v_1, \ldots, v_l)$ is a *cycle*, if $v_0 = v_l$. For cycles, each undirected edge $\{v_i, v_{i+1}\} \in E$ is treated as a directed edge, either (v_i, v_{i+1}) or (v_{i+1}, v_i).

A graph $G = (V, E)$ is

- *undirected*, if all edges $e \in E$ are undirected;
- *directed*, if all edges $e \in E$ are directed; and
- *acyclic*, if G contains no cycle.

Within this dissertation, DAG is the abbreviation for a directed acyclic graph. An undirected acyclic graph is a *tree* when there is exactly one u-v-path for each pair of nodes $u, v \in V$, $u \neq v$. A node $v \in V$ is a *leaf*, if it occurs in at most one edge. A tree with a distinguished node $r \in V$ is called a *rooted tree* and r is called its *root*, even if it occurs in at most one edge. A DAG with a node $r \in V$ such that there is exactly one r-v-path for each $v \in V$, $v \neq r$, is called a *rooted directed tree* with root r. In general, a *rooted* DAG is a DAG with distinguished node $r \in V$ and r is the *root* of the DAG. Furthermore, a node within a DAG that does not have any outgoing edge is called *terminal*, while a node with at least one outgoing edge is called *non-terminal*.

Finally, within a DAG $G = (V, E)$ each node $u \in V$ leads to a rooted directed acyclic subgraph $G_u = (V_u, E_u)$ where $v \in V_u$, if there is an u-v-path, $e \in E_u$, if e is part of an u-v-path for $e \in E$ and $v \in V_u$ with $v \neq u$, and u is the root. We use u to refer to the node u as well as to refer to the graph G_u.

1.3 Outline

The dissertation consists of three parts. In Part I we present our main contribution, the extension of the knowledge compilation map of Darwiche and Marquis. Part II considers various applications of the extended knowledge compilation map. The purpose of Part III is to provide insight into the implementation of a framework for the knowledge compilation map. With Part IV we conclude with a summary of the dissertation and the remaining open problems.

Part I

Chapter 2 In this chapter we discuss different kinds representations of Boolean functions and introduce the some important languages of the graphical representation of Boolean functions.

Chapter 1 Introduction

Chapter 3 This chapter follows the example of Darwiche and Marquis and sets up a knowledge compilation map for Boolean functions based on the graphical languages of Chapter 2.

Chapter 4 We pass the results of the map for Boolean functions on to Boolean-valued functions and discuss the representation of two generalizations of Boolean-valued functions.

Part II

Chapter 5 This chapter covers the identification of an adequate representation for semiring valuations.

Chapter 6 We provide a knowledge compilation for Bayesian networks that does not encode multi-state variables by Boolean ones, in contrast to the related approach of Chavira and Darwiche.

Chapter 7 The computation of the reliability and diagnostics of modular systems is the topic of this chapter.

Chapter 8 We consider two further applications of the knowledge compilation map, namely probabilistic model verification and the representation of solution configurations in semiring valuation algebras.

Part III

Chapter 9 The topic of this chapter is the body of a framework implementing the knowledge compilation map.

Chapter 10 Here we present some details of some selected algorithms.

Part IV

Chapter 11 We recapitulate the results of the dissertation.

Chapter 12 In the final chapter of the dissertation, we address the open problems concerning the knowledge compilation map and its applications.

Part I

Knowledge Compilation Map

Chapter 2

Representing Boolean Functions

The focus of this dissertation lies on the efficient computation of knowledge representations. In some cases being a medium for efficient computation works against knowledge representation as a means of human expression and communication. The remaining elements affect the efficient computation to a greater or lesser extent. Throughout the whole dissertation, we assume that knowledge is already represented in form of functions. Hence, we concentrate on the representation of functions and the consequences of different representation of the efficient computation.

For simplicity, we start with the representation of Boolean functions. As mentioned before, a Boolean function f is defined by

$$f : \mathbb{B}^r = \overbrace{\mathbb{B} \times \cdots \times \mathbb{B}}^{r} \to \mathbb{B}$$
$$\mathbf{v} = (v_1, \ldots, v_r) \mapsto f(\mathbf{v})$$

where $\mathbb{B} = \{0, 1\}$. Each $\mathbb{B}$ in the Cartesian product $\mathbb{B}^r$ may be the frame Ω_V of a variable V. I.e. f is a Boolean function in the Boolean variables $\mathbf{V} = \{V_1, \ldots, V_r\}$ with frame $\Omega_{V_i} = \mathbb{B}$, $1 \leq i \leq r$. Among the r-ary Boolean functions are

- the constant functions $f_\bot$ and $f_\top$ with $f_\bot(\mathbf{v}) = 0$ and $f_\top(\mathbf{v}) = 1$ for all $\mathbf{v} \in \Omega_\mathbf{V}$ and
- the functions f_{V_i} with $f_{V_i}(\mathbf{v}) = v_i$ for all $\mathbf{v} = (v_1, \ldots, v_i, \ldots, v_r) \in \Omega_\mathbf{V}$ and $1 \leq i \leq r$.

Note that the number of r-ary Boolean functions is equivalent to the number of subsets of $\Omega_\mathbf{V}$, i.e. there are 2^{2^r} r-ary Boolean functions. Our convention is to denote these functions by lower-case Roman letters such as f, g, or the like.

Chapter 2 Representing Boolean Functions

The basic functions $f_\bot$, $f_\top$, and f_{V_i} are only a small subset of $\mathbf{B}_r$. For an arbitrary function $f \in \mathbf{B}_r$, the question arises how to represent f efficiently. In the following, we present several methods for specifying and representing a Boolean function. These methods are called *languages*, according to Darwiche [2001a] and Darwiche and Marquis [2002], and are further examined on the basis of different qualities afterwards. Languages are denoted by typescript letters and words, e.g. L. As long as no confusion is anticipated, we omit the reference to the set of variables, otherwise we use L_V. The divers languages are classified in three different types: *explicit*, *textual*, and *graph-based*. We devote a section to each of these types, starting with explicit languages.

2.1 Explicit Languages

Probably the simplest language is the representation by a table of values. In case of Boolean functions, we call such a table a *truth table*. Hence, the language is the *language of truth tables*, and it is denoted by truth-table. Figure 2.1(a) shows the truth table of a Boolean function $f_\eta \in \mathbf{B}_4$ in the variables V_1, V_2, V_3, and V_4. In general, a truth table consists of $r + 1$ columns, one column for each variable V_i involved in f (resp. one column for each $\mathbb{B}$ in $\mathbb{B}^r$) and one column for the value of f. Apart from the header row, there are 2^r rows in a truth table for a Boolean function $f \in \mathbf{B}_r$, more precisely there is exactly one row for each complete assignment.

It is also possible to arrange the table in another way, as shown in Figure 2.1(b). Such a table is called *Karnaugh map*, *Veitch diagram*, *K-map*, or *KV-map*. Here, the variables are represented along two axes and the assignments are arranged such that the assignment of only one variable changes in going from one square to an adjacent square. The languages that employs only Karnaugh maps is the *language of Karnaugh maps*, and it is denoted by Karnaugh-map.

Another explicit representation of f_η is the *bit string* 1001101010010101. We obtain this string form the truth table of f_η (see Figure 2.1(a)) by reading the last column from bottom to the top and omitting the header. Note that a representation of this kind requires a convention about the position within the string and the corresponding complete assignment. We denote the *language of bit strings* by bit-string.

A common point of these three languages is the fact that both models and counter-models (complete assignments whose truth value is 1 and 0 respectively) are included. However, it

2.2 Textual Languages

V_1	V_2	V_3	V_4	f_η
0	0	0	0	1
0	0	0	1	0
0	0	1	0	1
0	0	1	1	0
0	1	0	0	1
0	1	0	1	0
0	1	1	0	0
0	1	1	1	1
1	0	0	0	0
1	0	0	1	1
1	0	1	0	0
1	0	1	1	1
1	1	0	0	1
1	1	0	1	0
1	1	1	0	0
1	1	1	1	1

(a) Truth Table

V_3V_4	V_1V_2			
	00	01	11	10
00	1	1	1	0
01	0	0	0	1
11	0	1	1	1
10	1	0	0	0

(b) Karnaugh Map

Figure 2.1: The Boolean function f_η represented by a truth table and a Karnaugh map.

is sufficient to consider either the models or the counter-models. By choosing the models, we represent f by the set $f^{-1}(1)$. In case of f_η, this leads to

$$f_\eta^{-1}(1) = \{(0,0,0,0), (0,0,1,0), (0,1,0,0), (0,1,1,1),$$
$$(1,0,0,1), (1,0,1,1), (1,1,0,0), (1,1,1,1)\}.$$

The *language of sets of models* is denoted by models-set. An obvious advantage of this representation, is the fact that it depends only on the number of models. By contrast, truth tables, Karnaugh maps, and bit strings always depend on the number of complete assignments which is exponential in the number of variables. Note that the number of models might be significantly smaller.

2.2 Textual Languages

As we have seen in Section 1.2.2, we can represent a Boolean function f in the variables $\mathbf{V}$ as a formula φ on $\mathbf{V}$ such that $[\![\varphi]\!] = f^{-1}(1)$. From this point of view, $\bot$ represents $f_\bot$,

Chapter 2 Representing Boolean Functions

$\top$ represents $f_\top$, and $V \in \mathbf{V}$ represents f_V. Together with the connectives $\neg$, $\vee$, and $\wedge$, this allows us to represent each $f \in \mathbb{B}_r$ in many different ways. The question arises how to obtain a formula representing f.

First, we represent each (complete) assignment $\mathbf{m}_i \in f^{-1}(1)$ by a term $\tau_i = \lambda_1 \wedge \cdots \wedge \lambda_s$. If a variable V is assigned to 1 in $\mathbf{m}_i$, we use the positive literal V, otherwise we use the negative one $\overline{V}$. Such a term τ_i represents the Boolean function f_{τ_i} with $f_{\tau_i}(\mathbf{m}_i) = 1$ and $f_{\tau_i}(\mathbf{v}) = 0$ for $\mathbf{v} \in \mathbb{B}^r$ with $\mathbf{v} \neq \mathbf{m}_i$. To obtain a formula representing $f^{-1}(1)$, we have to use the disjunction of these terms τ_i. In case of f_η, this leads to the formula

$$\begin{aligned} \eta_1 = & \left(\overline{V_1} \wedge \overline{V_2} \wedge \overline{V_3} \wedge \overline{V_4}\right) \vee \left(\overline{V_1} \wedge \overline{V_2} \wedge V_3 \wedge \overline{V_4}\right) \\ & \vee \left(\overline{V_1} \wedge V_2 \wedge \overline{V_3} \wedge \overline{V_4}\right) \vee \left(\overline{V_1} \wedge V_2 \wedge V_3 \wedge V_4\right) \\ & \vee \left(V_1 \wedge \overline{V_2} \wedge \overline{V_3} \wedge V_4\right) \vee \left(V_1 \wedge \overline{V_2} \wedge V_3 \wedge V_4\right) \\ & \vee \left(V_1 \wedge V_2 \wedge \overline{V_3} \wedge \overline{V_4}\right) \vee \left(V_1 \wedge V_2 \wedge V_3 \wedge V_4\right). \end{aligned}$$

A disjunction of terms where each term includes exactly one literal of each variable, like η_1, is called a *model representation* (MODS). However, f_η can also be represented by

$$\begin{aligned} \eta_2 = & \left(\overline{V_1} \wedge \overline{V_2} \wedge \overline{V_4}\right) \vee \left(V_1 \wedge \overline{V_2} \wedge V_4\right) \vee \left(V_2 \wedge \overline{V_3} \wedge \overline{V_4}\right) \vee (\wedge V_2 \wedge V_3 \wedge V_4) \\ & \vee (V_1 \wedge V_2 \wedge V_3 \wedge V_4). \end{aligned}$$

Note that the first terms include only three literals instead of four. In general, a disjunction of terms, like η_2, is called a *disjunctive normal form* (DNF) and MODS is a special case of DNF. Another special case of DNF it the *prime implicants* form (IP). A DNF φ is a IP, if each term ϑ with $\vartheta \models \varphi$ entails some term φ_i that appears in φ, i.e. $\vartheta \models \varphi_i$; and no term φ_i in φ entails another term φ_j in φ, i.e. $\varphi_i \not\models \varphi_j$ for $i \neq j$. The following formula η_3 is a IP representing f_η:

$$\eta_3 = \left(\overline{V_1} \wedge \overline{V_2} \wedge \overline{V_4}\right) \vee \left(V_1 \wedge \overline{V_2} \wedge V_4\right) \vee \left(V_2 \wedge \overline{V_3} \wedge \overline{V_4}\right) \vee (V_2 \wedge V_3 \wedge V_4).$$

The dual form of DNF, i.e. a conjunction of clauses, is called a *conjunctive normal form* (CNF). The following CNF η_4 also represents f_η:

$$\begin{aligned} \eta_4 = & \left(V_1 \vee V_2 \vee \overline{V_4}\right) \wedge \left(\overline{V_1} \vee V_2 \vee V_4\right) \wedge \left(\overline{V_2} \vee V_3 \vee \overline{V_4}\right) \wedge \left(\overline{V_2} \vee \overline{V_3} \vee V_4\right) \\ & \wedge \left(\overline{V_1} \vee \overline{V_2} \vee V_3 \vee V_4\right). \end{aligned}$$

Analog to DNF, there is a special case of CNF. This special case is called *prime implicates* form (PI). A CNF φ is a PI, if each clause ϑ with $\varphi \models \vartheta$ is entailed by a clause φ_i that appears in φ, i.e. $\varphi_i \models \vartheta$; and no clause φ_i in φ entails another clause φ_j in φ, i.e. $\varphi_i \not\models \varphi_j$ for $i \neq j$. For example, the following PI represents f_η:

$$\eta_5 = \left(V_1 \vee V_2 \vee \overline{V_4}\right) \wedge \left(\overline{V_1} \vee V_2 \vee V_4\right) \wedge \left(\overline{V_2} \vee V_3 \vee \overline{V_4}\right) \wedge \left(\overline{V_2} \vee \overline{V_3} \vee V_4\right).$$

Within these five formulae, only variables are negated. In general, a propositional formula, where only variables may be negated, is called a *negation normal form* (NNF). For example, f_η can be represented by the following NNF

$$\eta_6 = \left(\left((V_1 \vee V_2) \wedge \left(\overline{V_2} \vee V_3\right)\right) \wedge V_4\right) \vee \left(\left(\left(\overline{V_1} \wedge \overline{V_2}\right) \vee \left(V_2 \wedge \overline{V_3}\right)\right) \wedge \overline{V_4}\right).$$

And there are also propositional formulae without any restriction, e.g.

$$\eta_7 = \left(\left((V_1 \vee V_2) \wedge \neg \left(V_2 \wedge \overline{V_3}\right)\right) \wedge V_4\right) \vee \left(\neg \left((V_1 \vee V_2) \wedge \neg \left(V_2 \wedge \overline{V_3}\right)\right) \wedge \overline{V_4}\right)$$

which also represents f_η.

Of course, there are even more kinds of forms of propositional formulae. However, we omit them for now and turn towards more computer-oriented representations of Boolean functions.

2.3 Graph-based Languages

While the textual representation of propositional formulae is quite good for manual handling, it is advisable to use a graphical representation for computer-aided handling. In the following, we informally address a tree based and a DAG based representation. Then, we define the representation used in this dissertation, and we introduce several languages.

A native representation, which reflects the structure of a formula, is a directed tree. This tree is obtained by considering each occurring literal and each occurring logical connective as a node. Edges start at a logical connective and lead towards the elements connected by this connective. For example, Figure 2.2 shows different trees of the formula $V_1 \vee V_2 \vee V_3$. The different trees are obtained due to the associativity of $\vee$ (w.r.t. equivalence), since

$$V_1 \vee V_2 \vee V_3 \equiv (V_1 \vee V_2) \vee V_3 \equiv V_1 \vee (V_2 \vee V_3).$$

Chapter 2 Representing Boolean Functions

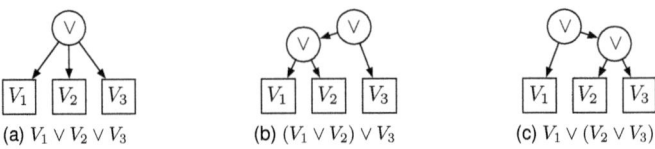

Figure 2.2: Different trees for the formula $V_1 \vee V_2 \vee V_3$.

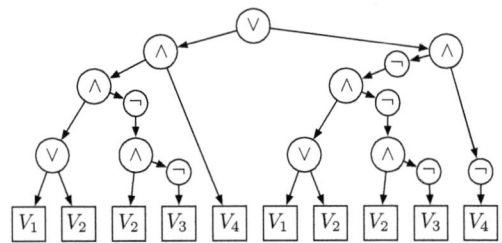

Figure 2.3: A tree representing $\eta_7 = \left(\left(\left(V_1 \vee V_2\right) \wedge \neg \left(V_2 \wedge \overline{V_3}\right)\right) \wedge V_4\right) \vee \left(\neg \left(\left(V_1 \vee V_2\right) \wedge \neg \left(V_2 \wedge \overline{V_3}\right)\right) \wedge \overline{V_4}\right)$

Figure 2.2(a) exploits the associativity by allowing an arbitrary (but finite) number of outgoing edges. Due to the commutativity of $\vee$ and $\wedge$, the order of the children is insignificant. In the following, we make use of this for both $\vee$ and $\wedge$ whenever possible.

After this preparatory work, it should be possible to obtain a tree from a formula. Note that $\overline{V}$ is an abbreviation for $\neg V$ with $V \in \mathbf{V}$. A tree representing η_7 is shown in Figure 2.3. Note that some parts of the tree occur twice, e.g. there are at least two nodes for each variable V_i, $1 \leq i \leq 4$. To reduce the number of nodes, we remove all but one node for each variable which leads to Figure 2.4(a). Now, we have two nodes labeled with $\vee$, where one edge is leading to the node labeled with V_1 and the other one is leading to node labeled with V_2. Obviously, these nodes represent the same formulae, namely $V_1 \vee V_2$. Hence, we choose one of them and remove the other one after redirecting the incoming edges to the chosen node. The same holds for the two nodes labeled with $\neg$ and connected with the node labeled with V_3. The result is shown in Figure 2.4(b). We repeat this until there are no more removable nodes. The final DAG is shown in Figure 2.4(c).

Now, let τ be the directed tree shown in Figure 2.3 and let γ be the DAG shown in Figure 2.4(c). The tree τ consists of 22 edges and 23 nodes, while the DAG γ consists of 16 edges and 13 nodes. It is obvious that a DAG obtained by reducing a tree as above has at

2.3 Graph-based Languages

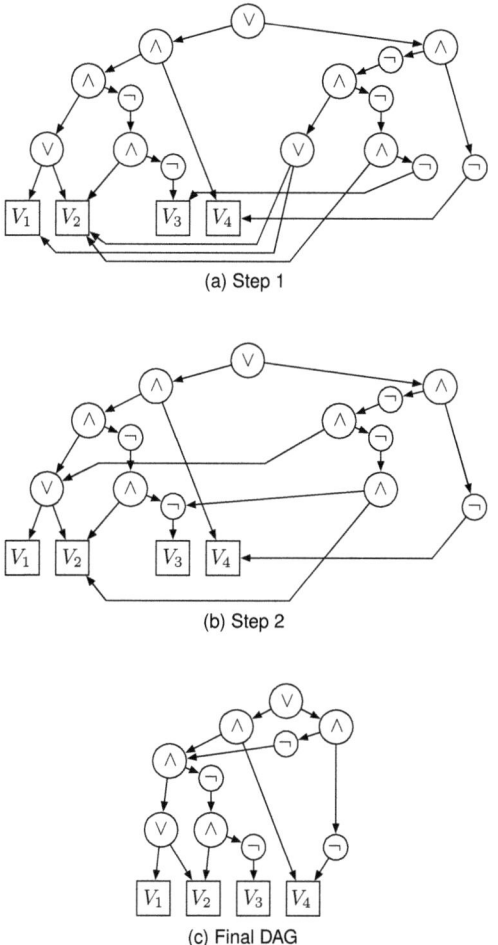

Figure 2.4: From a tree to a DAG.

Chapter 2 Representing Boolean Functions

most as many edges and nodes as the original tree. For some Boolean functions, the difference between the size of the tree and the size of the obtained reduced DAG is exponential. Among these functions are the *parity functions*.

There are two kinds of parity functions: the *odd* ones and the *even* ones. For $\mathbf{v} \in \mathbb{B}$, the odd parity function returns 1, if the number of occurrences of 1 within $\mathbf{v}$ is odd, otherwise it returns 0, while the even parity function returns 1, if the number of occurrences of 1 within $\mathbf{v}$ is even, otherwise it returns 0. Both functions can be represented inductively as follows:

(i) V_1 (resp. $\overline{V_1}$) represents the odd (resp. even) parity function on $\mathbf{V}_1 = \{V_1\}$.

(ii) $\left(V_1 \wedge \overline{V_2}\right) \vee \left(\overline{V_1} \wedge V_2\right)$ (resp. $(V_1 \wedge V_2) \vee \left(\overline{V_1} \wedge \overline{V_2}\right)$) represents the odd (resp. even) parity function on $\mathbf{V}_2 = \{V_1, V_2\}$.

(iii) Let φ represent the odd (resp. even) parity function on $\mathbf{V} = \{V_1, \ldots, V_{r-1}\}$, $r > 2$. Then, $(V_r \wedge \neg\varphi) \vee \left(\overline{V_r} \wedge \varphi\right)$ represents the odd (resp. even) parity function on $\mathbf{V}_3 = \{V_1, \ldots, V_{r-1}, V_r\}$.

The size of the corresponding tree or DAG representing V_1 is 0 while the size of $\overline{V_1}$ is 1. However, the next step compensates this difference between the two kinds of parity functions: The size of the tree based representation is 8 and the size of the DAG based representation is also 8 for both the odd and the even parity function. In terms of differences between the tree based and the DAG based approach, the interesting part is included in (iii). It is easy to see that the size of a tree representing $(V_r \wedge \neg\varphi) \vee \left(\overline{V_r} \wedge \varphi\right)$ is $8 + 2|\varphi| = 8(2^{r-1} - 1)$ whereas the size of a reduced DAG is $8 + |\varphi| = 8(r - 1)$. Summarized the size of the tree based approach is exponential in the number of variables, whereas the size of the DAG based approach is linear in the number of variables. As a matter of fact, we prefer the reduced DAG over the directed tree. Preliminary, we impose the following particularities on the DAG.

Definition 13. A *Propositional DAG* (PDAG) on the variables in $\mathbf{V}$ is a rooted directed acyclic graph of the following form[1]:

(i) Terminals are represented by □ and labeled with ⊥ (contradiction), ⊤ (tautology), or a symbol of a variable, e.g. V for $V \in \mathbf{V}$.

---

[1] Some authors use the same acronym PDAG for *Partially Directed Acyclic Graphs* Verma and Pearl [1992]. In graph theory, these structures are more commonly known as *mixed (acyclic) graphs* Gross and Yellen [2003], i.e. the ambiguity of using PDAG for *Propositional* DAGs is not severe.

2.3 Graph-based Languages

(ii) Non-terminals are represented by ◯ and labeled with ∨ (disjunction), ∧ (conjunction), or ¬ (negation).

    a) Non-terminals labeled with ∨ or ∧ have an arbitrary number of children.

    b) Non-terminals labeled with ¬ have exactly one child.

We use ⊥-terminal, ⊤-terminal, and V_i-terminal to refer to a terminal labeled with ⊥, ⊤, and $V_i \in \mathbf{V}$ respectively. Similarly, we use ∧-node, ∨-node, and ¬-node to refer to a non-terminal labeled with ∧, ∨, and ¬ respectively.

Figure 2.3 and Figures 2.4(a)-(c) depict such PDAGs. Note that a PDAG is simply a graphical notation of a propositional formula instead of a textual one. The language $\text{PDAG}_\mathbf{V}$ contains all possible PDAGs with respect to the set of variables $\mathbf{V}$. When no confusion is anticipated, we omit the reference to the set $\mathbf{V}$, i.e. we simply write PDAG instead of $\text{PDAG}_\mathbf{V}$. The set of variables included in a sub-PDAG α of φ is denoted by $vars(\alpha)$, and the height of φ, denoted by $h(\varphi)$, is the maximal *logical path length*, which is the length of the path minus the number of its ¬-nodes.

In the following, we use various preconditions on logical connectives to specify several properties of a PDAG. The properties of a PDAG are then used to distinguish sublanguages of PDAG. An overview of most important sublanguages is given in Figure 2.5. It divides them into five groups of languages:

(i) *propositional DAGs*;

(ii) *negation normal forms*;

(iii) *classic languages*;

(iv) *binary decision diagrams*;

(v) *further languages*.

Thereafter, we consider some structural reduction rules leading to smaller, representations.

Before we start with defining languages, we adapt the *closure principle* of Fargier and Marquis [2008].

Definition 14. Let L be language and let Δ be any finite subset of the non-terminals labeled with $\{\vee, \wedge, \neg\}$. Then, the *closure* $L[\Delta]$ is the set of graphs inductively defined by:

Chapter 2 Representing Boolean Functions

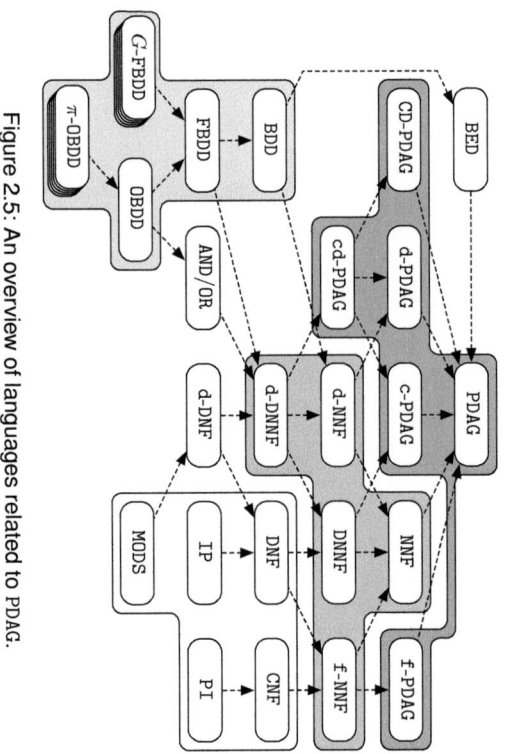

Figure 2.5: An overview of languages related to PDAG.

2.3 Graph-based Languages

- If $\varphi \in \mathtt{L}$, then $\varphi \in \mathtt{L}[\Delta]$.
- If $\vee \in \Delta$ and $\varphi_1, \ldots, \varphi_s \in \mathtt{L}[\Delta]$, then the $\vee$-node with children $\varphi_1, \ldots, \varphi_s$ is in $\mathtt{L}[\Delta]$.
- If $\wedge \in \Delta$ and $\varphi_1, \ldots, \varphi_s \in \mathtt{L}[\Delta]$, then the $\wedge$-node with children $\varphi_1, \ldots, \varphi_s$ is in $\mathtt{L}[\Delta]$.
- If $\neg \in \Delta$ and $\varphi \in \mathtt{L}[\Delta]$, then the $\neg$-node with child φ is in $\mathtt{L}[\Delta]$.

This adaption allows us to provide a formal definition of most languages. A language $\mathtt{L}$ is called *complete* w.r.t to the variables $\mathbf{V} = \{V_1, \ldots, V_r\}$, if and only if its members represent each Boolean function in $\mathbf{B}_r$. To avoid parentheses, we use $\mathtt{F}[\Delta_1][\Delta_2]$ to denote $(\mathtt{F}[\Delta_1])[\Delta_2]$ for $\Delta_1, \Delta_2 \subseteq \{\vee, \wedge, \neg\}$.

2.3.1 Propositional DAGs

This class inherits its name from its is least restrictive member, PDAG. Let $\mathtt{T}$ be the set of terminals labeled with $\bot$, $\top$, and $V \in \mathbf{V}$. In the proposed of closures notation (see above), it is defined as follows:

$\mathtt{PDAG} = \mathtt{T}[\neg, \vee, \wedge]$, the language of propositional DAGs (PDAG).

Note that it is possible to impose preconditions on the operations $\neg$, $\vee$, and $\wedge$. For now, we consider two preconditions.

Definition 15 (Decomposability: $\wedge$-node). A $\wedge$-node with children $\varphi_1, \ldots, \varphi_s$ is *decomposable*, if the sets of variables of φ_i are disjoint, i.e. $vars(\varphi_i) \cap vars(\varphi_j) = \emptyset$ for $i \neq j$.

In case that φ_i and φ_j share exactly one variable, e.g. V, we employ the *Shannon expansion*

$$((\varphi_i|V \wedge \varphi_j|V) \wedge V) \vee \left(\left(\varphi_i\middle|\overline{V} \wedge \varphi_j\middle|\overline{V}\right) \wedge \overline{V}\right)$$

to obtain an equivalent decomposable $\wedge$-node. If more than one variable is shared by φ_i and φ_j, we apply the Shannon expansion recursively on $\varphi_i|V \wedge \varphi_j|V$ and $\varphi_i\middle|\overline{V} \wedge \varphi_j\middle|\overline{V}$ to remove the shared variables one by one. Note that it is also possible to perform the Shannon expansion with subgraphs instead of variables. For example, if φ_i and φ_j share a single common subgraph ρ, we get

$$(\varphi_i|\rho \wedge \varphi_j|\rho \wedge \rho) \vee (\varphi_i|\neg\rho \wedge \varphi_j|\neg\rho \wedge \neg\rho)$$

Chapter 2 Representing Boolean Functions

assuming that $\varphi_i|\rho$, $\varphi_i|\neg\rho$, $\varphi_j|\rho$, $\varphi_j|\neg\rho$, and ρ do not share a common node. Otherwise, we have to ensure recursively that no common node is shared. Within the closure notation, we use the symbol $\times$ for decomposable $\wedge$-nodes.

Definition 16 (Determinism: $\vee$-node). A $\vee$-node with children $\varphi_1, \ldots, \varphi_s$ is *deterministic*, if the satisfying sets of φ_i are disjoint, i.e. $[\![\varphi_i]\!] \cap [\![\psi_j]\!] = \emptyset$ for $i \neq j$.

If φ_i and φ_j satisfy this precondition, they are called *logically contradictory*.

In case that φ_i and φ_j are not logically contradictory, we employ

$$\varphi_i \vee (\neg\varphi_i \wedge \varphi_j),$$

to obtain an equivalent deterministic $\vee$-node, since φ_i and $\neg\varphi_i \wedge \varphi_j$ are logically contradictory. Within the closure notation, we use the symbol $+$ for deterministic $\vee$-nodes.

Note that both decomposability and determinism are consistent with their definitions of Darwiche [1999, 2001a,b]. By adding the symbols $\times, +$ to the closure notation, we can define several languages for T:

c-PDAG $= \text{T}[\times, \vee, \neg]$, the language of *de̲composable* PDAGs;

d-PDAG $= \text{T}[\wedge, +, \neg]$, the language of *d̲eterministic* PDAGs;

cd-PDAG $= \text{T}[\times, +, \neg]$, the language of *de̲composable d̲eterministic* PDAGs.

We use c to refer to decomposability, since it affects only c̲onjunctions and d to refer to determinism, since it affects only d̲isjunctions. Note that c-PDAG and d-PDAG are sublanguages of PDAG, and cd-PDAG is a sublanguage of both c-PDAG and d-PDAG, since decomposable $\wedge$-nodes and deterministic $\vee$-nodes are special cases of $\wedge$-nodes and $\vee$-nodes. In accordance with Figure 2.2, the closure notation enables us to impose a restriction on the height of PDAG.

f-PDAG $= \text{T}[\neg][\wedge][\neg][\vee][\neg] \cup \text{T}[\neg][\vee][\neg][\wedge][\neg]$ is the language of *flat* PDAGs.

Flatness is consistent with its definition of Darwiche and Marquis [2002]. We use f to refer to f̲latness. These five languages are already introduced in Wachter and Haenni [2006a].

Up to now, decomposability is a precondition on $\wedge$-nodes and determinism is one on $\vee$-nodes. But it is also possible to apply decomposability to $\vee$-nodes and determinism to $\wedge$-nodes.

2.3 Graph-based Languages

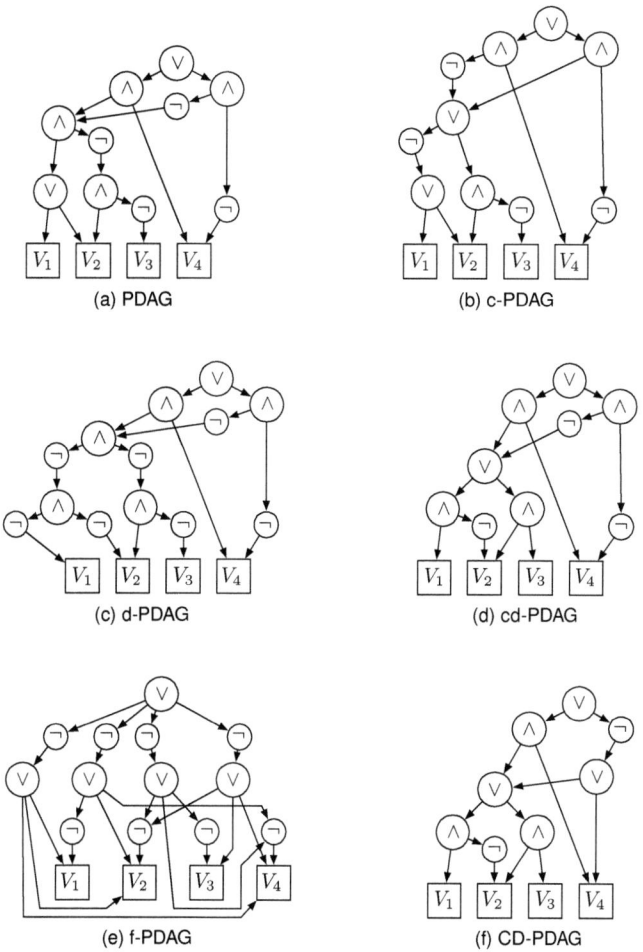

Figure 2.6: Different kinds of PDAGs representing f_η.

Chapter 2 Representing Boolean Functions

Definition 17 (Decomposability: ∨-node). A ∨-node with children $\varphi_1, \ldots, \varphi_s$ is *decomposable*, if the sets of variables of φ_i and φ_j are disjoint for $i \neq j$.

This definition is inspired by the equivalence:

$$\varphi \vee \psi \equiv \neg(\neg\varphi \wedge \neg\psi).$$

Analog, we adapt determinism.

Definition 18 (Determinism: ∧-node). A ∧-node with children $\varphi_1, \ldots, \varphi_s$ is *deterministic*, if $\neg\varphi_i$ and $\neg\varphi_j$ are logically contradictory for $i \neq j$.

The intuition for this is the equivalence

$$\varphi \wedge \psi \equiv \neg(\neg\varphi \vee \neg\psi).$$

Within the closure notation, we use the symbols $\overline{\times}$ for decomposable ∨-nodes and $\overline{+}$ for deterministic ∧-nodes. With these additional symbols, we define

CD-PDAG = $L[\neg, \times, \overline{\times}, +, \overline{+}]$, the language of *generally decomposable & generally deterministic PDAGs*.

It is obvious that cd-PDAG is a subset of CD-PDAG. However, as we will see later, they posses the same computational properties. Different kinds of PDAGs representing f_η are shown in Figure 2.6.

2.3.2 Negation Normal Forms

The name of this group of languages corresponds to its least restrictive member. In contrast to PDAG, this member is limited to *simple negations*, i.e. only terminals may be negated. This least restrictive language is

NNF = $T[\neg][\wedge, \vee]$, the language of *negation normal forms*.

Due to $\neg(\neg\varphi) \equiv \varphi$, $\overline{\overline{V}} \equiv V$ for $V \in \mathbf{V}$, and the *De Morgan's laws*

$$\neg(\varphi \wedge \psi) \equiv \neg\varphi \vee \neg\psi \qquad\qquad \neg(\varphi \vee \psi) \equiv \neg\varphi \wedge \neg\psi,$$

2.3 Graph-based Languages

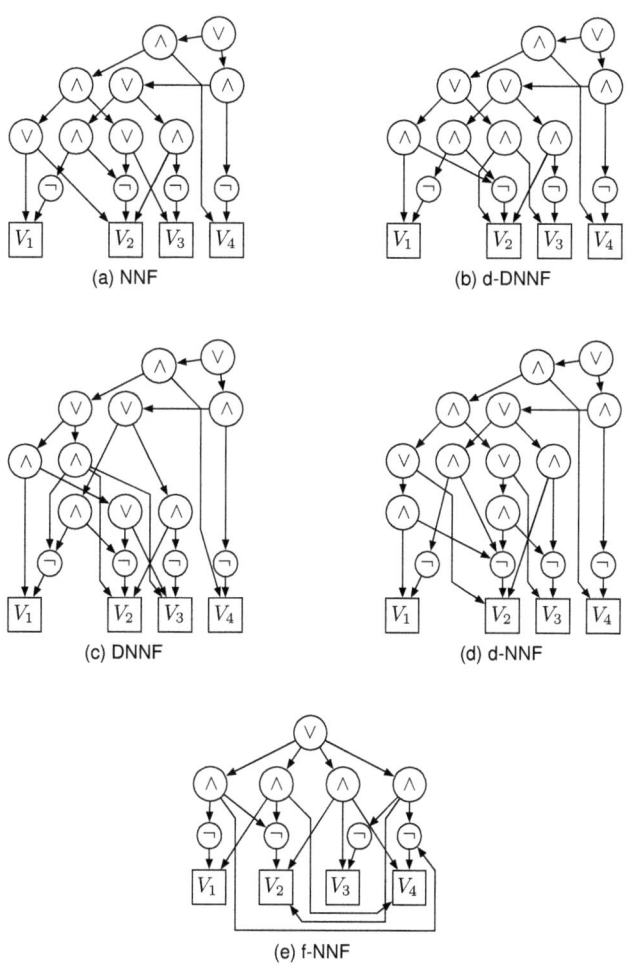

Figure 2.7: Different kinds of NNFs representing f_η.

Chapter 2 Representing Boolean Functions

we know that NNF is complete. Furthermore, NNF is a sublanguage of PDAG, since each $\varphi \in$ NNF is also a PDAG. By exchanging the connectives $\wedge$ or $\vee$ with $\times$ or $+$, or imposing a restriction on the height, we obtain further languages. The following ones will be further considered in this dissertation:

DNNF $=$ T$[\neg][\times, \vee]$, the language of *decomposable* NNFs;

d-NNF $=$ T$[\neg][\wedge, +]$, the language of *deterministic* NNFs;

d-DNNF $=$ T$[\neg][\times, +]$, the language of *deterministic decomposable* NNFs;

f-NNF $=$ T$[\neg][\wedge][\vee] \cup$ T$[\neg][\vee][\wedge]$, the language of *flat* NNFs.

Here, D denotes decomposability[2]. while the meaning of d (determinism) and f (flatness) remains the same as above. These languages are already studied in detail in Darwiche [1999, 2001a,b], Darwiche and Marquis [2002]. Figure 2.7 depicts different kinds of NNFs representing f_η.

2.3.3 Classic Languages

In Section 2.2, we reviewed some classic languages. Here, we are providing a more formal definition which allows to fit these languages into the concept of graphical propositional representation. In the following, let L denote the set of *literals*, i.e. the terminals labeled with $V \in \mathbf{V}$ and the $\neg$-nodes with such a terminal as child. Each element of L$[\wedge]$ is called a *term*, and each L$[\times]$ is called a *proper term*. Respectively, each element of L$[\vee]$ is called a *clause*, and each element of L$[\overline{\times}]$ is called a *proper clause*. According to Darwiche and Marquis [2002], proper terms and proper clause are also called *simple-conjunctions* and *simple-disjunctions* respectively. In case of L$[\times]$ and L$[\overline{\times}]$, we do not allow the Shannon expansion to ensure decomposability, i.e. either a $\wedge$-node or $\vee$-node is already decomposable or it does not belong to the corresponding language.

Definition 19. A $\vee$-node is called *smooth*, if its children mention the same variables, i.e. if $\beta_1, \ldots, \beta_n$ are the children of the $\vee$-node, then $vars(\beta_i) = vars(\beta_j)$ for all $i, j \in \{1, \ldots, n\}$.

Within the closure notation, we use a subscript s to indicate that the node is supposed to be smooth, e.g. $\vee_s$.

---
[2]According to the negation normal form, NNF, naming convention PDAG would be simply normal form, NF, since the simple-negation drops out. Then, DNF could be both a deterministic normal form and a disjunctive normal form (definition follows later on).

2.3 Graph-based Languages

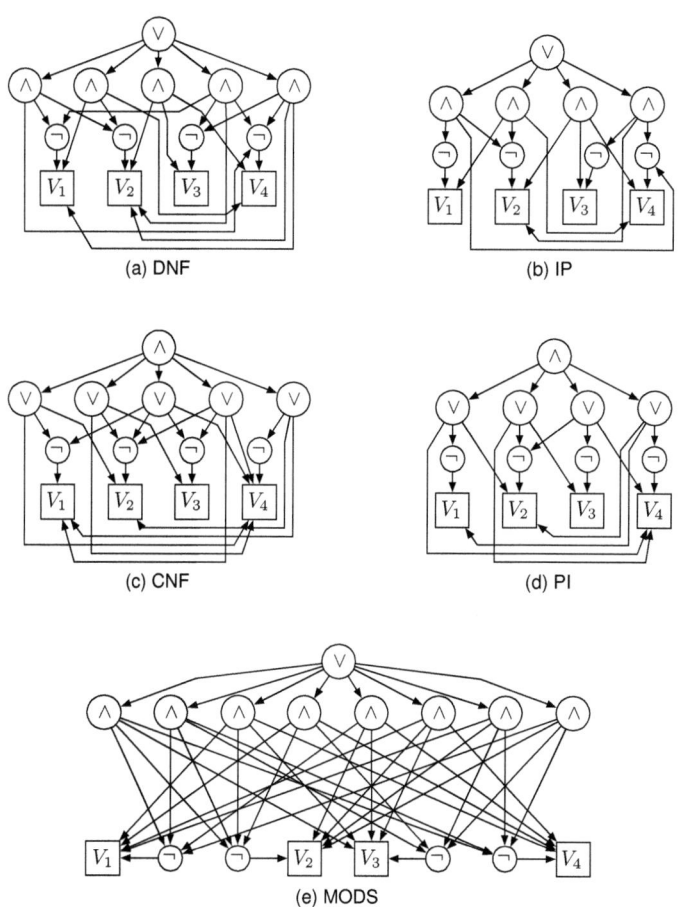

Figure 2.8: Different kinds of classic languages representing f_η.

Chapter 2 Representing Boolean Functions

According to this definition, we get

$\mathtt{DNF} = \mathtt{L}[\times][\vee] \cup \{\bot\text{-terminal}\}$, the language of *disjunctive normal forms* (DNF);

$\mathtt{MODS} = \mathtt{L}[\times][+_s] \cup \{\bot\text{-terminal}\}$, the language of *smooth deterministic* DNFs or *models*;

$\mathtt{CNF} = \mathtt{L}[\overline{\times}][\wedge] \cup \{\top\text{-terminal}\}$, the language of *conjunctive normal forms* (CNF).

Note that DNF is a sublanguage of DNNF. Furthermore, $\varphi \in \mathtt{MODS}$ contains one term for each model with respect to the variables $vars(\varphi)$. Beside these three languages, there are the following special cases of DNF and CNF, respectively:

IP, the language of *prime implicant* forms. $\varphi \in \mathtt{DNF}$ is a *prime implicant* form, if each term ϑ with $\vartheta \models \varphi$ entails some term φ_i that appears in φ, i.e. $\vartheta \models \varphi_i$; and no term φ_i in φ entails another term φ_j in φ, i.e. $\varphi_i \not\models \varphi_j$ for $i \neq j$.

PI, the language of *prime implicate* forms. $\varphi \in \mathtt{CNF}$ is a *prime implicate* form, if each clause ϑ with $\varphi \models \vartheta$ is entailed by a clause φ_i that appears in φ, i.e. $\varphi_i \models \vartheta$; and no clause φ_i in φ entails another clause φ_j in φ, i.e. $\varphi_i \not\models \varphi_j$ for $i \neq j$.

Figure 2.8 depicts different kinds of classic languages representing f_η. Note that some of them may look very complex for the human eye. However, keep in mind that the main purpose of the different languages is the representation for computer-aided calculations.

2.3.4 Binary Decision Diagrams

Again, this group is named after *binary decision diagrams* (BDD). According to Akers [1978], Bryant [1986], BDDs consist of three different kinds of components: a $\bot$-terminal, a $\top$-terminal, and *decision nodes*. A decision node is a non-terminal labeled with $V \in \mathbf{V}$ which has exactly two children, a 1-*child* φ and a 0-*child* ψ with $\varphi, \psi \in \mathtt{PDAG}$. Such a decision node is equivalent to the *decision* $(V \wedge \varphi) + (\overline{V} \wedge \psi)$. The textual representation of a decision is $v\langle\varphi, \psi\rangle$. Figure 2.9 shows the graphical representation of a decision node together with its children. We add this syntactical sugar to the definition of a PDAG and obtain:

Definition 20. A *Propositional DAG* (PDAG) on the variables in $\mathbf{V}$ is a rooted directed acyclic graph of the following form:

2.3 Graph-based Languages

Figure 2.9: Decision Node

(i) Terminals are represented by □ and labeled with ⊥ (contradiction), ⊤ (tautology), or a symbol of a variable, e.g. V for $V \in \mathbf{V}$.

(ii) Non-terminals are represented by ○ and labeled with ∨ (disjunction), ∧ (conjunction), ¬ (negation), or a variable $V \in \mathbf{V}$.

  a) Non-terminals labeled with ∨ or ∧ have an arbitrary number of children.

  b) Non-terminals labeled with ¬ have exactly one child.

  c) Non-terminals labeled with V have exactly two children: a 1-child and a 0-child.

This is the final definition of PDAG. Before we adapt the definitions of the previous languages, we have to consider decision nodes in combination with the preconditions of different connectives. As foreshadowed, a decision node contains a deterministic disjunction and a simple-negation, in addition to two conjunctions. Hence, among the preconditions only decomposability and smoothness have to be considered. A *decomposable* decision is denoted by $v\lfloor\varphi,\psi\rceil$, and it satisfies the condition $V \notin vars(\varphi) \cup vars(\psi)$. For both kinds of decisions, an additional index s indicates that smoothness is satisfied. For the closure notation, we use $v\langle\rangle$ and $v\lfloor\rceil$ as symbol for a decision node and a decomposable decision node. Again, subscript s indicates that the (decomposable) decision node is smooth. We use these symbols and adapt the definition of the closure notation.

Definition 21. Let L be a language over the variables $\mathbf{V} = \{V_1, \ldots, V_r\}$ and let Δ be any finite subset of

$$\{\vee, \vee_s, +, +_s, \overline{\times}, \wedge, \overline{\top}, \overline{\top}_s, \times, \neg, V_i\langle\rangle, V_i\lfloor\rceil, V_i\langle\rangle_s, V_i\lfloor\rceil_s\} \text{ with } 1 \leq i \leq r.$$

For $\varphi, \varphi_1, \ldots, \varphi_s \in L$, the *closure* $L[\Delta]$ is the set of graphs inductively defined by:

- If $\varphi \in L$, then $\varphi \in L[\Delta]$.

- If $\Delta \cap \{\vee, \vee_s, +, +_s, \overline{\times}\} \neq \emptyset$, then the ∨-node with children $\varphi_1, \ldots, \varphi_s$ is in $L[\Delta]$, if the corresponding preconditions are satisfied.

Chapter 2 Representing Boolean Functions

- If $\Delta \cap \{\wedge, \overline{\top}, \overline{\top}_s, \times\} \neq \emptyset$, then the $\wedge$-node with children $\varphi_1, \ldots, \varphi_s$ is in $L[\Delta]$, if the corresponding preconditions are satisfied.

- If $\neg \in \Delta$, then $\neg \varphi \in L[\Delta]$.

- If $\Delta \cap \{V_i\langle\rangle, V_i\lfloor\rfloor V_i\langle\rangle_s, V_i\langle\rangle_s\} \neq \emptyset$, then the V_i-node with children φ_1, φ_2 is in $L[\Delta]$, if the corresponding preconditions are satisfied.

Now, we can update the definition of PDAG, c-PDAG, d-PDAG, cd-PDAG, CD-PDAG, NNF, DNNF, d-NNF, and d-DNNF by adding the adequate type of decision. Let T be the set of terminals, as before, and let $V_I\langle\rangle$ be the abbreviation of $V_1\langle\rangle, \ldots, V_r\langle\rangle$. Then, we get:

$\text{PDAG} = \text{T}\,[\wedge, \vee, \neg, V_I\langle\rangle]$;

$\text{c-PDAG} = \text{T}\,[\times, \vee, \neg, V_I\lfloor\rfloor]$;

$\text{d-PDAG} = \text{T}\,[\wedge, +, \neg, V_I\langle\rangle,]$;

$\text{cd-PDAG} = \text{T}\,[\times, +, \neg, V_I\lfloor\rfloor]$;

$\text{CD-PDAG} = \text{T}\,[\times, \overline{\times}, +, \overline{\top}, \neg, V_I\lfloor\rfloor]$,

$\text{NNF} = \text{T}[\neg]\,[\wedge, \vee, V_I\langle\rangle]$,

$\text{DNNF} = \text{T}[\neg]\,[\times, \vee, V_I\lfloor\rfloor]$,

$\text{d-NNF} = \text{T}[\neg]\,[\wedge, +, V_I\langle\rangle]$, and

$\text{d-DNNF} = \text{T}[\neg]\,[\times, +, V_I\lfloor\rfloor]$.

Decision nodes are not useful for flat languages. Thus, we do not change the definition of these languages.

After this preliminary thoughts and adaptions, we are able to define the decision diagram languages. In the following, let $\Pi\,(1, \ldots, r)$ be the set of permutations of $\{1, \ldots, r\}$. Then, we get

$\text{BDD} = \{\bot\text{-terminal}, \top\text{-terminal}\}\,[V_I\langle\rangle]$, the language of *binary decision diagrams* (BDD);

$\text{FBDD} = \{\bot\text{-terminal}, \top\text{-terminal}\}\,[V_I\lfloor\rfloor]$, the language of *free* BDDs;

$\pi\text{-OBDD} = \{\bot\text{-terminal}, \top\text{-terminal}\}\,[V_{\pi(r)}\lfloor\rfloor] \cdots [V_{\pi(1)}\lfloor\rfloor]$, the language of π-*ordered* BDDs with $\pi \in \Pi\,(1, \ldots, r)$;

2.3 Graph-based Languages

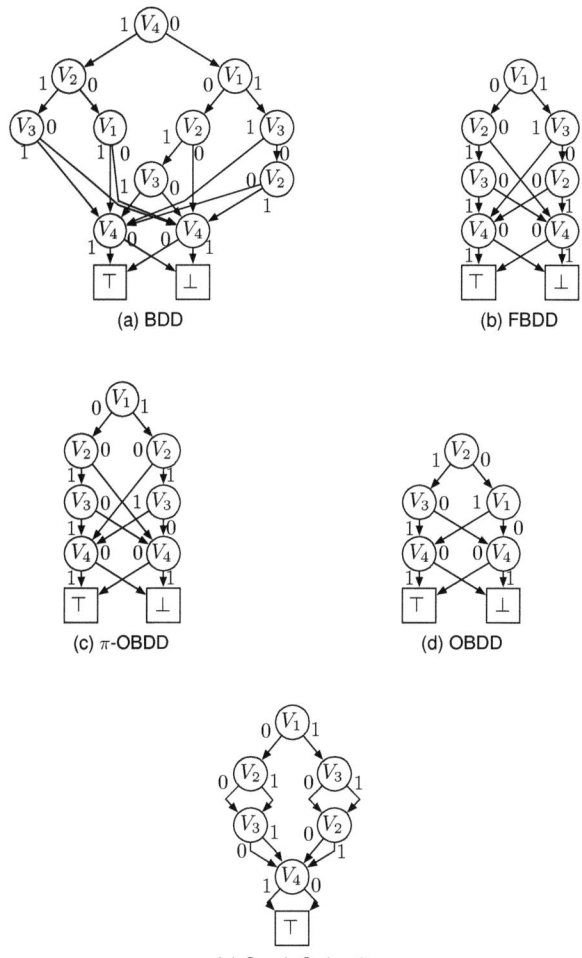

Figure 2.10: Different kinds of BDDs representing f_η. The permutation π used in (c) is obviously $\pi(i) = i$ which leads to $V_1 > V_2 > V_3 > V_4$. In (d) the order might be $V_2 > V_3 > V_1 > V_4$ or $V_2 > V_1 > V_3 > V_4$. Note that the FBDD shown in (b) meets the graph order G given in (e), i.e. (b) depicts also a G-FBDD.

Chapter 2 Representing Boolean Functions

$$\text{OBDD} = \bigcup_{\pi \in \Pi(1,\ldots,r)} \pi\text{-OBDD, the language of \textit{ordered} BDDs.}$$

Obviously, OBDD is the union of all π-OBDD, $\pi \in \Pi(1,\ldots,r)$, i.e. for each $\varphi \in$ OBDD there is a $\pi \in \Pi(1,\ldots,r)$ such that $\varphi \in \pi$-OBDD. On all paths from the root of $\varphi \in \pi$-OBDD to a terminal the appearing variables respect the order π, namely $V_{\pi(i)}$ appears before $V_{\pi(j)}$ for $i < j$. Hence, we may denote the order also in the following way: $V_{\pi(1)} > \cdots > V_{\pi(r)}$. It is possible to carry the idea of ordering forward to FBDD. Again, we require that the appearance of variables on a path respects on order. However, this order may vary from path to path. E.g. each $\varphi \in$ FBDD respects the *graph-order* that is defined by φ itself. More formally, a graph-order G is a FBDD where each variable occurs exactly once on each path and G has exactly one terminal, a ⊤-terminal. A FBDD φ respects the graph-order G if the appearance of variables on a path from the root to a terminal in φ is consistent with the appearance of variables on the corresponding path in G. Such a φ is called *graph-driven* FBDD guided by G. Hence, we define:

G-FBDD, the language of *graph-driven* FBDDs guided by G.

Analog to the relationship between OBDD and π-OBDD, FBDD is the union of all G-FBDD's, i.e.

$$\text{FBDD} = \bigcup_{G \text{ graph-order}} G\text{-FBDD}.$$

To emphasize the fact that there is not only a single language of π-OBDDs or a single language G-FBDDs, they are represented with several layers in Figure 2.5. Figure 2.10 depicts different kinds of BDDs representing f_η.

According to Wegener [2000], further BDD-like languages exist in the literature. They can be classified into to three groups. The first group contains variants where the properties decomposability, ordering, π-ordering, or G-ordering are relaxed. The second group consists of variants, which include ∨- or ∧-nodes or nodes representing the exclusive disjunction. Some of non-deterministic variants also use a *partition* of $\mathbb{B}^r$, e.g. *partioned* OBDD. The third group contains the *randomized* variants of BDDs. Wegener [2000] provides a good survey of the different languages. Note that some of these language may also be incorporated in the concept of PDAGs. To some extent this would not even require additional preconditions.

2.3 Graph-based Languages

2.3.5 Further Languages

So far, we only considered the tip of the iceberg. There are many other languages that could also be considered. For example, there are further logical connectives. Luckily, they can be reduced to the connectives $\neg$, $\vee$ and $\wedge$. Among these connectives are the following ones:

- *exclusive disjunction* $\oplus$ with $\varphi \oplus \psi \equiv (\varphi \wedge \neg\psi) + (\neg\varphi \wedge \psi)$;
- *equivalence* $\Leftrightarrow$ with $\varphi \Leftrightarrow \psi \equiv (\varphi \wedge \psi) + (\neg\varphi \wedge \neg\psi)$;
- *nand* $\overline{\wedge}$ with $\varphi \overline{\wedge} \psi \equiv \neg(\varphi \wedge \psi)$;
- *nor* $\overline{\vee}$ with $\varphi \overline{\vee} \psi \equiv \neg(\varphi \vee \psi)$;
- *existential quantification* $\exists$ over a variable $V \in \mathbf{V}$, where $\exists V.\varphi$ is equivalent to $\varphi|V \vee \varphi|\overline{V}$; and
- *universal quantification* $\forall$ over a variable $V \in \mathbf{V}$, where $\forall V.\varphi$ is equivalent to $\varphi|V \wedge \varphi|\overline{V}$.

Obviously, the possible preconditions on these new connectives correspond to the preconditions on $\neg$, $\vee$, and $\wedge$.

Additionally, it is also possible to extend the meaning of decision for a language L by labeling the non-terminal with $\rho \in$ L instead of $V \in \mathbf{V}$. For $\varphi, \psi \in$ L, a decision based on $\rho \in$ L is represents the Boolean function $(f_\varphi \wedge f_\rho) \vee (f_\psi \wedge \neg f_\rho)$.

It is also possible to link BDDs by logical connectives as mentioned above. Such a language is

> BED = $\{\top, \bot\}[\vee, \wedge, \neg, V_1\langle\rangle, \ldots, V_r\langle\rangle]$, the language of *Boolean expression diagrams*, consider Andersen and Hulgaard [1997], Hulgaard et al. [1999].

A BED consists of labeled nodes with exactly two children. Amongst others, the label corresponds to the logical connectives $\vee$, $\wedge$, and $\neg$. In case of $\neg$, the second child is redundant..

A very similar language is composed of *AND/OR (search) graphs*, consider Dechter and Mateescu [2007]. It is denoted by

AND/OR, the language of *AND/OR (search) graphs*.

Like a PDAG, an AND/OR graph arises from a tree by merging certain nodes according to some specified rules. The *AND/OR (search) tree* itself is based on a *pseudo tree* which

Chapter 2 Representing Boolean Functions

contains exactly one node for each variable. Informally, the root of the AND/OR tree is a decision node labeled with the same variable as the root of the pseudo tree, its children are ∧-nodes. The children of the ∧-nodes are decision nodes labeled with the successors of the root pseudo tree. This alteration between ∧- and decision nodes continues until all leaves of the pseudo tree are reached. The children of the lowest decision nodes correspond to the value of the Boolean function of the corresponding assignment, i.e. a ⊤- or a ⊥-terminal. Note that if the pseudo tree is a chain, i.e. if there is no branching point, then we obtain a π-OBDD where π corresponds to the pseudo tree. From this point of view, AND/OR is a super-language of OBDD. On the other side, AND/OR is a sublanguage of d-DNNF, since both the ∧- and decision nodes are decomposable due to the setup of the pseudo tree.

In addition to BED and AND/OR, which are related to BDD, we also consider a language that is related to one of the classic ones. More exactly, this language is a sublanguage of DNF. It is

d-DNF = T[+] ∪ {⊥}, the language of *determinisitc* or *orthogonal* DNFs or *disjoint Sum-of-Products*,

where T is the set of proper terms. Note that d-DNF = d-DNNF ∩ DNF. d-DNF plays an important role in reliability theory, consider Rai et al. [1995], Rauzy et al. [2003]. The IP shown in Figure 2.8(b) is also a d-DNF.

Of course, there are further languages. For example, Pipatsrisawat and Darwiche [2008] introduce new languages by combining the existing language DNNF and d-DNNF with the idea of AND/OR graphs. The arising languages are $DNNF_T$ and SDNNF, the union of all $DNNF_T$, and their deterministic variants $d\text{-}DNNF_T$ and d-SDNNF. Two further languages arise from DNF and CNF by replacing literals with so-called *horn clauses* and *horn terms*, respectively. A horn clause is a (proper) clause with exactly one positive literal, and a horn term is a (proper) term with exactly one positive literal.

2.3.6 Structural Reduction Rules for Graph-based Languages

After having defined about two dozen languages, it is time to consider some structural reduction rules. These rules are applied not only to transform a tree into a graph, but also to reduce the graph obtained by combining one or more graphs. The prime benefit is a reduced size. Under certain circumstances, we even obtain a canonical structure, i.e. there is

2.3 Graph-based Languages

a unique representation for each Boolean function. According to Bryant [1986] the canonical structure is based on two concepts: *isomorphism* and *redundancy*.

Informally, isomorphism allows to use a single node instead of several structurally equivalent ones, and redundancy allows to replace a node φ by an equivalent one that is included in φ. Let φ, ψ be two PDAGs, we define isomorphism as follows.

Definition 22. The nodes φ and ψ are *isomorphic*, iff one of the conditions given below holds.

- φ and ψ are terminals with the same label, either $\bot$ or $\top$ or $V \in \mathbf{V}$.
- φ and ψ are $\neg$-nodes with the same child $\gamma \in$ PDAG.
- φ and ψ are either two $\wedge$- or two $\vee$-nodes with the same children $\gamma_1, \ldots, \gamma_t \in$ PDAG, where the order of the children may vary for φ and ψ.
- φ and ψ are V-nodes with the same 0-child $\gamma_0 \in$ PDAG and the same 1-child $\gamma_1 \in$ PDAG.

In addition, a $\wedge$-node and a $\vee$-node with no child are isomorphic to a $\top$-terminal and a $\bot$-terminal, respectively.

If φ and ψ are isomorphic, it is sufficient to use φ (or ψ) and to direct all incoming edges of ψ to φ (or vice versa).

While isomorphism is a concept between at least two nodes, redundancy concerns only a single node. The definition of redundancy is:

Definition 23. The node φ is *redundant*, if one of the conditions below holds.

- φ is a $\neg$-node and its child is (a) a $\bot$-terminal, or (b) a $\top$-terminal, or (c) a $\neg$-node with child $\psi \in$ PDAG.
- φ is a $\wedge$-node or $\vee$-node with exactly one child.
- φ is a V-node and the 0-child and the 1-child are the same $\psi \in$ PDAG.

A redundant $\neg$-node is replaced by (a) a $\top$-terminal, (b) a $\bot$-terminal, or (c) its child ψ. A redundant $\wedge$-node or $\vee$-node with one child is replaced by its child. Finally, a redundant V-node is replaced by its common child ψ.

Chapter 2 Representing Boolean Functions

φ is a	$c_\wedge^+(\varphi)$	$c_\wedge^-(\varphi)$	$c_\vee^+(\varphi)$	$c_\vee^-(\varphi)$
$\bot$-terminal	$\{\varphi\}$	$\emptyset$	$\emptyset$	$\emptyset$
$\top$-terminal	$\emptyset$	$\emptyset$	$\{\varphi\}$	$\emptyset$
V-terminal	$\{\varphi\}$	$\emptyset$	$\{\varphi\}$	$\emptyset$
$\neg$-node	$c_\vee^-(\varphi_0)$	$c_\vee^+(\varphi_0)$	$c_\wedge^-(\varphi_0)$	$c_\wedge^+(\varphi_0)$
$\wedge$-node	$\{\varphi\} \cup \bigcup_{i=1}^{t} c_\wedge^+(\varphi_i)$	$\bigcup_{i=1}^{t} c_\wedge^-(\varphi_i)$	$\{\varphi\}$	$\emptyset$
$\vee$-node	$\{\varphi\}$	$\emptyset$	$\{\varphi\} \cup \bigcup_{i=1}^{t} c_\vee^+(\varphi_i)$	$\bigcup_{i=1}^{t} c_\vee^-(\varphi_i)$
V-node	$\{\varphi\}$	$\emptyset$	$\{\varphi\}$	$\emptyset$

Table 2.1: The recursive definition of the four different closures $c_\wedge^+(\varphi)$, $c_\wedge^-(\varphi)$, $c_\vee^+(\varphi)$, and $c_\vee^-(\varphi)$. φ_0 refers to the child of a $\neg$-node, and $\varphi_1, \ldots, \varphi_t$ refer to the children of a $\wedge$- and a $\vee$-node respectively.

For PDAGs, more precisely, for $\wedge$- and $\vee$-nodes, there is an enhanced concept of redundancy. Under certain circumstances, a $\wedge$-node might be replaced by a $\bot$-terminal, and a $\vee$-node might be replaced by a $\top$-terminal. The idea of *enhanced redundancy* is to consider the *positve* and *negative closure* of a $\wedge$- or $\vee$-node φ. If the intersection of the closures is not empty, φ can be replaced as suggested before. The closures differ for $\wedge$- and $\vee$-nodes, i.e. there are two positive closures, $c_\wedge^+$ and $c_\vee^+$, and two negative ones, $c_\wedge^-$ and $c_\vee^-$. Their recursive definition is given in Table 2.1, and it allows us to define enhanced redundancy.

Definition 24. A $\wedge$-node φ is *enhanced redundant*, if

$$\top\text{-terminal} \in c_\wedge^-(\varphi), \bot\text{-terminal} \in c_\wedge^+(\varphi), \text{ or } c_\wedge^+(\varphi) \cap c_\wedge^-(\varphi) \neq \emptyset.$$

A $\vee$-node φ is *enhanced redundant*, if

$$\top\text{-terminal} \in c_\vee^+(\varphi), \bot\text{-terminal} \in c_\vee^-(\varphi), \text{ or } c_\vee^+(\varphi) \cap c_\vee^-(\varphi) \neq \emptyset.$$

An enhanced redundant $\wedge$-node may be replaced by a $\bot$-terminal, while an enhanced redundant $\vee$-node may be replaced by a $\top$-terminal.

For $\wedge$- and $\vee$-nodes, there is another concept going beyond isomorphism and (both kinds of) redundancy. We call this concept *inflation*. It allows to reduce the number of children of both $\wedge$- and $\vee$-nodes, and it is defined as follows.

Definition 25. A ∧-node is *inflated*, if a child ψ occurs more than once or if ψ is a ⊤-terminal. A ∨-node is *inflated*, if a child ψ occurs more than once or if ψ is a ⊥-terminal.

In both cases, we may omit all but one occurrence of ψ. In addition, all occurrences of ⊤-terminal within a ∧-node and ⊥-terminal within a ∨-node may be omitted. Note that the enhanced redundancy rule is applied before the inflation rule as long as a node has more than one child.

To perform the structural reduction, we start with the terminals and the non-terminals without a child (isomorphism). Further nodes are considered as soon as all their children have been considered. For example, let φ be such a node and let φ_i be the reduced children. At first, we check if φ is redundant. In case that φ is a ∧- or ∨-node which is not redundant, we also scan φ for enhanced redundancy. If φ is neither redundant nor enhanced redundant, we test if it is isomorphic to an already reduced node. Note that in case that φ is a ∧- or ∨-node, we possibly reduce the number of children, if φ is inflated, and look for an isomorphic node afterwards.

From now on, we consider only reduced representations, i.e. representations that are free of isomorphism, (both kinds of) redundancy, and inflation. We also assume that the languages only contain reduced representations. Hence, π-OBDD and G-FBDD become *canonical* languages as shown by Bryant [1986] and Wegener [2000], i.e. each of them contains a unique representation for each Boolean function. The sole exception to this assumption is the representation of a graph order.

2.4 Recapitulation: Representing Boolean Functions

This chapter covered different representation techniques for Boolean functions. These techniques are divided into three groups. The first group are the explicit languages. Most explicit language contain an entry for each complete assignment. We have also seen that it is sufficient to represent the satisfying set $f^{-1}(1)$ of a Boolean function f. The two remaining groups exploit this fact. One of this groups concentrates on a textual representation, while the other one concentrates on a graph-based representation. Within these two groups, preconditions on the logical connectives ¬, ∧, and ∨ together with different orders of the variables are used to differentiate the various languages. Our contribution in this area are PDAG, c-PDAG, d-PDAG, f-PDAG, cd-PDAG and CD-PDAG.

Chapter 3

Knowledge Compilation Map for Boolean Functions

After having introduced various languages in the previous chapter it is time to compare them. The comparison is divided into three parts. First, we analyze if a language offers a more compact representation for all Boolean functions than another one. The compactness of a language is called *succinctness*. Thereafter, we determine which kind of information a language offers in time polynomial in the size of the representation of one or more Boolean functions. This is often referred to *query answering*, where the *query* is the kind of information we are asking for. Finally, we examine which combinations, called *transformations*, of one or more Boolean functions are performed, again in time polynomial in the size of the representation of the involved functions.

The idea behind the knowledge compilation map is the following. Depending on the application, we come up with a set of queries and transformations, which the chosen language should support in time polynomial in the size of the representation. Thus, if more than one language qualifies, the most succinct language provides the most compact representation. This is then the most appropriate language for the considered application. The following subsections discuss the succinctness of the languages, then, the possible queries, and finally, the possible transformations.

Note that replacing the non-leaves of $\varphi \in$ PDAG by corresponding logical gates leads to a *digital circuit* implementing f_φ. We prefer to make a distinction between PDAGs and digital circuits to emphasize their respective purposes. Digital circuits are mainly used to *implement* Boolean functions, whereas PDAGs are useful to *represent*, answer *queries* about, and *transform* Boolean functions. As suggested by Darwiche and Marquis [2002], we use exactly

Chapter 3 Knowledge Compilation Map for Boolean Functions

these three topics to set up a knowledge compilation map. The following map considers only reduced graph-based languages shown in Figure 3.1. These languages are sufficient for a computer-oriented representation. Note that for a small number of variables the explicit representations might also be useful.

3.1 Succinctness

With respect to two languages L_1 and L_2, the intuitive idea of succinctness is to figure out whether Boolean functions are represented more compactly by elements of L_1 or by elements of L_2. The following definition corresponds to the one given by Darwiche and Marquis [2002], Wachter and Haenni [2006a].

Definition 26. Let L_1 and L_2 be two languages. L_1 is *equally or more succinct than* L_2 (or L_1 is *at least as succinct as* L_2), denoted by $L_1 \preceq L_2$ iff for every $\varphi_2 \in L_2$, there is a $\varphi_1 \in L_1$ such that $\varphi_1 \equiv \varphi_2$ and $|\varphi_1|$, the size of φ_1, is polynomial in $|\varphi_2|$, the size of φ_2.

The relation $\preceq$ is clearly a partial order over all possible sublanguages of PDAG. In the following, let L_1 and L_2 be languages. Furthermore, L_1 is *strictly more succinct* than L_2, denoted by $L_1 \prec L_2$, iff $L_1 \preceq L_2$ and $L_2 \not\preceq L_1$. L_1 and L_2 are *equally succinct*, denoted by $L_1 \equiv L_2$, iff $L_1 \preceq L_2$ and $L_2 \preceq L_1$. They are *incomparable* iff $L_1 \not\preceq L_2$ and $L_2 \not\preceq L_1$. If the relation between L_1 and L_2 is unknown, it is denoted by $L_1 ? L_2$.

Note that if L_1 is a super-language of L_2, then we have $L_1 \preceq L_2$ automatically. Accordingly, Figure 2.5 depicts already some succinctness results, since an edge from L_2 and L_1 represents $L_1 \preceq L_2$. The transitivity of $\preceq$ allows to omit an edge between L_1 and L_2 if they are already connected by a directed path which does not contain this edge. Due to *De Morgan's laws*, we obtain the following result which is useful to simplify the picture even more.

Proposition 1.1. *The following groups consist of equally succinct languages:*

(i) PDAG, BED, c-PDAG, d-PDAG, *and* NNF*;*

(ii) f-PDAG *and* f-NNF*;*

(iii) cd-PDAG *and* CD-PDAG.

In addition to these three groups of equally succinct languages, there is a forth group. Unlike the previous result, this one is not based on the *De Morgan's laws*.

3.1 Succinctness

	decomposability	determinism	flatness	general decomposability & general determinism	simple-negation	simple-conjunction	simple-disjunction	smoothness	prime implicants	prime implicates	decision	ordering	π-ordering	G-ordering
PDAG														
c-PDAG	•													
d-PDAG		•												
cd-PDAG	•	•												
f-PDAG			•											
CD-PDAG				•										
NNF					•									
DNNF	•				•									
d-NNF		•			•									
d-DNNF	•	•			•									
f-NNF			•		•									
DNF	○		○		○	•								
MODS	○	○	○		○	•			•					
CNF			○		○		•							
IP	○		○		○	○			•					
PI			○		○		○			•				
BDD		○			○						•			
FBDD	•	○			○						•			
π-OBDD	○	○			○						○	○	•	○
OBDD	○	○			○						○	•		
G-FBDD	○	○			○						•			•
BED														
AND/OR	○	○			○									
d-DNF	○	•	○		○	•								

Table 3.1: PDAG and some of its sublanguages according to the 13 properties. • means that a language satisfies the corresponding property, and ○ means that this property is implied by other properties or other particularities in the definition of the language.

Chapter 3 Knowledge Compilation Map for Boolean Functions

	PDAG	cd-PDAG	DNNF	d-DNNF	FBDD	G-FBDD	OBDD	π-OBDD	DNF	CNF	d-DNF	IP	PI	MODS
PDAG	≤	≤	≤	≤	≤	≤	≤	≤	≤	≤	≤	≤	≤	≤
cd-PDAG	≰*	≤	≰*	≤	≤	≤	≤	≤	≰*	≰*	≤	?	?	≤
DNNF	≰*	?	≤	≤	≤	≤	≤	≤	≤	≰*	≤	≤	?	≤
d-DNNF	≰*	?	≰*	≤	≤	≤	≤	≤	≰*	≰*	≤	?	?	≤
FBDD	≰	≰	≰	≰	≤	≤	≤	≤	≰	≰	?	≰	≰	≤
G-FBDD	≰	≰	≰	≰	≰	≤	≰	≰	≰	≰	?	≰	≰	≤
OBDD	≰	≰	≰	≰	≰	≰	≤	≤	≰	≰	?	≰	≰	≤
π-OBDD	≰	≰	≰	≰	≰	≰	≰	≤	≰	≰	?	≰	≰	≤
DNF	≰	≰	≰	≰	≰	≰	≰	≰	≤	≰	≤	≤	≰	≤
CNF	≰	≰	≰	≰	≰	≰	≰	≰	≰	≤	?	≰	≤	≤
d-DNF	≰	≰	≰	≰	≰	≰	≰	≰	≰*	≰	≤	?	≰	≤
IP	≰	≰	≰	≰	≰	≰	≰	≰	≰	≰	?	≤	≰	≰
PI	≰	≰	≰	≰	≰	≰	≰	≰	≰	≰	?	≰	≤	?
MODS	≰	≰	≰	≰	≰	≰	≰	≰	≰	≰	≰	≰	≰	≤

Table 3.2: Succinctness relationships of the considered languages. The symbol * means that the result holds unless the polynomial hierarchy collapses.

Proposition 1.2. *The languages* OBDD *and* AND/OR *are equally succinct.*

The proofs are included in the appendix. To simplify the picture, the idea is to use the most characteristic member of a group to address the whole group, i.e. we use PDAG as a general term for the first group, f-PDAG as a general term for the second group, cd-PDAG as the general term for the third one; and OBDD as a general term for OBDD and AND/OR. For the remaining discussion of succinctness, f-PDAG, d-NNF, and BDD are omitted, since they do not allow any queries in time polynomial in the size, as we will see in the following section. The same remark holds for PDAG, but it is kept as the common roof of all considered languages. From the 24 languages in Figure 2.5, 14 languages remain for further analysis. The whole analysis is summarized by the following proposition, its proof is included in the appendix.

Proposition 1.3. *The results on succinctness relationships between the considered languages hold as shown in Figure 3.1 and Table 3.2 respectively.*

Note that some of the edges in Figure 3.1 are conditioned on the polynomial hierarchy not collapsing, Table 3.2 clarifies which ones. A solid arrow means that the source language is strictly less succinct then the target language, e.g. cd-PDAG ≺ PDAG. A dashed edge with

3.1 Succinctness

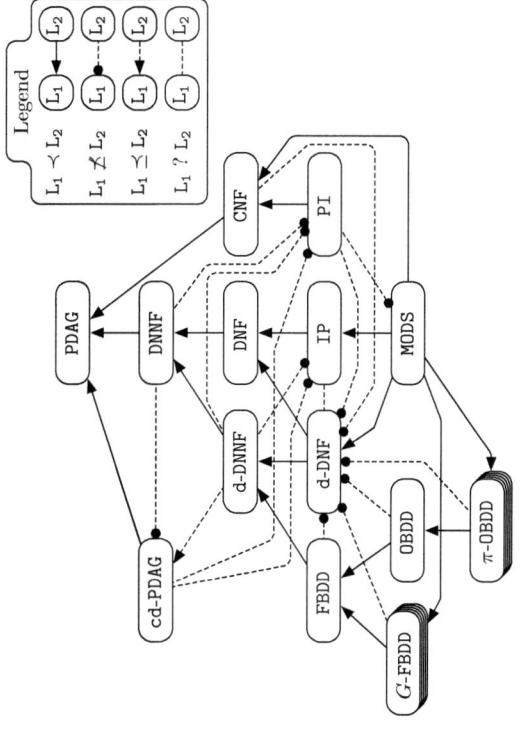

Figure 3.1: The succinctness relationships of the considered languages. Some of the edges are conditioned on the polynomial hierarchy not collapsing, Table 3.1 clarifies which ones.

Chapter 3 Knowledge Compilation Map for Boolean Functions

a bullet on one end means that the language at the end with the bullet is not at least as succinct as the language at the other end of the edge, e.g. cd-PDAG $\not\preceq$ DNNF. The only unknown relation between d-DNF and IP is depicted by an undirected dashed edge. Due to the transitivity of $\preceq$, two languages are incomparable, iff they don't share an edge and there is no directed path along edges with triangular heads connecting them.

It is also very important to take a close look at relations involving G-FBDD and π-OBDD. Both of them involve a set of languages, one language for each graph-order G and ordering π respectively. Let L$_1$ be either a G-FBDD or a π-OBDD, and let L$_2$ be another language (possibly G'-FBDD or π'-OBDD). The entries L$_1 \preceq$ L$_2$ and L$_2 \preceq$ L$_1$ hold for each graph-ordering G or ordering π, while the entries L$_1 \not\preceq$ L$_2$ and L$_2 \not\preceq$ L$_1$ hold at least for one graph-ordering G or ordering π. Hence, G_1-FBDD $\not\preceq G_2$-FBDD and π_1-OBDD $\not\preceq \pi_2$-OBDD are consequences of G-FBDD $\not\preceq$ FBDD and π-OBDD $\not\preceq$ OBDD for some graph orders G_1, G_2 and some variable orders π_1, π_2. The open questions are discussed in Section 3.4.

3.2 Queries

The succinctness of a language is not the only factor to consider when choosing an appropriate target compilation language for a particular application. The second crucial factor is the set of *queries* supported in polynomial time, its discussion follows below. The third factor is the set of *transformations* supported in polynomial time, which we discuss in the next section. Form now on, we say *polytime* to express that the time is polynomial in the size of the involved PDAGs.

As pointed out by Darwiche and Marquis [2002], there is a trade-off between the succinctness of the target language and the set of queries that is supported in polytime, i.e. more succinct languages support less queries in polytime, and vice versa. In other words, if a language L supports a query in polytime, all sublanguages of L also support this query in polytime. The considered queries can be classified into *simple* and *complex* ones. The former are *predicates* returning simply *yes*/*no* or 1/0, whereas the latter are general functions with more complex ranges. Within this dissertation, we discuss the complexity of the predicates and complex queries as shown in Table 3.3. In the following, the predicates are described shortly, and, afterwards, we briefly characterize the complex queries. For this let φ, ψ be PDAGs and let $\lambda_1, \ldots, \lambda_t$ be literals.

3.2 Queries

Predicate		Notation
IN	*inconsistency*	$\varphi \equiv \bot$
VA	*validity*	$\varphi \equiv \top$
CE	*clause entailment*	$\varphi \models \lambda_1 \vee \cdots \vee \lambda_t$
IM	*term implication*	$\lambda_1 \wedge \cdots \wedge \lambda_t \models \varphi$
SE	*sentential entailment*	$\varphi \models \psi$
SI	*sentential inconsistency*	$\varphi \models \neg\psi$
SV	*sentential validity*	$\neg\varphi \models \psi$
EQ	*equivalence*	$\varphi \equiv \psi$
CP	*complement*	$\varphi \equiv \neg\psi$
PEQ	*probabilistic equivalence*	$\varphi \stackrel{\epsilon}{\equiv} \psi$
PCP	*probabilistic complement*	$\varphi \stackrel{\epsilon}{\equiv} \neg\psi$

(a) Predicates

Complex Query		Notation
CT	*model counting*	$|[\![\varphi]\!]|$
WCT	*weighted model counting*	$|[\![\varphi]\!]|_\mathcal{R}$
PR	*probability computation*	$P(\varphi)$
CA	*minimal cardinality*	$\mathrm{card}_{\max}(\varphi)$
MAX	*maximum*	$\max_\mathcal{R}(\varphi)$
ARG	*argument(s) of the maximum*	$\mathrm{argmax}_\mathcal{R}(\varphi)$
MS	*model selection*	$[\![\varphi]\!]_1$
$\overline{\mathrm{MS}}$	*counter model selection*	$[\![\neg\varphi]\!]_1$
ME	*model enumeration*	$[\![\varphi]\!]$
$\overline{\mathrm{ME}}$	*counter model enumeration*	$[\![\neg\varphi]\!]$

(b) Complex Queries

Table 3.3: The predicates and complex queries. $\varphi, \psi \in$ PDAG are general PDAGs, and $\lambda_1, \ldots, \lambda_t \in$ PDAG are literals that share no variable.

Chapter 3 Knowledge Compilation Map for Boolean Functions

3.2.1 Predicates

Inconsistency (IN) tests if the $[\![\varphi]\!]$ has no elements, whereas *validity* (VA) tests if $[\![\varphi]\!]$ has exactly $2^{|vars(\varphi)|}$ elements. *Sentential entailments* (SE) checks if $[\![\varphi]\!] \subseteq [\![\psi]\!]$. The same holds for *clause entailment* (CE) and *term implication* (IM) with $\psi = \lambda_1 \vee \cdots \vee \lambda_t$ and $\varphi = \lambda_1 \wedge \cdots \wedge \lambda_t$ respectively. In addition to sentential entailment, we also consider *sentential inconsistency* (SI), $[\![\varphi]\!] \subseteq [\![\neg\psi]\!]$, and *sentential validity* (SV), $[\![\neg\varphi]\!] \subseteq [\![\psi]\!]$. Both are very similar to sentential entailment, except that ψ and φ respectively are negated. The relation between *equivalence* (EQ) and *complement* (CP) is similar to the relation of the three sentential queries. Equivalence tests if $[\![\varphi]\!] = [\![\psi]\!]$, whereas complement tests if $[\![\varphi]\!] = [\![\neg\psi]\!]$. In addition to those accurate predicates, there are probabilistic versions of equivalence and complement. Those predicates permits an error ϵ with $0 < \epsilon < 1$. More precisely, a positive *probabilistic equivalence* (PEQ) (*probabilistic complement* (PCP)) test with error ϵ means that φ and ψ are equivalent (complementary) with probability $1 - \epsilon$, whereas a negative test result always means that φ and ψ are not equivalent (not complementary). If we specify a time limit or a number of runs instead of an error, the probabilistic predicates become complex queries. In this case, they return the probability that φ and ψ are equivalent (complementary), according to Blum et al. [1980], Jain et al. [1991], Darwiche and Huang [2002], Wachter and Haenni [2006b].

Apparently, inconsistency is a special case of clause entailment and validity is a special case of term implication. In addition, clause entailment is a special case of sentential entailment, and it can be derived from sentential inconsistency. On the other side, term implication is also a special case of sentential entailment, and it can be derived from sentential validity. Furthermore, the equivalence test is equivalent to the conjunction of two sentential entailment test, whereas the complement test is equivalent to the conjunction of a sentential inconsistency and a sentential validity test. Note that both inconsistency and validity are also special cases of the equivalence and the complement test.

3.2.2 Complex Queries

The first query among the complex ones is *model counting* (CT), which computes the number of models of φ, i.e. $|[\![\varphi]\!]|$. It is easy to see, that model counting can be used to derive an inconsistency test and a validity test. The generalization of model counting is *weighted model counting* (WCT). For this query, each variable has to be equipped with two values

3.2 Queries

from a *complemented commutative semiring* $\mathcal{R}$, one value for its positive literal and one for its negative literal. Informally, a ∧-node is replaced by multiplication, a ∨-node by addition, and a ¬-node is replaced by the *complementary* value of its child as defined in $\mathcal{R}$. For model counting, the values of $\mathcal{R}$ are the natural numbers $\mathbb{N}_{\not\models}$ and the operators are the usual addition and multiplication. The value of each literal is 1, and the complementary value of φ is $2^{|vars(\varphi)|} - |[\![\varphi]\!]|$. *Probability computation* (PEQ) is another special case of weighted model counting. Here, the values of $\mathcal{R}$ corresponds to the interval $[0, 1]$. Again, the operators are the usual addition and multiplication. The weight of the positive literal corresponds to the probability of the variable and the complementary value of φ is $1 - \mathbf{P}(\varphi)$. In this case, it is sufficient to specify only one weight for each variable, since the other is its complementary value. Note that both the probabilistic equivalence and the probabilistic complement test are special cases of weighted model counting. Both cases compute the weights of φ and ψ respectively ¬ψ and compare the outcome.

Probability computation is based on two assumptions. First, all variables are random variables and have a probability distribution. Second, all variables are independent of each other. If the second assumption is violated, we may follow the theory of *probabilistic argumentation*[1]. According to Haenni et al. [2000], Haenni [2005], we eliminate the variables without probability distribution and compute the probability of the obtained formula. For example, consider φ with $vars(\varphi) = \mathbf{V}$ where all variables $\mathbf{W} \subseteq \mathbf{V}$ have a probability distribution and the variables in $\mathbf{U} = \mathbf{V} \setminus \mathbf{W}$ don't have one. First, we eliminate the variables of $\mathbf{U}$ from φ and obtain $\exists \mathbf{U}.\varphi$. Then, we compute the probability $P(\exists \mathbf{U}.\varphi)$.

The *minimal cardinality* query (CA) returns the minimal number of negative literals within a model of φ or undefined if φ is inconsistent. It's generalization is the maximum query (MAX) which returns the maximal weight of a model of φ or undefined if φ is inconsistent. As above, this query requires a commutative semiring $\mathcal{R}$. However, $\mathcal{R}$ must not contain negative elements. In addition, a *total order* $\leq$ has to be defined on $\mathcal{R}$. Informally, a ∧-node corresponds to the multiplicative operation of the semiring, whereas a ∨-node corresponds to additive operation of the semiring. In this case, the multiplicative operation is either maximization or

---
[1]This is a theory of formal reasoning which aims at unifying the classical fields of logical and probabilistic reasoning. The principal idea is to evaluate the credibility of a hypothesis by non-additive *probabilities of provability* (or *degrees of support*). This is a natural extension of the classical concepts of probability (in probability theory) and provability (in logic) Haenni [2005]. The non-additivity of this measure is an important characteristic to distinguish properly between uncertainty and ignorance, but the particularity of the model in this dissertation always causes the resulting probabilities of provability to degenerate into ordinary (additive) probabilities. The embedding into the theory of probabilistic argumentation has no practical significance for the method and goals of this dissertation, but it allows inference to be seen from a totally new perspective.

Chapter 3 Knowledge Compilation Map for Boolean Functions

minimization. Unfortunately, it is only possible to handle simple-negations. We use CA to illustrate this. For CA, the semiring consists of the natural numbers and the operations $\min$ (addition) and $+$ (multiplication). The V-terminals get the value 0 and their negations get the value 1. Now, let φ be a $\wedge$-node with two children: a $\neg$-node of a V_1-terminal and a V_2-terminal. Obviously, the minimal cardinality of φ is 1. Can we use this result to get the minimal cardinality of $\neg\varphi$? As we mentioned before, this is not possible. $\neg\varphi$ has three models and the cardinalities of these models are 0, 1, and 2. Sometimes the maximum (or minimum) itself is not the goal of an application, but the models which lead the maximal (or minimal) weights. This is handled by argument(s) of maximum, again in conjunction with a totally ordered commutative semiring $\mathcal{R}$ with non-negative elements. This query returns the list of models φ with the maximal weight or undefined if φ is inconsistent.

It is also possible that an application is interested in a single model or counter model, or in all models or counter models of φ in general. *Model selection* (MS) and *counter model selection* ($\overline{\text{MS}}$) handle the request of a single model and counter model respectively, while *model enumeration* (ME) and *counter model enumeration* ($\overline{\text{ME}}$) handle exactly the request of enumerating of models and counter models respectively. Note the the selection queries can only return a model or counter model if there is one, otherwise they return undefined.

We simply say that a language L $\subseteq$ PDAG *supports* a query, if L supports this query in polytime with respect to the size $|\varphi|$ for all $\varphi \in$ L (in the case of maximum, model, or counter-model enumeration, the reference size is both $|\varphi|$ and $|\ [\![\varphi]\!]\ |_\mathcal{R}$, $|\ [\![\varphi]\!]\ |$, or $|\ [\![\neg\varphi]\!]\ |)^2$. Obviously, if query Q1 is a special case of query Q2, it means that any language L supporting Q2 also supports Q1. The correlations between queries, as mentioned above, are depicted in Figure 3.2 as solid arrowheads. The other kind of arrowheads will be explained later on. Since WCT and its special cases CT, PR, and PEQ are closely related problems, they are all supported as soon as one of them is supported. This is indicated by grouping them together. The same remark holds for MAX and its special case CA. Note that φ is inconsistent, iff MS returns undefined. Accordingly, φ is valid, iff $\overline{\text{MS}}$ returns undefined. Furthermore, φ is inconsistent, iff CA or MAX return undefined.

Further correlations are obtained if the transformation of *term conditioning* is supported, see Darwiche and Marquis [2002]. These relations are marked by an hallow arrowheads in Figure 3.2. It is important to recognize that neither ME nor ARG can be used to replace IN, since their runtime is polynomial in the size of the representation and the number of models. The same remark holds for $\overline{\text{ME}}$ with VA instead of IN and for MAX with CA/MAX. In Figure 3.2,

---
[2]The authors of Darwiche and Marquis [2002] prefer to say that L *satisfies* the corresponding query.

3.2 Queries

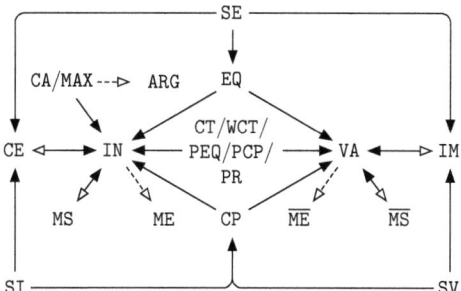

Figure 3.2: Correlations between queries.

this difference in the reference size is expressed by dashed arrows. The definition and discussion of term conditioning follows in the next section. We write TC to denote that a language supports term conditioning.

Proposition 1.4. *If a language supports TC and IN, then it also supports CE, ME, and MS.*

Proposition 1.5. *If a language supports TC and VA, then it also supports IM, $\overline{ME}$, and $\overline{MS}$.*

Proposition 1.6. *If a language supports TC and MAX, then it also supports ARG.*

As we see in the next section, every considered PDAG sublanguage supports TC. Darwiche and Marquis [2002] show that TC is supported by all NNF sublanguages. The argumentation can easily be extended towards PDAG sublanguages. With this, we are now ready for the main statement of this section.

Proposition 1.7. *The results on the supported queries hold as shown in Table 3.4.*

The set of supported queries of a language L is denoted by queries(L). With respect to appropriate languages, this propoistion leads us to the conclusion that PDAG, f-PDAG, and d-NNF are not qualified, since no queries are supported. This is the reason for omitting the succinctness analysis of f-PDAG and d-NNF. Note that equally succinct languages are grouped as suggested before. Some parts of the table corresponds to the results presented by Darwiche and Marquis [2002]. The open questions are discussed in Section 3.4.

59

Chapter 3 Knowledge Compilation Map for Boolean Functions

Queries	IN CE MS ME	VA IM $\overline{\text{MS}}$ $\overline{\text{ME}}$	CT WCT PR PEQ PCP	EQ	CP	SE	SI	SV	CA MAX ARG
PDAG	o	o	o	o	o	o	o	o	o
f-PDAG	o	o	o	o	o	o	o	o	o
cd-PDAG	√	√	√	?	?	o	o	o	?
d-NNF	o	o	o	o	o	o	o	o	o
DNNF	√	o	o	o	o	o	o	o	√
d-DNNF	√	√	√	?	?	o	o	o	√
BDD	o	o	o	o	o	o	o	o	o
FBDD	√	√	√	?	?	o	o	o	√
G-FBDD	√	√	√	√	√	√	√	√	√
OBDD	√	√	√	√	√	o	o	o	√
π-OBDD	√	√	√	√	√	√	√	√	√
DNF	√	o	o	o	o	o	√	o	√
CNF	o	√	o	o	o	o	o	√	o
d-DNF	√	√	√	?	?	?	√	?	√
IP	√	√	o	√	?	√	√	?	√
PI	√	√	o	√	?	√	?	√	?
MODS	√	√	√	√	√	√	√	?	√

Table 3.4: Subsets of PDAG and their supported queries. The symbol √ means "supports", o means "does not support unless P = NP", and ? means "unknown".

3.3 Transformations

The third factor to consider when choosing an appropriate target compilation language is the set of *transformations* supported in polytime. Darwiche and Marquis [2002] point out that sublanguages do in general not inherit the tractability of transformations, in contrast to the queries which are inherited. The reason for this is the prerequisite that the output of a transformation is given in the same language as the input.

In the following, let $\mathbf{W} \subseteq \mathbf{V}$ be a subset of variables, and let $X \in \mathbf{V}$ be a single variable. Furthermore, we use $\varphi, \psi, \varphi_1, \ldots, \varphi_t \in \mathtt{PDAG}$ for general PDAGs. The considered main transformations are:

- *Term Conditioning*: $\varphi|\psi$ where ψ is a proper term;
- *Existential Forgetting*: $\exists \mathbf{W}.\varphi$;
- *Universal Forgetting*: $\forall \mathbf{W}.\varphi$;
- *Conjunction*: $\bigwedge_{i=1}^{t} \varphi_i = \varphi_1 \wedge \cdots \wedge \varphi_t$;
- *Disjunction*: $\bigvee_{i=1}^{t} \varphi_i = \varphi_1 \vee \cdots \vee \varphi_t$;
- *Negation*: $\neg \varphi$.

The idea of *term conditioning* (TC) is to transform φ according to a proper term ψ into a new PDAG $\varphi|\psi$, such that $\psi \wedge \varphi|\psi \equiv \psi \wedge \varphi$ and $vars(\psi) \cap vars(\varphi|\psi) = \emptyset$. Essentially, this involves two replacements. First, each V-terminal, $V \in \mathbf{V}$, in φ is replaced by $\top$ (resp. $\bot$), if V occurs as a positive (resp. negative) literal in ψ. Second, each V-node, $V \in \mathbf{V}$, in φ is replaced by its 1-child (resp. 0-child), if V occurs as a positive (resp. negative) literal in ψ. According to Darwiche and Marquis [2002], term conditioning preserves all relevant properties like decomposability, determinism, or flatness. Obviously, this is also true for simple-negation. However, G-ordering is not preserved, since conditioning $\varphi \in G$-FBDD on a term ψ results in $\varphi|\psi \in G|\psi$-FBDD. Note that π-ordering (and the corresponding G_π-ordering) is preserved by term-conditioning. I.e. apart from G-FBDD, term conditioning is supported by the entire family of PDAG sublanguages. If the term ψ represents a complete assignment $\mathbf{x}$, i.e. ψ contains all variables, then $\varphi|\psi$ represents the value of $f_\varphi(\mathbf{x})$, where a $\top$-terminal means 1 and a $\bot$-terminal means 0. Note that term conditioning can be extended to a more general form of conditioning with respect to sub-PDAGs of φ instead of literals. This is also possible for G-FBDD, since it does not violate the graph ordering G.

Chapter 3 Knowledge Compilation Map for Boolean Functions

The essential idea of both existential and universal forgetting is to generate a new PDAG such that the specified variables are no longer included. First, there is existential forgetting $\exists \mathbf{W}.\varphi$. Its satisfying set $[\![\exists \mathbf{W}.\varphi]\!]$ is supposed to be the projection of $[\![\varphi]\!]$ to the restricted set of variables $\mathbf{U} = \mathbf{V} \setminus \mathbf{W}$. Note that for each model $\mathbf{m}$ of $\exists \mathbf{W}.\varphi$ there is at least one assignment $\mathbf{a}$ of the variables in $\mathbf{W}$ such that $\mathbf{m}$ and $\mathbf{a}$ together are a model of φ. A special case is the existential forgetting of a single variable, i.e. $\mathbf{W} = \{V\}$. One way to realize this is by $\varphi|V \vee \varphi|\neg V$, whereas existential forgetting in general is realized by a sequence of existential forgetting of single variables. In the literature, existential forgetting was originally called *elimination of middle terms* by Boole [1854], but it is also common to call it *projection, variable elimination*, or *marginalization*, see Kohlas [2003]. Note that $\mathbf{W}$ may be *deterministic* with respect to φ, i.e. for all assignments $\mathbf{w_i}, \mathbf{w_j}$ with $\mathbf{w_i} \neq \mathbf{w_j}$ we have $\varphi|\mathbf{w_i} \wedge \varphi|\mathbf{w_j} \equiv \bot$, according to Wachter and Haenni [2007b]. This leads to two other special cases of the existential forgetting: one for deterministic variables $\mathbf{W}$ in general, and one for a single deterministic variable $\mathbf{W} = \{V\}$.

Second, there is universal forgetting $\forall \mathbf{W}.\varphi$. Hence, its satisfying set $[\![\forall \mathbf{W}.\varphi]\!]$ is supposed to be the projection $\left(\bigcap_{\mathbf{w} \in \Omega_\mathbf{W}} [\![\varphi|\mathbf{w}]\!]\right)$ to the restricted set of variables $\mathbf{U} = \mathbf{V} \setminus \mathbf{W}$. Note that for each model $\mathbf{m}$ of $\exists \mathbf{W}.\varphi$ and each assignment $\mathbf{a}$ of the variables in $\mathbf{W}$, the two assignments together $\mathbf{m}$ and $\mathbf{a}$ together are a model of φ. Obviously, $[\![\forall \mathbf{W}.\varphi]\!] \subseteq [\![\exists \mathbf{W}.\varphi]\!]$. Again, a special case is the universal forgetting of a single variable, i.e. $\mathbf{W} = \{V\}$. One way to realize this is by $\varphi|V \wedge \varphi|\neg V$, whereas universal forgetting in general is realized by a sequence of universal forgetting of single variables. Note that $\mathbf{W}$ may be *decomposable* with respect to φ, i.e. for all assignments $\mathbf{w_i}, \mathbf{w_j}$ with $\mathbf{w_i} \neq \mathbf{w_j}$ we have $vars(\varphi|\mathbf{w_i}) \cap vars(\varphi|\mathbf{w_j}) = \emptyset$. This leads to two other special cases of the universal forgetting: one for decomposable variables $\mathbf{W}$ in general, and one for a single decomposable variable $\mathbf{W} = \{V\}$.

Note that existential forgetting corresponds to the elimination of existential quantifiers in *quantified boolean formulae*, whereas universal forgetting corresponds to the elimination of universal quantifiers in quantified boolean formulae.

The transformations conjunction, disjunction, and negation are as defined before. In addition, there is one special case for each of the two transformations conjunction and disjunction. This special case assumes $t = 2$, i.e. $\varphi_1 \wedge \varphi_2$ and $\varphi_1 \vee \varphi_2$ respectively.

Table 3.5 lists all the considered transformations together with their notation. If a language $L \subseteq$ PDAG supports a transformation in polytime with respect to the size $|\varphi|$ for all $\varphi \in L$,

3.3 Transformations

we simply say that L *supports* this transformation[3]. Note that each transformation also has to ensure that the logical connectives within the representation of the result satisfy the preconditions imposed by the concrete language. The whole analysis is summarized by the following proposition, its proof is included in the appendix.

Proposition 1.8. *The results on the supported transformations hold as shown in Table 3.6.*

The set of supported transformations of a language L is denoted by transformations(L). Note that equally succinct languages are grouped as suggested above, and again that some parts of the table corresponds to the results presented by Darwiche and Marquis [2002].

---

[3]Darwiche and Marquis [2002] prefer to say that L it is *closed under* the corresponding operator.

Chapter 3 Knowledge Compilation Map for Boolean Functions

Transformation		Restriction	Notation
TC	term conditioning	ψ term	$\varphi \mid \psi$
$FO_{\exists}$	existential forgetting		$\exists \mathbf{W} \cdot \varphi$
$FO_{\exists}^d$	deterministic existential forgetting	$\mathbf{W}$ deterministic	$\exists_d \mathbf{W} \cdot \varphi$
$SFO_{\exists}$	existential singleton forgetting		$\exists V \cdot \varphi$
$SFO_{\exists}^d$	deterministic existential singleton forgetting	V deterministic	$\exists_d V \cdot \varphi$
$FO_{\forall}$	universal forgetting		$\forall \mathbf{W} \cdot \varphi$
$FO_{\forall}^c$	decomposable universal forgetting	$\mathbf{W}$ decomposable	$\forall_c \mathbf{W} \cdot \varphi$
$SFO_{\forall}$	universal singleton forgetting		$\forall V \cdot \varphi$
$SFO_{\forall}^c$	decomposable universal singleton forgetting	V decomposable	$\forall_c V \cdot \varphi$
AND	conjunction		$\varphi_1 \wedge \cdots \wedge \varphi_t$
AND_2	binary conjunction		$\varphi \wedge \psi$
OR	disjunction		$\varphi_1 \vee \cdots \vee \varphi_t$
OR_2	binary disjunction		$\varphi_1 \vee \varphi_2$
NOT	negation		$\neg \varphi$

Table 3.5: The transformations. $\psi, \varphi, \varphi_1, \ldots, \varphi_t \in$ PDAG are general PDAGs, $\mathbf{W} \subseteq \mathbf{V}$ is a set of variables, and $V \in \mathbf{V}$ is a single variable.

3.3 Transformations

	TC	FO$_\exists$	FO$_\exists^d$	SFO$_\exists$	SFO$_\exists^d$	FO$_\forall$	FO$_\forall^c$	SFO$_\forall$	SFO$_\forall^c$	AND	AND$_2$	OR	OR$_2$	NOT
PDAG	√	○	○	√	√	?	?	√	√	√	√	√	√	√
f-PDAG	√	○	○	√	√	?	?	○	√	•	•	•	•	√
cd-PDAG	√	○	?	○	√	?	?	√	√	√	√	√	○	√
d-NNF	√	○	?	√	√	?	?	√	√	√	√	√	√	○
DNNF	√	√	√	√	√	?	?	○	√	○	○	○	○	?
d-DNNF	√	○	√	○	√	?	?	○	√	○	○	○	○	?
BDD	√	○	?	√	√,?	?	?	√	√	√	√	√	√	√
FBDD	√	•	?	√	○	?	?	○	√	•	○	•	○	√
G-FBDD	×	×	×	×	×	×	×	×	×	•	○	•	○	√
OBDD	√	•	?	√	√	?	?	×	√	•	○	•	○	√
π-OBDD	√	•	?	√	√	?	?	√	√	•	○	•	√	√
DNF	√	√	√,?	√	√	?	?	√	√	•	√	√	√	•
CNF	√	○	√,?	√,?	√,?	?	?	√,?	√,?	√	√,?	•	?	•
d-DNF	√	?	√,?	√,?	√,?	?	?	√,?	√,?	?	?	?	?	?
IP	√	•	√,?	•	√	?	?	√,?	√,?	•	√	•	•	•
PI	√	√	√	√	√	?	?	√,?	√,?	•	•	•	√	•
MODS	√	√	√	√	√	?	?	√	√	√	√	•	•	•

Table 3.6: Subsets of the PDAG and their supported transformations. √ means "supports", • means "does not support", ○ means "does not support unless P = NP", and ? means "unknown". × indicates a clash between the transformation and the language.

Chapter 3 Knowledge Compilation Map for Boolean Functions

3.4 Recapitulation: Knowledge Compilation Map for Boolean Functions

In this chapter, we build a knowledge compilation map for Boolean functions. The languages included are the graph-based languages from the previous chapter. In the first section, we studied the succinctness relationship of the different languages. A language L_1 is at least as succinct a language L_2, if each Boolean function f can be represented in L_1 such that the size is polynomial in the size of the representation of f in L_2. This analysis enabled us to group several languages together which simplified the following steps. Besides the relations including at least one of the omitted languages d-NNF and BDD, there are open questions. The following relations still have to be verified:

cd-PDAG $\preceq$ IP;	cd-PDAG $\preceq$ PI;
DNNF $\preceq$ cd-PDAG;	DNNF $\preceq$ PI;
d-DNNF $\preceq$ cd-PDAG;	d-DNNF $\preceq$ IP;
d-DNNF $\preceq$ PI;	FBDD $\preceq$ d-DNF;
G-FBDD $\preceq$ d-DNF;	OBDD $\preceq$ d-DNF;
π-OBDD $\preceq$ d-DNF;	CNF $\preceq$ d-DNF;
d-DNF $\preceq$ IP;	IP $\preceq$ d-DNF;
PI $\preceq$ d-DNF;	and PI $\preceq$ MODS.

Due to sublanguage relationships a verification (or falsification) of one these relations may imply further results. For example, the verification of d-DNNF $\preceq$ cd-PDAG implies DNNF $\preceq$ cd-PDAG. Furthermore, d-DNF $\preceq$ IP implies d-DNNF $\preceq$ IP which in turn implies cd-PDAG $\preceq$ IP. Similarly, d-DNNF $\preceq$ PI implies both cd-PDAG $\preceq$ PI and DNNF $\preceq$ PI. Besides that PI $\preceq$ d-DNF implies CNF $\preceq$ d-DNF. For the decision diagrams, we have that π-OBDD $\preceq$ d-DNF implies OBDD $\preceq$ d-DNF which in turn implies FBDD $\preceq$ d-DNF. Finally, G-FBDD $\preceq$ d-DNF also implies FBDD $\preceq$ d-DNF.

The second section covers the extraction of information from a Boolean function. At first, we reviewed and introduced the queries. Afterwards, we tested each language L for the queries performable in time polynomial in the size of the representation in L. The open questions are indicated by '?' in Table 3.4. Two facts are very helpful: First, if a language supports a certain query all its sub-languages also support this query. Second, the correlations (see

3.4 Recapitulation: Knowledge Compilation Map for Boolean Functions

Figure 3.2) between the different queries support deriving further results.

The third section covers obtaining new Boolean functions from existing ones. Again, the transformations are reviewed and introduced, before each language L is tested for the transformations performable in time polynomial in the size of the representation of the involved Boolean functions in L. A '?' in Table 3.6 indicates the open problems with respect to the considered transformations.

Besides these open problems, it is also possible to extend the knowledge compilation map by adding additional languages, queries, or transformations. Adding a new language L involves three steps:

(i) L has to be inserted into the succinctness relationship, i.e. for each language L′ in the knowledge compilation map we have to test both $L \preceq L'$ and $L' \preceq L$.

(ii) For each query Q in the knowledge compilation map, we have to analyze whether or not L supports Q.

(iii) For each transformation T in the knowledge compilation map, we have to analyze whether or not L supports T.

When adding a new query or a new transformation, we have to check which language supports the new query or the new transformation. For example, we have shown that AND/OR and OBDD are equally succinct. The fact that each AND/OR graph can be transformed into an OBDD in time polynomial in the size of the original graph, allowed us to handle these language under the name OBDD.

Chapter 4

Extending the Knowledge Compilation Map

The previous chapter constructed a knowledge compilation map for Boolean functions. However, knowledge is not always nicely expressible using Boolean variables only. In the following, we introduce different kinds of generalized Boolean functions. Let f be a function with domain D and codomain C, i.e.

$$f : D \to C$$
$$d \mapsto f(d) = c.$$

For a (r-ary) Boolean function, we have the domain $D = \mathbb{B}^r = \overbrace{\mathbb{B} \times \cdots \times \mathbb{B}}^{r}$ and the codomain $C = \mathbb{B}$. Each $\mathbb{B}$ in the domain corresponds to a frame $\Omega_{V_i} = \{0, 1\}$ of a Boolean variable V_i, $1 \leq i \leq r$. We consider two generalizations of Boolean-functions:

(i) Permitting multi-state variables with finite frames instead of Boolean variables, leads to $D = \Omega_\mathbf{V} = \Omega_{V_1} \times \cdots \times \Omega_{V_r}$. As mentioned before, such a function is called a Boolean-valued function. We will study such functions with domain $D = \Omega_\mathbf{V}$.

(ii) Compared with a Boolean-valued function, the codomain could also be something more complicated, e.g. $C = \mathbb{B}^s$ instead of $C = \mathbb{B}$.

As we will see later on that representing Boolean-valued functions and sets or partitions thereof covers the representation of knowledge based on variables with finite frames. In the following, each of this three topics is considered. In addition, we also discuss an alternative way for representing the third one. Now, let's start with Boolean-valued functions.

Chapter 4 Extending the Knowledge Compilation Map

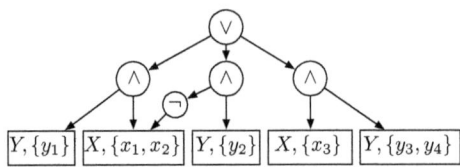

Figure 4.1: An MDAG representing the Boolean-valued function corresponding to the formula $((Y, \{y_1\}) \wedge (X, \{x_1, x_2\})) \vee (\neg (X, \{x_1, x_2\}) \wedge (Y, \{y_2\})) \vee ((X, \{x_3\}) \wedge (Y, \{y_3, y_4\}))$.

4.1 Boolean-Valued Functions

The representation of Boolean-valued functions is covered partly in the literature. Wegener [2000] studies the representation of Boolean-valued functions in the context of decision diagrams and concludes that an adapted representation is

> "... useful if the considered function has a natural description with multivalued [here: multi-state] variables."
>
> [Wegener, 2000, Section 9.1, page 216]

The adapted decision diagrams are called *multivalued decision diagrams* (MDD). In the following, we adjust the considered graphical propositional languages to represent Boolean-valued functions. The common roof is the adjustment of PDAG which is defined as follows:

Definition 27. A *multi-state DAG* (or *multivalued*) (MDAG) is a rooted directed acyclic graph of the following form:

(i) Terminals are represented by □ and labeled with ⊥ (contradiction), ⊤ (tautology) or a tuple (V, Ω) consisting of a variable $V \in \mathbf{V}$ and a subset $\Omega \subset \Omega_V$;

(ii) Non-terminals are represented by ○ and labeled with ∧ (conjunction), ∨ (disjunction), ¬ (negation), or a variable $V \in \mathbf{V}$;

    a) Non-terminals labeled with ∧ or ∨ have at least one child;

    b) Non-terminals labeled with ¬ have exactly one child;

    c) Non-terminals labeled with V have exactly $|\Omega_V|$ children, for each $v \in \Omega_V$ there is a v-child.

4.1 Boolean-Valued Functions

Figure 4.1 depicts an MDAG representing the Boolean-valued function corresponding to the formula

$$((Y, \{y_1\}) \wedge (X, \{x_1, x_2\}))$$
$$\vee (\neg (X, \{x_1, x_2\}) \wedge (Y, \{y_2\}))$$
$$\vee ((X, \{x_3\}) \wedge (Y, \{y_3, y_4\})).$$

The definition from above is more flexible than the previous one by Wachter and Haenni [2007a], where Ω is supposed to be a singleton, i.e. it contains exactly one state of the variable. As mentioned in Section 1.2.2, $(V = v)$ is equivalent to $(V, \{v\})$. A (V, Ω)-terminal denotes a leaf labeled with (V, Ω) and means that the state of variable V is an element of Ω. Hence, the negation of a (V, Ω)-terminal is equivalent to a $(V, \Omega_V \setminus \Omega)$-terminal. From this point of view, simple negations are already included in the set of all terminals $\{(V, \Omega)\text{-terminal} \mid V \in \mathbf{V}, \Omega \subseteq \Omega_V\}$ labeled with a variable $V \in \mathbf{V}$ and $\Omega \subseteq \Omega_V$. Furthermore, *(multi-state) terms* and *(multi-state) clauses* contain multi-state terminals with $\emptyset \neq \Omega \neq \Omega_V$ for $V \in \mathbf{V}$. In the following, we consider only the multi-state languages depicted in Table 4.1. We do not include the multi-state variants of the languages IP and PI.

The structural reduction rules also apply to MDAGs. In addition to the previous rules, there is an enhanced version of isomorphism.

Definition 28. A terminal labeled with (V, Ω_V) is *enhanced isomorphic* to a $\top$-terminal, whereas a terminal labeled with $(V, \emptyset)$ is *enhanced isomorphic* to a $\bot$-terminal.

For following the discussion, we only consider reduced representations, i.e. representation which are also free of enhanced isomorphism in addition to the previous requirements. The idea is to set up a knowledge compilation map for MDAG based on the adapted versions of the queries and transformations. Besides handling of multi-state variable instead of Boolean variables, the queries and transformations depend on the satisfying set. For a representation φ of a Boolean-valued function f_φ, the satisfying set is $[\![\varphi]\!] = f_\varphi^{-1}(1)$, analog to the definition of the satisfying set of a representation of a Boolean function. In addition, we assume that the term within term conditioning consists of (V, Ω)-terminals with $|\Omega| = 1$. The new transformation *general term conditioning* (TC_*) compensates this restriction. Since general term conditioning is closely related to existential forgetting, we also introduce *deterministic general term conditioning* (TC_*^d). For this we suppose that the variables within the term are deterministic.

Chapter 4 Extending the Knowledge Compilation Map

Multi-state Language	Definition	Boolean Counterpart
MDAG	$T[\wedge, \vee, \neg, v_I \langle \rangle]$	PDAG
cd-MDAG	$T[\times, +, \neg, v_I \lfloor \rfloor]$	cd-PDAG
f-MDAG	$T[\neg][\wedge][\neg][\vee][\neg] \cup T[\neg][\vee][\neg][\wedge][\neg]$	f-PDAG
cn-MDAG	$T[\times, \vee, v_I \lfloor \rfloor]$	DNNF
cdn-MDAG	$T[\times, +, v_I \lfloor \rfloor]$	d-DNNF
MDNF	$L[\times][\vee] \cup \{\bot\text{-terminal}\}$	DNF
d-MDNF	$L[\times][+] \cup \{\bot\text{-terminal}\}$	d-DNF
MMODS	$L[\times][+_s] \cup \{\bot\text{-terminal}\}$	MODS
MCNF	$L[\overline{\times}][\wedge] \cup \{\top\text{-terminal}\}$	CNF
MDD	$\{\bot\text{-terminal}, \top\text{-terminal}\}[v_1 \langle \rangle, \ldots, v_r \langle], \rangle$	BDD
FMDD	$\{\bot\text{-terminal}, \top\text{-terminal}\}[v_1 \lfloor \rfloor, \ldots, v_r \lfloor \rfloor,]$	BDD
G-FMDD	FMDD guided by graph order G	G-FBDD
π-OMDD	$\{\bot\text{-terminal}, \top\text{-terminal}\}[\pi(r) \lfloor \rfloor] \cdots [\pi(1) \lfloor \rfloor]$	π-OBDD
OMDD	$\bigcup_{\pi \in \Pi(1,\ldots,r)} \pi\text{-OBDD}$	OBDD

Table 4.1: Multi-state languages and their Boolean counterpart for the variables $\mathbf{V} = \{V_1, \ldots, V_r\}$, where T is the set of terminals labeled with $\bot$, $\top$, and (V, Ω) with $V \in \mathbf{V}$ and $\Omega \subseteq \Omega_V$, and L is the set consisting of the terminals labeled with (V, Ω) with $V \in \mathbf{V}$ and $\Omega \subseteq \Omega_V$ and the $\neg$-nodes with such a terminal as child. Note that c stands for decomposability, d for determinism, n for negation-free (instead of simple-negation), and f for flat.

4.1 Boolean-Valued Functions

Based on the proposition below, we already obtain some results for the knowledge compilation map of Boolean-valued functions.

Proposition 1.9. *The results from* PDAG *are handed over to* MDAG *as follows:*

- Succinctness: *For each pair of multi-state languages* M, M', *together with their Boolean counterparts* P, P' *(see Table 4.1), we have*

$$P \npreceq P' \Rightarrow M \npreceq M'$$
$$\left(M \preceq M' \Rightarrow P \preceq P'\right).$$

- Queries: *For each multi-state language* M *together with its Boolean counterpart* P, *and for each query* Q, *we have*

$$Q \notin \text{queries}(P) \Rightarrow Q \notin \text{queries}(M)$$
$$\left(Q \in \text{queries}(M) \Rightarrow Q \in \text{queries}(P)\right).$$

- Transformations: *For each multi-state language* M *together with its Boolean counterpart* P, *and for each transformation* T, *we have*

$$T \notin \text{transformations}(P) \Rightarrow T \notin \text{transformations}(M)$$
$$\left(T \in \text{transformations}(M) \Rightarrow T \in \text{transformations}(P)\right).$$

This proposition is a direct consequence of the fact that each Boolean function is also a Boolean-valued one. It permits the transfer of the corresponding results from the Boolean to the multi-state map. For the remaining parts of the multi-state knowledge compilation map, we have to consider the corresponding proofs of the Boolean map. In the majority of cases, the "Boolean" proof also leads to a "multi-state" proof. This leads to the following result for the succinctness relations.

Proposition 1.10. *For each pair of multi-state languages* M, M', *together with their Boolean counterparts* P, P', *we have*

$$M_1 \preceq M_2 \Leftrightarrow P_1 \preceq P_2.$$

I.e. the succinctness relationship of two multi-state languages matches the succinctness relationship of their Boolean counterparts. There is a similar result for queries, namely:

Chapter 4 Extending the Knowledge Compilation Map

Proposition 1.11. *For each multi-state language* M *together with its Boolean counterpart* P*, we have*

$$queries(\texttt{M}) = queries(\texttt{P}).$$

In other words, a multi-state language supports the same queries as its Boolean counterpart. The result on transformations is more complex.

Proposition 1.12. *For each multi-state language*

$$\texttt{M} \in \{\texttt{MDAG}, \texttt{cd-MDAG}, \texttt{dn-MDAG}, \texttt{cn-MDAG}, \texttt{cdn-MDAG}, \texttt{MDD}, G\text{-FMDD}\}$$

together with its Boolean counterpart P*, we have*

$$trans(\texttt{M}) = trans(\texttt{P}). \tag{4.1}$$

As long as the variable V (with $\varphi \in$ M) in $\exists V.\varphi$, $\exists_d V.\varphi$, $\forall V.\varphi$, and $\forall_c V.\varphi$ has only two states, this result also holds for the remaining languages. For a variable V with more than two states, the transformations $\texttt{SFO}_\exists$, $\texttt{SFO}_\exists^d$, $\texttt{SFO}_\forall$, *and* $\texttt{SFO}_\forall^c$ *are only supported by the languages* f-MDAG, FMDD, OMDD, π-OMDD, MDNF, MCNF, d-MDNF, MMODS *as shown in Table 4.2.*

The transformations $\texttt{TC}_*$ and $\texttt{TC}_*^d$ are closely related to $\texttt{FO}_\exists$ and $\texttt{FO}_\exists^d$ respectively. Therefore, they are not mentioned explicitly.

4.2 Generalizations of Boolean-valued Functions

Consider a function f with domain $D = \Omega_1 \times \cdots \times \Omega_r$ where each Ω_i is a finite frame of a variable. If f is a Boolean-valued function, its codomain would be $\mathbb{B} = \{0, 1\}$. Now we will analyze what happens if the codomain is changed. For this purpose, we consider two ways. On one hand, the codomain could be $\mathbb{B}^s$ instead of $\mathbb{B}$. On the other hand, the codomain could be an arbitrary (possibly infinite) set C.

4.2 Generalizations of Boolean-valued Functions

	$\|\Omega_V\|=2$				$\|\Omega_V\|>2$			
	SFO$_\exists$	SFO$_\exists^d$	SFO$_\forall$	SFO$_\forall^c$	SFO$_\exists$	SFO$_\exists^d$	SFO$_\forall$	SFO$_\forall^c$
MDAG	✓	✓	✓	✓	✓	✓	✓	✓
f-MDAG	✓	✓	✓	✓	?	?	?	?
cd-MDAG	∘	✓	∘	✓	∘	✓	∘	✓
dn-MDAG	✓	✓	✓	✓	✓	✓	✓	✓
cn-MDAG	✓	✓	∘	✓	✓	✓	∘	✓
cdn-MDAG	∘	✓	∘	✓	∘	✓	∘	✓
MDD	✓	✓	✓	✓	✓	✓	•	✓
FMDD	∘	?	∘	✓	•	?	•	✓
OMDD	✓	✓	✓	✓	•	?	•	?
π-OMDD	✓	✓	✓	✓	✓	?	✓	?
MDNF	✓	✓	✓	✓	✓	✓	•	?
MCNF	✓	✓	✓	✓	•	?	✓	✓
d-MDNF	?	✓	?	✓	?	✓	?	?
MMODS	✓	✓	✓	✓	✓	✓	?	?

Table 4.2: Subsets of the MDAG and their supported kinds of singleton forgetting transformations. ✓ means "supports", • means "does not support", ∘ means "does not support unless P = NP", and ? means "unknown". $\mathcal{G}$-FMDD is omitted because of a clash between the definitions of the transformations and the language itself.

Chapter 4 Extending the Knowledge Compilation Map

4.2.1 Functions with Codomain $\mathbb{B}^s$

Consider the function

$$f : \Omega_1 \times \cdots \times \Omega_r \to \overbrace{\mathbb{B} \times \cdots \times \mathbb{B}}^{s}$$
$$(v_1, \ldots, v_r) \mapsto f(v_1, \ldots, v_r) = (w_1, \ldots, w_s).$$

which can be easily represented by a tuple $(f_1, \ldots, f_s)$ of r-ary Boolean-valued functions with $f_i(v_1, \ldots, v_r) = w_i$. The tuple of the representations is called a *multi-rooted* DAG. Analog to Wegener [2000], each representation of the function f_i within the tuple is called a *shared* MDAG, since it may share nodes with the representations of other functions f_j, $j \neq i$, of the same tuple or another one.

Instead of a tuple $(f_1, \ldots, f_s)$, there is another way to represent the function f. For this new representation, we introduce a variable $V \notin \mathbf{V}$ with $\Omega_V = \{1, \ldots, s\}$. The variable V is used to select one of the functions f_i within the tuple, hence V is called *selector variable*. Now, a (multi-state) decision node $v\langle f_1, \ldots, f_s\rangle$ represents f. More exactly, this means that we represent the function

$$f : \Omega_{V_1} \times \cdots \times \Omega_{V_r} \to \mathbb{B}^s$$

by the Boolean-valued function

$$f' : \Omega_{V_1} \times \cdots \times \Omega_{V_r} \times \Omega_V \to \mathbb{B}.$$

For $\mathbf{v} \in \Omega_{V_1} \times \cdots \times \Omega_{V_r}$, we get $f(\mathbf{v}) = (f'(\mathbf{v}, 1), \ldots, f'(\mathbf{v}, s))$. The advantage of this representation is that there is no need to construct a new knowledge compilation map for functions with co-domain $\mathbb{B}^s$, since this kind of generalization is reducible to Boolean-valued functions again. In addition, it also allows us to transfer the meaning of the queries and transformations to functions with codomain $\mathbb{B}^s$.

4.2.2 Functions with arbitrary Codomain C

Consider the function

$$f : \Omega_{V_1} \times \cdots \times \Omega_{V_r} \to C$$
$$(v_1, \ldots, v_r) \mapsto f(v_1, \ldots, v_r) = c$$

4.2 Generalizations of Boolean-valued Functions

with an arbitrary (possibly infinite) set C. Due to the fact that $\Omega_\mathbf{V} = \Omega_{V_1} \times \cdots \times \Omega_{V_r}$ is finite, the range of f, $f(\Omega_\mathbf{V}) = \{f(\mathbf{v}) | \mathbf{v} \in \Omega_\mathbf{V}\} = \{c_1, \ldots, c_t\}$, is also finite (even if C is infinite). To transfer the queries and transformations, we follow a similar strategy as above and represent f by a tuple of Boolean-valued functions.

Consider the Boolean-valued functions f_i, $1 \leq i \leq t$, with $f_i(\mathbf{v}) = 1$ if and only iff $f(\mathbf{v}) = c_i$. Note that $[\![f_i]\!] \cap [\![f_j]\!] = \emptyset$ for $i \neq j$ and $\bigcup_{i=1}^{t} [\![f_i]\!] = \Omega_\mathbf{V}$, i.e. we have a partition of $\Omega_\mathbf{V}$ consisting of the blocks $[\![f_i]\!]$, $1 \leq i \leq t$. As before, we could represent f by $(f_1, \ldots, f_t)$ with $f_i(\mathbf{v}) = 1 \Leftrightarrow f(\mathbf{v}) = c_i$. Again, we could also introduce a new variable $V \notin \mathbf{V}$ with $\Omega_V = \{1, \ldots, t\}$. Then, the (multi-state) decision node $v\langle f_1, \ldots, f_t\rangle$ represents f. More precisely, the Boolean-valued function f' defined by

$$f' : \Omega_{V_1} \times \cdots \times \Omega_{V_r} \times \Omega_V \to \mathbb{B}$$
$$(v_1, \ldots, v_r, i) \mapsto f'(v_1, \ldots, v_r, i)$$

represents the function f where $f'(v_1, \ldots, v_r, i) = 1$ if and only if $f(v_1, \ldots, v_r) = c_i$, i.e. $f'(\mathbf{v}, i) = f_i(\mathbf{v})$. Again, V is called *selector variable*. The difference between the representation of a function with codomain $\mathbb{B}^s$ and the representation of a function with arbitrary codomain C, it the fact that V is deterministic with respect to the second representation. Thus, the representation f' is automatically deterministic, if each f_i is deterministic.

4.2.3 Alternative Representation

In the context of decision diagrams, there is another approach to represent a function f with an arbitrary (possibly infinite) set C (this includes $\mathbb{B}^s$). As in the previous subsection, the range of f, $f(\Omega_\mathbf{V}) = \{f(\mathbf{v}) | \mathbf{v} \in \Omega_\mathbf{V}\} = \{c_1, \ldots, c_t\}$, is finite (even if C is infinite). We represent f by a decision diagram. Instead of the $\bot$- and the $\top$-terminal, we use a terminal labeled with c_i for each $c_i \in f(\Omega_\mathbf{V})$. Then, we represent f by the diagram, where a path corresponding to $\mathbf{v} \in \Omega_\mathbf{V}$ ends in the terminal labeled with c_i if and only if $f(\mathbf{v}) = c_i$. For Boolean case, i.e. $\Omega_\mathbf{V} = \mathbb{B}^r$, this kind of representation is called *multiterminal BDD* (MTBDD) or *algebraic decision diagram* (ADD) according to Wegener [2000]. For multi-state variables, we obtain *multiterminal MDDs* (MTMDD). Of course, it is also possible to require preconditions on a MTBDD and a MTMDD. Although the combination of MTBDD and MDD is not discussed in detail, most of its properties (succinctness, supported queries and transforma-

Chapter 4 Extending the Knowledge Compilation Map

tions) are easily obtained by considering the knowledge compilation map for Boolean-valued functions.

4.3 Example

For $\Omega_X = \Omega_Y = \{0, 1, 2\}$, consider the two functions f and g,

$$f : \Omega_X \times \Omega_Y \to \mathbb{B}^2, \qquad\qquad g : \Omega_X \times \Omega_Y \to \mathbb{N}$$

as defined in Figure 4.2(a). While f is a generalization of Boolean-valued functions of the first kind, g is one of the second kind. In the following, let x be a state of X and y be a state of Y, in other words, $x \in \Omega_X$ and $y \in \Omega_Y$. First, we concentrate on f, and afterwards on g. Finally, we also provide the alternative representation and discuss the different approaches.

We choose OMDDs as representation for a fair comparison with ordered MTMDDs (OMT-MDD). To improve readability, the $\bot$-terminal and edges leading towards it are omitted in the OMDDs

Functions with codomain $\mathbb{B}^s$: As suggested, we represent f by two (shared) OMDDs f_1, f_2 such that $f(x, y) = (f_1(x, y), f_2(x, y))$, see Figure 4.2(b). By adding a decision node for the variable A with $\Omega_A = \{1, 2\}$ to choose between f_1 and f_2 on top of f_1 and f_2, we obtain the function $f' : \Omega_X \times \Omega_Y \times \Omega_A \to \mathbb{B}$ as depicted in Figure 4.2(c) such that $f(x, y) = (f'(x, y, 1), f'(x, y, 2))$.

Functions with arbitrary codomain C: There are two similar representations for g. The first one is the tuple (g_0, g_1, g_2, g_3) such that $g(x, y) = i$ if and only if $g_i(x, y) = 1$, see Figure 4.2(d). By adding a decision node for the variable B with $\Omega_B = \{0, 1, 2, 3\}$ to choose between g_i on top of g_i, $0 \le i \le 3$, we obtain the function $g' : \Omega_X \times \Omega_Y \times \Omega_B \to \mathbb{B}$ with $g'(x, y, i) = 1$ if and only if $g(x, y) = i$ as depicted in Figure 4.2(e).

Alternative representation: g is also represented by the OMTMDD of Figure 4.2(f).

Up to now, we considered the two approaches for representing f and the three approaches to represent g but not the relation between f and g. Obviously, $f(x, y) = (b_1, b_2)$ with $b_i \in \mathbb{B}$ is a bit representation of the values of g where b_1 is the most and b_2 is the least significant bit. Hence, the representations of f are also representations of g and vice versa. In general, this relation might be less obvious. For example, if the values of g are enumerated and f

4.3 Example

X	Y	f	g
0	0	(0,1)	1
0	1	(1,0)	2
0	2	(0,0)	0
1	0	(1,1)	3
1	1	(1,1)	3
1	2	(0,0)	0
2	0	(1,0)	2
2	1	(0,1)	1
2	2	(1,1)	3

(a) The functions f and g

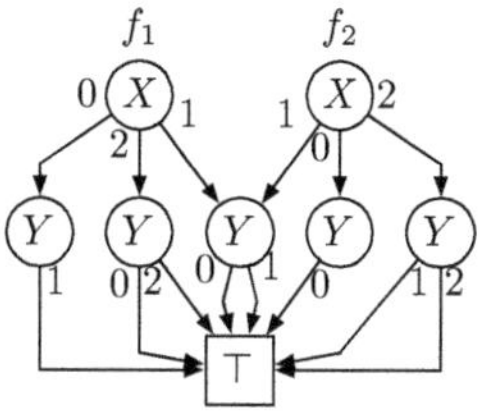

(b) Representing f by (f_1, f_2)

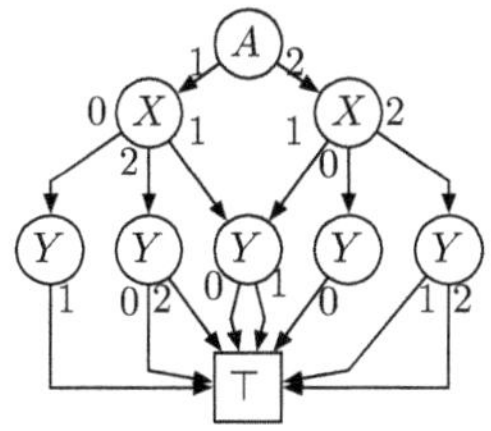

(c) Representing f by f'

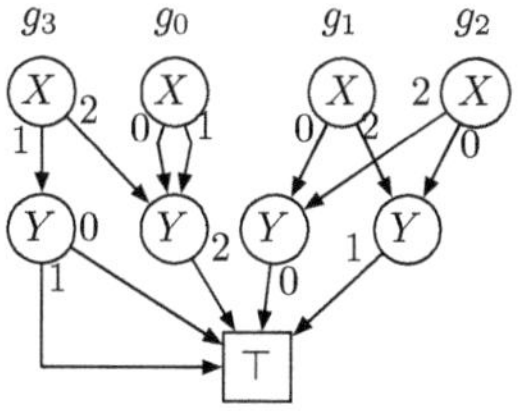

(d) Representing g by $(g_0, \ldots, g_3)$

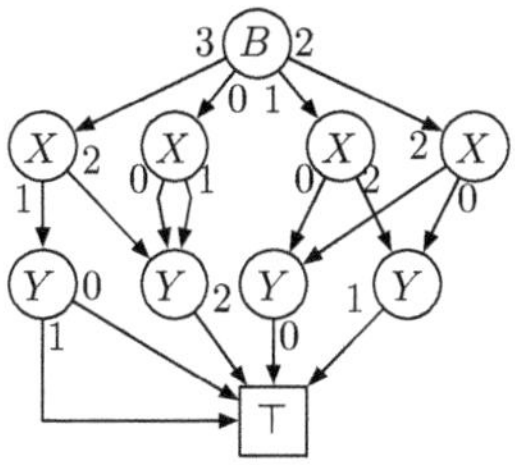

(e) Representing g by g'

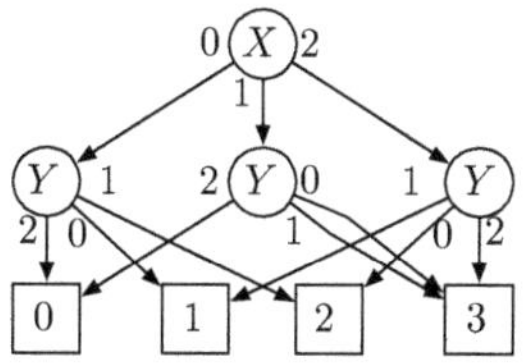

(f) Representing g by a MTMDD

Figure 4.2: The functions f and g and their different representations. The $\bot$-terminal and edges directed towards it are omitted due to readability.

represents the bits of the enumeration instead of the value itself. While all representations have their advantages and disadvantages, the interesting question 'which of them is more useful?' remains unanswered.

4.4 Recapitulation: Extending the Knowledge Compilation Map

In this chapter, we generalized the results of the knowledge compilation map to Boolean-valued functions. For this, we split the existential and universal quantification of a single variable into two cases to obtain a more precise result. In the first case, we considered the quantification of a variable with two states. Here, the different quantification queries are supported by a language for representing Boolean-valued functions, if the queries are supported by the corresponding language for representing Boolean functions. The second case covers the quantification of a variable with more than two states. In this case only some languages for representing Boolean-valued functions coincide with their corresponding language for Boolean functions regarding the different quantification queries for single variables. For the remaining languages, we obtain different results due to the fact that the transformation disjunction (OR) is not supported.

In the next step, we considered generalizations of Boolean-valued functions and showed that they can be reduced to a tuple of Boolean-valued functions or even a single Boolean-valued function with an additional selector variable. In addition, an alternative approach is discussed where the terminals of an MDD contain the values of the function, which leads to a MTMDD. This new map can also be used to find an appropriate representation for a functions f and g with $f : \Omega_\mathbf{V} \to \mathbb{B}^s$ or $g : \Omega_\mathbf{V} \to C$.

Part II

Applying the Knowledge Compilation Map

Chapter 5

Semiring Valuation Algebras

To cover a whole range of application areas in a single generic framework, we start with a special kind of the theory of *valuation algebras* introduced by Kohlas [2003]. The basic elements of a valuation algebra are *valuations*, which can be regarded as pieces of information about the possible values of some variables. Thus, if $\mathbf{V}$ denotes the set of all variables relevant to a problem, then each valuation φ refers to a finite set of variables $d(\varphi) \subseteq \mathbf{V}$, called its *domain*. For an arbitrary set $\mathbf{W} \subseteq \mathbf{V}$ of variables, $\Phi_\mathbf{W}$ denotes the set of all valuations φ with $d(\varphi) = \mathbf{W}$. With this notation, we can write

$$\Phi = \bigcup_{\mathbf{W} \subseteq \mathbf{V}} \Phi_\mathbf{W} \qquad (5.1)$$

to denote the set of all possible valuations over $\mathbf{V}$. For the variables $\mathbf{V}$, we define the three primitive operations of a valuation algebra as follows[1]:

- *Labeling*: $\Phi \to \mathcal{P}(\mathbf{V})$, $\varphi \mapsto d(\varphi) = \mathbf{W}$, if $\varphi \in \Phi_\mathbf{W}$;
- *Combination*: $\Phi \times \Phi \to \Phi$, $(\varphi, \psi) \mapsto \varphi \otimes \psi$;
- *Variable elimination*: $\Phi \times \mathbf{V} \to \Phi$, $(\varphi, V) \mapsto \varphi^{-V}$.

These operations lead to the following definition.

Definition 29 (Kohlas [2003]). A tuple $(\Phi, \mathcal{P}(\mathbf{V}), d, \otimes, -)$ is a *valuation algebra*, if it satisfies the following set of axioms:

  (i) *Commutative Semigroup:* Φ is associative and commutative under $\otimes$.

---
[1] The more general definition given in Kohlas [2003] considers arbitrary distributive lattices. In this case, we must replace the operation of variable elimination by marginalization.

Chapter 5 Semiring Valuation Algebras

(ii) *Labeling*: If $\varphi, \psi \in \Phi$, then $d(\varphi \otimes \psi) = d(\varphi) \cup d(\psi)$.

(iii) *Variable Elimination*: If $\varphi \in \Phi$ and $V \in d(\varphi)$, then $d(\varphi^{-V}) = d(\varphi) - \{V\}$.

(iv) *Commutativity of Elimination*: If $\varphi \in \Phi_\mathbf{V}$ and $V, W \in d(\varphi)$, then $(\varphi^{-V})^{-W} = (\varphi^{-W})^{-V}$.

(v) *Combination*: If $\varphi, \psi \in \Phi$ with $V \notin d(\varphi)$ and $V \in d(\psi)$, then $(\varphi \otimes \psi)^{-V} = \varphi \otimes \psi^{-V}$.

Instances of valuation algebras are large in number and occur in very different contexts. For an extensive list of valuation algebra instances, we refer to Kohlas [2003].

5.1 Semiring Valuations

An important class of valuation algebras, which actually covers a majority of the known instances, results from the notion of *semiring valuations*. For this, let the elements $V \in \mathbf{V}$ be variables with finite frames Ω_V. By convention, we define the frame of the empty variable set as $\Omega_\emptyset = \{\diamond\}$. Furthermore, we write $\mathbf{v}^{\downarrow \mathbf{W}}$ for the projection of an assignment $\mathbf{v} \in \Omega_\mathbf{V}$ to a subset $\mathbf{W} \subseteq \mathbf{V}$. In particular, we have $\mathbf{v}^{\downarrow \emptyset} = \diamond$.

Definition 30 (Kohlas [2004]). A *semiring valuation* φ is a function

$$\varphi : \Omega_\mathbf{V} \to A$$

from the set of assignments $\Omega_\mathbf{V}$ to the set of values A of a commutative semiring $(A, +, \times)$.

Figure 5.1 depicts such a semiring valuation. Note that as a valuation algebra the domain of φ is $\mathbf{V}$, whereas as a function its domain is $\Omega_\mathbf{V}$. Obviously, φ corresponds to a generalized Boolean-valued function of the kind $f : \Omega_\mathbf{V} \to C$ where C is the set of values of a commutative semiring. With respect to the set Φ of all semiring valuations over the variables $\mathbf{V}$, the operations of combination and variable elimination are defined in terms of the semiring operations $+$ and $\times$ as follows:

Combination: For $\mathbf{v} \in \Omega_{d(\varphi) \cup d(\psi)}$, let

$$\varphi \otimes \psi (\mathbf{v}) = \varphi \left(\mathbf{v}^{\downarrow d(\varphi)}\right) \times \psi \left(\mathbf{v}^{\downarrow d(\psi)}\right).$$

X	Y	φ
0	0	a_0
0	1	a_1
0	2	a_2
1	0	a_3
1	1	a_4
1	2	a_5
2	0	a_6
2	1	a_7
2	2	a_8

Figure 5.1: A semiring valuation φ with $a_i \in A$ and $d(\varphi) = \{X, Y\}$ where $\Omega_X = \Omega_Y = \{0, 1, 2\}$.

Variable Elimination: For $V \in d(\varphi)$ with $\Omega_V = \{v_1, \ldots, v_t\}$, and $\mathbf{u} \in \Omega_{d(\varphi) \setminus \{V\}}$, let

$$\varphi^{-V}(\mathbf{u}) = \varphi(\mathbf{u}, v_1) + \cdots + \varphi(\mathbf{u}, v_t) = \sum_{i=1}^{r} \varphi(\mathbf{u}, v_i).$$

The most important property of semiring valuations is described in the following theorem.

Theorem 2 (Kohlas [2004], Kohlas and Wilson [2006]). *For labeling, combination and variable elimination as defined above, a set Φ of semiring valuations, closed w.r.t. combination and variable elimination, satisfies the axioms of a valuation algebra.*

The insight that every semiring induces a valuation algebra foreshadows the richness of formalisms that are covered by this theory. For the *Boolean semiring* $(\mathbb{B}, \vee, \wedge)$, semiring valuations correspond to Boolean-valued functions. Furthermore, when all frames Ω_V for the variables $V \in \mathbf{V}$ are binary, i.e. $\Omega_V = \mathbb{B}$ and $\Omega_{\mathbf{V}} = \mathbb{B}^r$, then the valuations are Boolean functions.

5.2 Local Computation

The computational interest in valuation algebras arises from the following notion of an *inference problem* and the generality of the resulting solution. For a given set of valuations $\{\varphi_1, \ldots, \varphi_n\}$, called the *knowledge base*, the inference problem consists in eliminating from

Chapter 5 Semiring Valuation Algebras

the *joint valuation* $\varphi = \varphi_1 \otimes \cdots \otimes \varphi_n$ with $d(\varphi) = \mathbf{V}$ all variables that do not belong to some set $\mathbf{Q} \subseteq \mathbf{V}$ of *query variables*. More formally, this means to computate

$$\varphi^{-\mathbf{V}\setminus\mathbf{Q}} = (\varphi_1 \otimes \cdots \otimes \varphi_n)^{-\mathbf{V}\setminus\mathbf{Q}}.$$

Note that the transitivity of the variable elimination allows us to eliminate sets of variables, e.g. $\mathbf{V} \setminus \mathbf{Q}$, without further specifying the ordering (see axiom (iv)).

To solve the inference problem efficiently, it is clear that an explicit computation of the joint valuation is normally not feasible[2]. *Local computation* methods counteract this problem by organizing the computations in such a way that the maximal domain size remains reasonably bounded. In the following, we restrict our attention to one such algorithm called *fusion algorithm*[3] according to Shenoy [1992] and refer to Schneuwly et al. [2004] for a broad discussion of related local computation schemes.

To describe the fusion algorithm, we consider first the elimination of a single variable V from a set of valuations $\Psi \subseteq \Phi$, which is defined by

$$\mathrm{Fus}_V(\Psi) = \{\psi_V^{-V}\} \cup \{\varphi \in \Psi \mid V \notin d(\varphi)\}$$

with $\psi_V = \otimes \{\varphi \in \Psi \mid V \in d(\varphi)\}$. The fusion algorithm follows then from a repeated application of this basic operation to all variables in $\mathbf{V} \setminus \mathbf{Q} = \{V_1, \ldots, V_k\}$. The order in which the variables are eliminated dues not influence the result itself but the time required to compute the result. Fortunately, there are good heuristics that provide decent orders Haenni and Lehmann [2000]. This leads to the following general solution for the inference problem:

$$\begin{aligned}\varphi^{-\mathbf{V}\setminus\mathbf{Q}} &= (\varphi_1 \otimes \cdots \otimes \varphi_n)^{-\{V_1,\ldots,V_k\}} \\ &= \otimes \mathrm{Fus}_{V_k}(\cdots(\mathrm{Fus}_{V_1}(\{\varphi_1,\ldots,\varphi_n\}))\cdots).\end{aligned}$$

We refer to Kohlas [2003] for a proof and further considerations regarding the complexity of this generic inference algorithm.

---

[2] In most cases, the complexity of valuation algebra operations tends to increase exponentially with the size of the involved domains.
[3] Other names for exactly the same type of algorithm are *bucket elimination* Dechter [1999] or simply *variable elimination* Zhang and Poole [1996]. The algorithm is also closely related to the *collect algorithm* Kohlas [2003]

5.3 Representing Semiring Valuations

An optimized representation of the valuations is important to further speed up the fusion algorithm, i.e. to go beyond the capacities offered by local computation. Fortunately, the knowledge compilation map addresses exactly this problem. While Chavira and Darwiche [2007] consider a particular instance of semiring valuations with Boolean variables, we consider semiring valuations in general. The following analysis is based on the assumption that both operations $+$ and $\times$ of a semiring can be performed in time polynomial in the size of the chosen representation of the semiring valuations.

In general, a semiring valuation φ is represented by a table similar to truth table. The difference is that instead of the Boolean values 0 and 1 the right-most column contains elements of the set A. Hence, the idea is to replace this representation by a more appropriate one. For this, the two essential operations of combination and variable elimination have to be analyzed in order to determine the required queries and transformations. The labeling operation is negligible, since it can be achieved easily. This is the common starting point for two approaches.

5.3.1 Approach A

In the following, we assume that the valuations, e.g.

$$\varphi : \Omega_\mathbf{V} \to A, \qquad \psi : \Omega_\mathbf{W} \to A,$$
$$\mathbf{v} \mapsto \varphi(\mathbf{v}) = a, \qquad \mathbf{w} \mapsto \psi(\mathbf{w}) = b,$$

are represented by sets of pairs consisting of a Boolean-valued function and a semiring value, e.g. $\{(f_i, a_i)\}$, $\{(g_j, b_j)\}$. The satisfying sets of the functions partition the domain of the functions, here $\Omega_\mathbf{V}$ and $\Omega_\mathbf{W}$, such that there is one block for each value in the range of the valuation. I.e. $f_{i_1} \wedge f_{i_2} \equiv \bot$ and $a_{i_1} \neq a_{i_2}$ for $i_1 \neq i_2$ as well as $g_{j_1} \wedge g_{j_2} \equiv \bot$ and $b_{j_1} \neq b_{j_2}$ for $j_1 \neq j_2$. Let us now discuss the combination and variable elimination. Note that grouping pairs might also be required for a valuation arising form a combination or variable elimination. Hence, grouping is discussed after combination and variable elimination.

Combination: It is quite obvious that $\varphi \otimes \psi$ essentially consists of all combined entries $(f_i \wedge g_j, a_i \times b_j)$, except of the ones with $f_i \wedge g_j \equiv f_\bot$. In our terminology, $f_i \wedge g_j$ corresponds

Chapter 5 Semiring Valuation Algebras

to the transformation AND_2, and the test $f_i \wedge g_j \equiv f_\perp$ corresponds to the query IN. Hence, both AND_2 and IN are required for the combination of two semiring valuations. Obviously, the combination of three or more valuations requires the transformation AND instead of AND_2. It is important to keep in mind that the representation of the resulting valuation might have more than one entry for the same semiring value a, e.g. $4 \times 3 = 2 \times 6$. To take care of these entries, it is necessary to group them, which is discussed after variable elimination.

Variable Elimination: For the elimination of a variable $V \in d(\varphi)$ from φ, it is possible to express φ^{-V} in terms of a similar operation as above. For this, let $\varphi|v$ denote the result of conditioning φ on a value $v \in \Omega_V$. The idea is to delete from each Boolean-valued function f_i the part which is inconsistent with $V = v$, and then project all remaining function to $\mathbf{V} \setminus \{V\}$. This can be achieved by conditioning each f_i on v. Note that $f_i|(V, \{v\})$ may become equivalent to $\perp$ for some $i \in \{1, \ldots, s\}$ where $s = |\{(f_i, a_i)\}|$. Conditioning a Boolean-valued functions corresponds to the transformation term conditioning TC.

In the Boolean case, i.e. for $\Omega_V = \{0, 1\}$, let $I, J \subseteq \{1, \ldots, s\}$ contain the indices of each $f_i|(V, \{0\}) \neq f_\perp$ resp. $f_i|(V, \{1\}) \neq f_\perp$. With this, we obtain φ^{-V} by computing all combined entries $(f_i|(V, \{0\}) \wedge f_j|(V, \{1\}), a_i + a_j)$ for $i \in I$ and $j \in J$. Note that we may again get and delete some functions $f_i|(V, \{0\}) \wedge f_j|(V, \{1\})$ equivalent to $f_\perp$. Eliminating a Boolean variable from semiring valuations requires thus TC, AND_2, and IN.

For non-Boolean variables, this gets more complicated. Consider the variable V with $\Omega_V = \{v_1, \ldots, v_t\}$. For $j \in \{1, \ldots, t\}$, let $I_j \subseteq \{1, \ldots, s\}$ contain the indices of each $f_i|(V, \{v_j\}) \neq f_\perp$. Then, we get the combined entries $(f_{i_1}|(V, \{v_1\}) \wedge \cdots \wedge f_{i_t}|(V, \{v_t\}), a_{i_1} + \cdots + a_{i_t})$ for $i_j \in I_j$. Obviously, eliminating a non-Boolean variable from semiring valuations requires AND instead of AND_2 in addition to TC and IN. Note also that eliminating more than one variable also requires AND, even if all variables are Boolean ones.

Again, we have to keep in mind that the representation of the resulting valuation might have more than one entry for the same semiring value a, e.g. $4 + 3 = 2 + 5$. To take care of these entries, it is necessary to group them, which is discussed below.

Grouping: As mentioned before the representation of a valuation, resulting from combination or variable elimination, might have more than one entry for the same semiring

5.3 Representing Semiring Valuations

value a. Consider the valuation φ represented by $\{(f_i, a_i)\}$ where $f_{i_1} \wedge f_{i_2} \equiv \bot$ for all $i_1 \neq i_2$ and $a_{i_1} = a_{i_2}$ for some $i_1 \neq i_2$. To obtain a valuation that satisfies the assumption $a_{j_1} \neg a_{j_2}$ for all $j_1 \neq j_2$ we have to replace these pairs by a single pair. E.g. if there are (f_{k_j}, a_{k_j}) with $a_{k_j} = a$ for $1 \leq j \leq s$ and $s \geq 2$, then, we replace (f_{k_j}, a_{k_j}), $1 \leq j \leq s$, by $(f_{k_1} \vee \cdots \vee f_{k_s}, a)$. Obviously the transformation OR is required. Note that the transformation OR_2 is sufficient, if s is at most 2.

In the end, the queries and transformations required for the fusion algorithm are IN, TC, AND, and OR. Note that in some cases, AND_2 or OR_2 might be sufficient instead of AND or OR. Hence, we are looking for languages that support at least IN, TC, AND_2, and OR_2.

According to our results of the previous part, the query IN is supported by a dozen languages. All of these languages support the transformation TC. However, only three languages are valuable candidates:

- G-FMDD and π-OMDD support IN, TC, AND_2 and OR_2 (but not AND and OR) in polynomial time;

- MDNF supports IN, TC, AND_2 and OR (but not AND) in polynomial time.

Figures 4.2(b)-(e) show four π-OMDD based representations of the semiring valuation g defined in Figure 4.2(a). Note that in terms of their succinctness, G-FMDD, π-OMDD, and MDNF are incomparable. Nevertheless, π-OMDDs are often much smaller than corresponding MDNFs, which is why π-OMDD (resp. π-OBDD) is recommended by Wachter et al. [2007] to be used as representation language for semiring valuations. Note also that the proposed rule-based representation for *Bayesian networks* proposed in Poole and Zhang [2003] is very close to using DNFs.

5.3.2 Approach B

In the previous chapter, we mentioned an alternative representation for functions $f : \Omega_V \to C$. This representation is the combination of MTBDD and MDD. For a semiring C, we consider π-OMTMDD, the language of π-*ordered multiterminal multivalued decision diagrams* (π-OMTMDD). A π-OMTMDD is an OMDD where the labels of the terminals are arbitrary values of the semiring C. Chavira and Darwiche [2007] suggest a special kind of π-OMTMDDs, namely ADDs with a fixed variable order, as representation for Bayesian networks with

Chapter 5 Semiring Valuation Algebras

Boolean variables, an instance of semiring valuations. The revers order used in the elimination processes ensures that when a variable is eliminated from an ADD, it appears at the bottom of the ADD, which is more efficient.

For this approach, we assume, that a valuation is represented by a π-OMTMDD. Again, we have to consider three things:

(i) How to perform combinations? This corresponds to the transformations AND$_2$ and AND. According to the knowledge compilation map, AND$_2$ is supported while AND is not supported by π-OMTMDD.

(ii) How to perform variable eliminations? Obviously, this corresponds to SFO$_\exists$ and FO$_\exists$. However, the ordering ensures that a variable is at the bottom when it is eliminated. Let φ be a node of the variable V with $\Omega_V = \{v_1, \ldots, v_t\}$ which is eliminated next. The children of φ are the terminals τ_i labeled with values $c_i \in C$. Note that $\tau_i = \tau_j$, and, hence, $c_i = c_j$, is possible for some $i, j \in \{1, \ldots, t\}$. To eliminate V, we replace φ by a terminal labeled with $\sum_{i=1}^{t} c_i$. In a similar way, it is also possible to eliminate more than one variable at once.

(iii) How to perform grouping? This is already covered by the structural reduction rules, see Section 2.3.6.

Figure 4.2 (f) shows a π-OMTMDD representing the semiring valuation g defined in Figure 4.2(a). From this point of view, π-OMTMDD is another valuable candidate for representing semiring valuations. The drawback of π-OMTMDD is the same as the one of MDNF, namely that the transformation AND is not supported.

5.4 Recapitulation: Semiring Valuation Algebras

This chapter reviewed the generic theory of valuation algebra with focus on semiring valuations. Additionally, it covered the results of Wachter and Haenni [2007b]. From a computational point of view, we considered the fusion algorithm to demonstrate the advantages of local computation. To further improve the speed of the fusion algorithm, we determined languages for representing semiring valuations by analyzing the combination of valuations and the variable elimination. It turned out that the query IN and the transformations TC, AND, and OR are required. According to those requirements, we identified three valuable candidates, namely MDNF, G-FMDD, and π-OMDD. Unfortunately, none of the candidates supports all

5.4 Recapitulation: Semiring Valuation Algebras

requirements. G-FMDD and π-OMDD only support AND$_2$ and OR$_2$ in addition to TC and IN. On the other side, MDNF supports support AND$_2$ and OR in addition to TC and IN. Inspired by Chavira and Darwiche [2007], we also considered π-OMTMDD which requires only the transformation AND. However, it supports only AND$_2$. In summary, we identified four candidates. G-FMDD and π-OMDD are lacking the transformations AND and OR, while MDNF and π-OMTMDD are lacking the transformation AND.

Chapter 6

Bayesian Networks

According to Pearl [1988], a *Bayesian network* is a compact graphical model of a complex probability distribution over a set of variables $\Delta = \{X_1, \ldots, X_n\}$. It consists of two parts: a DAG representing the direct influences among the variables, and a set of conditional probability tables (CPT) quantifying the strengths of these influences. The whole BN represents the exponentially sized *joint probability distribution* over its variables in a compact manner by

$$P(X_1, \ldots, X_n) = \prod_{i=1}^{r} P(X_i | parents(X_i)),$$

where $parents(X_i)$ denotes the parents of node X_i in the DAG. Figure 6.1 depicts a small Bayesian network with three variables $X, Y,$ and Z.

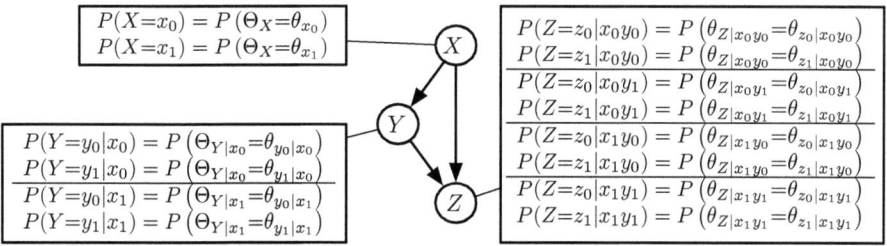

Figure 6.1: Example of a Bayesian network.

93

Chapter 6 Bayesian Networks

6.1 Logical Representation

Consider a variable $X \in \Delta$ with $parents(X) = \{Y_1,\ldots,Y_u\} = \mathbf{Y}$, $\Omega_X = \{x_1,\ldots,x_t\}$, and the corresponding CPT. Since X has u parents and each parent has at least two states, the CPT has $|\Omega_\mathbf{Y}| \geq 2^u$ conditional probability distributions, i.e. one conditional probability distribution $P(X|\mathbf{y})$ for each instantiation $\mathbf{y} \in \Omega_\mathbf{Y}$ of $\mathbf{Y}$. For each $P(X|\mathbf{y})$, we introduce an auxiliary variable $\Theta_{X|\mathbf{y}}$ with $\Omega_{\Theta_{X|\mathbf{y}}} = \{\theta_{x_1|\mathbf{y}},\ldots,\theta_{x_t|\mathbf{y}}\}$. Then, $\Theta_{X|\mathbf{y}}$ allows us to logically express the state of X w.r.t. $\mathbf{y}$. E.g. $\Theta_{X|\mathbf{y}} = \theta_{x_1|\mathbf{y}}$ means that x_1 is the X given $\mathbf{y}$. Assuming that the variables $\Theta_{X|\mathbf{y}}$ represent probabilistically independent events, we define their respective marginal probabilities by $P(\Theta_{X|\mathbf{y}}=\theta_{x|\mathbf{y}}) = P(X=x|\mathbf{y})$, as shown in Figure 6.1. The auxiliary variables allow us to represent logically represent the each CPT. Finally, the disjunction of these logical representations of the CPTs is a logically representation of the whole Bayesian Network.

To see how the proposed logical representation of the Bayesian network works, take a closer look at one particular instantiation $\mathbf{y}$ of $parents(X)$. The idea is that if $\mathbf{y}$ happens to be the true state of $parents(X)$, then $\Theta_{X|\mathbf{y}}=\theta_{x|\mathbf{y}}$ is supposed to logically imply $X=x$. This logical relationship between $Y_1=y_1,\ldots,Y_u=y_u$, $\Theta_{X|\mathbf{y}}=\theta_{x|\mathbf{y}}$ with $\mathbf{y} = y_1\cdots y_u \in \Omega_\mathbf{Y}$ and $X=x$ is expressed by the implication in the following logical expression. By taking the conjunction of all such implications over all instantiations $\mathbf{y}$, we obtain a logical representation ψ_X of the node X with its relationship to its parents:

$$\psi_X = \bigwedge_{\substack{\mathbf{y}\in\Omega_\mathbf{Y} \\ \mathbf{y}=y_1\cdots y_u}} \bigwedge_{x\in\Omega_X} \psi_{x,\mathbf{y}} \quad \text{where}$$

$$\psi_{x,\mathbf{y}} = [Y_1=y_1] \wedge \cdots \wedge [Y_u=y_u] \wedge [\Theta_{X|\mathbf{y}}=\theta_{x|\mathbf{y}}] \to [X=x].$$

A logical representation ψ_Δ of the whole BN is the conjunction

$$\psi_\Delta = \bigwedge_{X\in\Delta} \psi_X$$

over all network variables $X \in \Delta$. This sentence includes two types of variables, the ones linked to the CPT entries and the network variables. The respective sets of variables are denoted by Θ and Δ, respectively. Note that ψ_X and therewith ψ_Δ is a MCNF (or CNF), as each of its implications can be written as a clause. For the Bayesian network given in Figure 6.1, we have $\Theta = \{\Theta_X, \Theta_{Y|x_0}, \Theta_{Y|x_1}, \Theta_{Z|x_0y_0}, \Theta_{Z|x_0y_1}, \Theta_{Z|x_1y_0}, \Theta_{Z|x_1y_1}\}$, $\Delta = \{X,Y,Z\}$, and ψ_Δ as shown in Figure 6.2.

$$\psi_\Delta = \bigwedge \begin{pmatrix} \left.\begin{array}{l}[\Theta_X=\theta_{x_0}]\to[X=x_0]\\ [\Theta_X=\theta_{x_1}]\to[X=x_1]\end{array}\right\} \text{from } \psi_X \\ \left.\begin{array}{l}[X=x_0]\wedge[\Theta_{Y|x_0}=\theta_{y_0|x_0}]\to[Y=y_0]\\ [X=x_0]\wedge[\Theta_{Y|x_0}=\theta_{y_1|x_0}]\to[Y=y_1]\\ [X=x_1]\wedge[\Theta_{Y|x_1}=\theta_{y_0|x_1}]\to[Y=y_0]\\ [X=x_1]\wedge[\Theta_{Y|x_1}=\theta_{y_1|x_1}]\to[Y=y_1]\end{array}\right\} \text{from } \psi_Y \\ \left.\begin{array}{l}[X=x_0]\wedge[Y=y_0]\wedge[\Theta_{Z|x_0y_0}=\theta_{z_0|x_0y_0}]\to[Z=z_0]\\ [X=x_0]\wedge[Y=y_0]\wedge[\Theta_{Z|x_0y_0}=\theta_{z_1|x_0y_0}]\to[Z=z_1]\\ [X=x_0]\wedge[Y=y_1]\wedge[\Theta_{Z|x_0y_1}=\theta_{z_0|x_0y_1}]\to[Z=z_0]\\ [X=x_0]\wedge[Y=y_1]\wedge[\Theta_{Z|x_0y_1}=\theta_{z_1|x_0y_1}]\to[Z=z_1]\\ [X=x_1]\wedge[Y=y_0]\wedge[\Theta_{Z|x_1y_0}=\theta_{z_0|x_1y_0}]\to[Z=z_0]\\ [X=x_1]\wedge[Y=y_0]\wedge[\Theta_{Z|x_1y_0}=\theta_{z_1|x_1y_0}]\to[Z=z_1]\\ [X=x_1]\wedge[Y=y_1]\wedge[\Theta_{Z|x_1y_1}=\theta_{z_0|x_1y_1}]\to[Z=z_0]\\ [X=x_1]\wedge[Y=y_1]\wedge[\Theta_{Z|x_1y_1}=\theta_{z_1|x_1y_1}]\to[Z=z_1]\end{array}\right\} \text{from } \psi_Z \end{pmatrix}$$

Figure 6.2: The representation of the Bayesian network given in Figure 6.1 with $\Theta = \{\Theta_X, \Theta_{Y|x_0}, \Theta_{Y|x_1}, \Theta_{Z|x_0y_0}, \Theta_{Z|x_0y_1}, \Theta_{Z|x_1y_0}, \Theta_{Z|x_1y_1}\}$, $\Delta = \{X, Y, Z\}$.

6.2 Computing Posterior Probabilities

The goal of a Bayesian network is the computation of the posterior probability $P(\mathbf{q}|\mathbf{e}) = P(\mathbf{q},\mathbf{e})/P(\mathbf{e})$ of a query event $\mathbf{q} \in \Omega_\mathbf{Q}$ given the observed evidence $\mathbf{e} \in \Omega_\mathbf{E}$. In order to use the logical representation ψ to compute the posterior probability $P(\mathbf{q}|\mathbf{e}) = P(\mathbf{q},\mathbf{e})/P(\mathbf{e})$ of a query event $\mathbf{q} \in \Omega_\mathbf{Q} = \Omega_{Q_1} \times \cdots \times \Omega_{Q_r}$ given the evidence $\mathbf{e} \in \Omega_\mathbf{E} = \Omega_{E_1} \times \cdots \times \Omega_{E_s}$, it is sufficient to look at the simpler problem of computing prior probabilities $P(\mathbf{x})$ of arbitrary conjunctions $\mathbf{x} \in \Omega_\mathbf{X} = \Omega_{X_1} \times \cdots \times \Omega_{X_t}$ to obtain corresponding numerators $P(\mathbf{q},\mathbf{e})$ and denominators $P(\mathbf{e})$. Our solution for this consists of the following three steps:

(i) Condition ψ on $\mathbf{x} \in \Omega_\mathbf{X}$ to obtain $\psi|\mathbf{x}$.

(ii) Eliminate (forget) from $\psi|\mathbf{x}$ the variables Δ. The resulting logical representation of $[\psi|\mathbf{x}]^{-\Delta}$ consists of variables from Θ only.

(iii) Compute the probability of the event represented by $[\psi|\mathbf{x}]^{-\Delta}$ to obtain $P(\mathbf{x}) = P([\psi|\mathbf{x}]^{-\Delta})$. For this, we assume that the variables $\Theta_{X|\mathbf{y}} \in \Theta$ are probabilistically independent and that

$$P\left(\Theta_{X|\mathbf{y}}=\theta_{x|\mathbf{y}}\right) = P\left(X=x|\mathbf{y}\right)$$

Chapter 6 Bayesian Networks

are the respective marginal probabilities for $\theta_{x|y} \in \Omega_{\Theta_{X|y}}$ and $x \in \Omega_X$.

The following theorem states that the essential step to solve this problem is to forget the propositions Δ from ψ_Δ (or any equivalent form of it) conditioned on x.

Theorem 3. $P(\mathbf{x}) = P\left([\psi_\Delta|\mathbf{x}]^{-\Delta}\right)$.

This guarantees that the computed values are correct. To ensure that this computation requires only polynomial time, we need to compile ψ_Δ into an appropriate member ψ of a language that simultaneously supports the query PR and the transformations TC and FO$_\exists$. These are the essential operations in the above 3-step procedure. According to Table 3.4 and Table 3.6, there is no such language. However, the following theorem allows us to replace FO$_\exists$, not supported by cdn-MDAG, by FO$_\exists^d$, supported by cdn-MDAG.

Theorem 4. Δ *is a deterministic set of variables with respect to* ψ_Δ.

A consequence of this simple theorem is that Δ is also a deterministic set of variables with respect to $\psi \in$ cdn-MDAG. Hence, we conclude that cdn-MDAG is the most suitable target compilation language for Bayesian networks, since it supports PR, TC, and FO$_\exists^d$, and thus allows to compute posterior probabilities in polynomial time.

6.3 Beyond Context Specific Independence

Bayesian networks were mainly designed to exploit *conditional* (or *structural*) *independencies*, which allows the (global) joint probability function to be replaced by several (local) CPTs. The locality of the CPTs in turn is responsible for the success of Bayesian networks as an efficient computational tool for probabilistic inference. For details consider Shenoy and Shafer [1988].

The exploitation of another type of independence relations, *contextual* or *context-specific independences* (CSI), has been proposed by Boutilier et al. [1996][1]. CSI deals with local independence relations *within* (rather than *between*) the given CPTs. A *context* within a CPT is a partial parent assignment.

---

[1] The notion of context-specific independence first appeared in the influence diagram literature Smith et al. [1993]. Note that some authors prefer to use *contextual strong independence* as an alternative name with the same acronym Wong and Butz [1999]. Other similar notions are *asymmetric independence* Geiger and Heckerman [1991] and *probabilistic causal irrelevance* Galles and Pearl [1997].

Most approaches exploiting CSI suggest a tree-structured CPT representation, but different names such as *CPT-trees*, according to Boutilier et al. [1996], *probability trees*, introduced by Cano et al. [2000], or *multi-resolution binary trees*, see Bellot and Bessière [2003], are in use for essentially the same concept. All these techniques share a common goal, namely to merge CPT entries with the same value for a specific context. Note that such a simplified CPT may still include the same value more than once.

More advanced CPT representations allow a complete partitioning of the parent assignments, in which each value occurs exactly once. According to Poole and Zhang [2003], a simple idea to achieve this it to represent the partitions by logical rules. Chavira and Darwiche [2007] provide a more efficient approach, namely the use of algebraic decision diagrams. Technically speaking, this method exceeds CSI insofar as it considers the entire local structure to simplify a given CPT, thus possibly spanning over various contexts.

Wachter et al. [2007] follow this approach and shift the analysis from Bayesian networks into the generic framework of semiring valuation algebras. From this point of view, each CPT is a semiring valuation where the semiring is composed of the real numbers $\mathbb{R}$ together with the normal addition $+$ and the normal multiplication $\times$. Valuations of this particular type are often called *probability potentials* according to Shenoy and Shafer [1990].

As we have seen in the previous chapter, MDNF, G-FMDD, and π-OMDD, and π-OMTMDD are the candidates for representing semiring valuation algebras. Due to the fact that a CPT is a semiring valuation, these are also the candidates for representing CPTs.

6.4 Recapitulation: Bayesian Networks

In this chapter, we shortly reviewed Bayesian Networks and showed how they may be represented logically. On the theoretical side, based on the knowledge compilation map, we provide a precise explanation of why cdn-MDAGs are apparently the most suitable logical representations for Bayesian networks. This is mainly a consequence of the fact that some of the involved variables are deterministic. On the practical side, we provide precise step-by-step instructions to implement a new encoding and inference method for Bayesian networks in terms of a few simple operations for cdn-MDAGs. In addition, it is also possible to speed up inference by optimizing the representation of CPTs. Since each CPT is a semiring valuation, there are four valuable candidates for representing a CPT as shown in the previous chapter.

Chapter 7

Reliability and Diagnostic of Modular Systems

Wachter et al. [2006] show that the knowledge compilation map is also useful to compute the reliability of a modular system and to find possible diagnoses explaining the cause of a defect within a system.

In the following, we assume that each involved part of the system is either working or not. I.e. it is sufficient to consider the knowledge compilation map for Boolean functions.

A (non-modular) *system* $\mathcal{S} = (\mathbf{C}, f)$ consists of several *components* $\mathbf{C} = \{C_1, \ldots, C_r\}$, $r \geq 1$, and a *structure function* f. To represent a component's state of operation, we use C_i not only to denote the component itself, but also for an associated Boolean variable. Suppose that $C_i = 1$ if C_i is working and $C_i = 0$ is C_i is faulty.

The structure function is a Boolean function $f : \mathbb{B}^r \to \mathbb{B}$, which connects the components' states of operation with the state of operation of the entire system, i.e. we have $f(c_1, \ldots, c_r) = 1$ iff the system is working. In reliability theory, f is often restricted to be *coherent* or *monotone* (non-decreasing in each argument) where forgetting is feasible, but we refrain from doing so here. Note that $\neg f = 1 - f$ is the complementary structure function of the system's failure state.

Since explicitly specifying f becomes impracticable if r is large, we may do better by exploiting the modular structure of a system. Thus, we define a *modular system* $\mathcal{M} = (\mathbf{C}, \mathbf{M}, T, \mathbf{L})$ to consist of components $\mathbf{C} = \{C_1, \ldots, C_r\}$, $r \geq 1$, *modules* $\mathbf{M} = \{M_0, \ldots, M_s\}$, $s \geq 0$, an *organizing tree* T, and *local structure functions* $\mathbf{L} = \{\ell_0, \ldots, \ell_s\}$ according to Kohlas [1987].

Chapter 7 Reliability and Diagnostic of Modular Systems

The organizing tree T is supposed to be directed and rooted, and we suppose the elements of $\mathbf{C}$ to be the leaves, the elements of $\mathbf{M}$ to be the non-leaves, and M_0 to be the root of the organizing tree. With $\mathbf{N} = \mathbf{C} \cup \mathbf{M}$ we denote the complete set of nodes of T. The *successor set* $succ(M_i) \subseteq \mathbf{N}$ of a module $M_i \in \mathbf{M}$ contains all its direct descendants in T. Note that the tree structure ensures each single component and each single module to appear in at most one successor set.

The local structure function of each module $M_i \in \mathbf{M}$ is a Boolean function

$$\ell_i : \mathbb{B}^{|succ(M_i)|} \to \mathbb{B},$$

which describes the state of operation of the module in terms of its constituents $succ(M_i)$. Note that the particular case $\mathbf{M} = \{M_0\}$ implies ℓ_0 to be the (non-local) structure function of the corresponding (non-modular) system $\mathcal{S} = (\mathbf{C}, \ell_0)$. Conversely, every system $\mathcal{S}' = (\mathbf{C}, f)$ is equivalent to the modular system $\mathcal{M}' = (\mathbf{C}, \{M_0\}, T, \{f\})$, where T is the tree with root M_0 and $succ(M_0) = \mathbf{C}$.

In general, any modular system $\mathcal{M} = (\mathbf{C}, \mathbf{M}, T, \mathbf{L})$ unambiguously defines the (non-local) structure function of a corresponding (non-modular) system $\mathcal{S}$ with the same components $\mathbf{C}$. To show this connection, let us define the unfolded (non-local) structure function of a component or module $N \in \mathbf{N}$ by

$$f(N) = \begin{cases} C_i, & \text{if } N = C_i \in \mathbf{C}, \\ \ell_i(f(N_1), \ldots, f(N_t)), & \text{if } N = Mi \in \mathbf{M}, \end{cases}$$

with $succ(M_i) = \{N_1, \ldots, N_t\}$. Thus $f(M_i)$ is the structure function of module M_i with respect to the restricted set of components appearing in its own subtree. The modular system $\mathcal{M} = (\mathbf{C}, \mathbf{M}, T, L)$ is then equivalent to the system $\mathcal{S} = (C, f(M_0))$.

For example, consider an aircraft consisting of two modules S (steering) and G (gear). Module G is further decomposed in two submodules E (engine) and F (fuel). Module S has two steering components S_1 and S_2, module E has three components E_1 (left engine), E_2 (right engine), and E_3 (rear engine), and module F has two components F_1 (fuel tank 1) and F_2 (fuel tank 2). The structure and behavior of the system is described by the *reliability block diagram* (RBD) shown in Figure 7.1, where $2/3$ stands for a "2-out-of-3"-relationship. RBDs represent the system's *success state* and are mostly constructed bottom-up. RBDs are graphical representations of the components and modules (represented as *blocks*) of

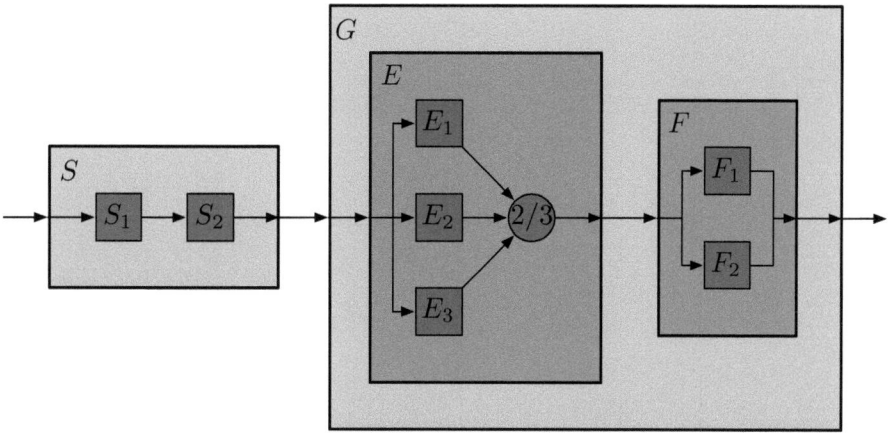

Figure 7.1: The RBD of the aircraft example.

the system and of how they are reliability-wise arranged. This means that the success state of the system or module is represented in terms of the success states of its individual components. Note that this may differ from how the components are physically connected.

In terms of the above formal setting, the airworthiness of the aircraft leads to a the modular system $\mathcal{M} = (\mathbf{C}, \mathbf{M}, T, \mathbf{L})$ with

$$\mathbf{C} = \{S_1, S_2, E_1, E_2, E_3, F_1, F_2\},$$
$$\mathbf{M} = \{A, S, G, E, F\},$$
$$\mathbf{L} = \{\ell_A, \ell_S, \ell_G, \ell_E, \ell_F\},$$

and the organizing tree T shown in Figure 7.2. The root node A represents the state of operation of the entire aircraft and can be thought of as the overall module that makes up the system.

To be in accordance with the above RBD, the corresponding local structure functions are as

Chapter 7 Reliability and Diagnostic of Modular Systems

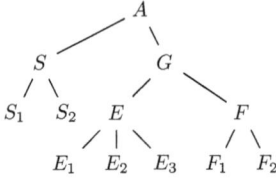

Figure 7.2: The organizing tree in the aircraft example.

follows:

$$\ell_A(S, G) = S \wedge G,$$
$$\ell_S(S_1, S_2) = S_1 \wedge S_2,$$
$$\ell_G(E, F) = E \wedge F,$$
$$\ell_E(E_1, E_2, E_3) = (E_1 \wedge E_2) \vee (E_1 \wedge E_3) \vee (E_2 \wedge E_3),$$
$$\ell_F(F_1, F_2) = F_1 \vee F_2.$$

By plugging the local structure functions recursively into each other, we obtain the following "global" structure function $f(A)$ for the entire aircraft:

$$f(A) = S_1 \wedge S_2 \wedge [(E_1 \wedge E_2) \vee (E_1 \wedge E_3) \vee (E_2 \wedge E_3)] \wedge (F_1 \vee F_2).$$

In the following two sections, we demonstrate how to use the knowledge compilation map to determine the appropriate language for computing the reliability of a modular system and the posterior probabilities of possible diagnoses.

Before we continue, note that modular systems are closely related to Bayesian networks and, hence, to semiring valuations. Obviously, each structure function $\ell : \Omega \to \mathbb{B}$ can be regarded as a CPT of a Bayesian network and the organizing tree T corresponds to the DAG of a Bayesian network. The properties of a modular system are reflected in the fact that each values within a CPT is either 0 or 1, and the fact that the underlying network is a tree. From this point of view, it is possible to use the results from the previous chapters. However, the properties of modular systems offer further improvements.

7.1 Reliability

Reliability is commonly defined as the probability of an item (component, module, system) to operate for a given amount of time without failure. Of course, the reliability of a modular system depends primarily on the reliability of its modules, which themselves depend on the reliability of their components. To make a reliability analysis of a modular system $\mathcal{M} = (\mathbf{C}, \mathbf{M}, T, \mathbf{L})$, suppose that the components fail *independently* of each other, and let the probability that a component $C \in \mathbf{C}$ is properly working for a given amount of time be denoted by $P(C)$. This is the typical starting point of a *static* analysis. Obviously, we have to require that the representation of a modular systems supports at least the query PR which allows to compute the probabilities in time polynomial in the size of the representation. Hence, we represents a modular system in the language cd-PDAG. According to the knowledge compilation map cd-PDAG is the most succinct language that supports PR. In a *dynamic* setting, $P(C)$ is simply replaced by a time-dependent probability $P(C, t)$. This can easily be incorporated into the probability computation of a cd-PDAG just by including t as an additional parameter.

To compute the reliability of the modular system $\mathcal{M}$ efficiently, let each local structure function ℓ_i of M_i be represented by a local cd-PDAG λ_i, where the successors of M_i are the leaves of λ_i. The tree structure ensures that each single component and each single module appears in at most one successor set. Starting from λ_0, this allows us to recursively replace in each λ_i the leaves labeled with a module by the cd-PDAG of the corresponding local structure function, while both decomposability and determinism are preserved due to the tree structure of the modular system. Formally, let

$$\varphi(N) = \begin{cases} C\text{-terminal}, & \text{if } N \in \mathbf{C}, \\ \lambda_i(\varphi(N_1), \ldots, \varphi(N_t)), & \text{if } N = M \in \mathbf{M}, \end{cases}$$

be the non-local cd-PDAG of each node $n \in N$. With $\lambda_i(\varphi(N_1), \ldots, \varphi(N_t))$ we denote the cd-PDAG obtained from a module M with $succ(M) = \{N_1, \ldots, N_t\}$ by replacing each leaf N_j of λ_i by $\varphi(N_j)$. In this way, we obtain a non-local cd-PDAG $\varphi(M)$ for each module $M \in \mathbf{M}$, i.e. $\varphi(M_0)$ is the cd-PDAG representation of M_0's structure function $f(M_0)$. Finally, to obtain the overall reliability of the entire modular systems, all we have to do is to compute the probability $P(M_0) = P(\varphi(M_0))$.

Again, consider the aircraft from the previous section and its description as a modular sys-

Chapter 7 Reliability and Diagnostic of Modular Systems

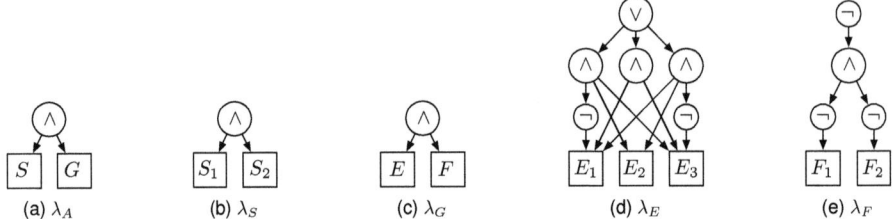

Figure 7.3: The cd-PDAGs λ_i representing the local structure functions ℓ_i with $1 \leq i \leq 5$.

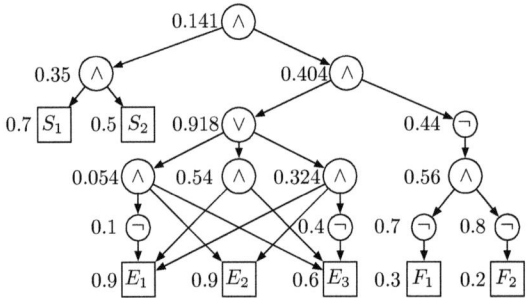

Figure 7.4: The cd-PDAG φ_A of the entire aircraft and the calculation of its probability. Note that the values are rounded to the third place.

tem. The cd-PDAGs λ_i of the local structure functions ℓ_i are shown in Figure 7.3, and the global cd-PDAG $\varphi(A)$ of the entire modular system is shown in Figure 7.4. Note that $\varphi(A)$ is obtained from λ_A by replacing the leaves labeled with S and G by $\varphi(S)$ and $\varphi(G)$, respectively. Similarly, $\varphi(G)$ is obtained from λ_G by replacing the leaves labeled with E and F by $\varphi(E)$ and $\varphi(F)$, respectively, and so on.

The calculation of the aircraft's reliability $P(A) = 0.141$ is also shown in Figure 7.4 (up to up 3 decimal places). It is based on the following success probabilities of the components: $P(E_1) = P(E_2) = 0.9$, $P(E_3) = 0.6$, $P(S_1) = 0.7$, $P(S_2) = 0.5$, $P(F_1) = 0.3$, and $P(F_2) = 0.2$. These values are arguably not very realistic, but they are suitable for our illustrative purposes.

7.2 Diagnostics

Let us now turn our attention to the problem of finding possible diagnoses if the system or parts of it are observed to be malfunctioning. The method is based on the reliability analysis of the previous section. The goal is to compute conditional probabilities of a module or component being broken given some observations about the state of operation of one or several parts of the system (including the entire system). Computing such conditional probabilities is generally the spirit of a Bayesian analysis, which is now applied to the diagnostic problem.

As before, the discussion is focused on the static case, where each component $C \in \mathbf{C}$ has an fixed success probability $P(C)$. Furthermore, we suppose the Boolean function of a modular system $\mathcal{M}$ to be represented by the cd-PDAG $\varphi(M_0)$ of its top-level module M_0, as explained in the previous section. Note that the cd-PDAG $\varphi(N)$ of any module or component $N \in \mathbf{N}$ is contained in $\varphi(M_0)$ as a subgraph (see example in Figure 7.4). We use $\varphi(\neg N)$ to denote the ¬-node with child $\varphi(N)$, thus representing the negation of $\varphi(N)$.

Now let $\{N_{obs}^1, \ldots, N_{obs}^k\} \subseteq \mathbf{N}$ be the observed modules or components, and let $obs_i \in \{N_{obs}^i, \neg N_{obs}^i\}$ denote whether N_{obs}^i is working or not. Furthermore, suppose that $Q \in \mathbf{N}$ is the component or module under investigation. In this dissertation, we only consider the case of single queries, but this is not a conceptual restriction. The conditional probability that Q is working, is calculated by

$$P(Q|obs_1, \ldots, obs_k) = \frac{P(Q, obs_1, \ldots, obs_k)}{P(obs_1, \ldots, obs_k)}.$$

To see how to compute $P(Q|obs_1, \ldots, obs_k)$ using the given cd-PDAG $\varphi(M_0)$, let us first restrict our discussion to the particular case of a single observation $obs \in \{N_{obs}, \neg N_{obs}\}$. Note that the cd-PDAGs $\varphi(Q)$ and $\varphi(N_{obs})$ are both sub-PDAGs of $\varphi(M_0)$, while $\varphi(\neg N_{obs})$ is easily obtained from $\varphi(N_{obs})$ by adding a ¬-node on top. The posterior success probability of Q can thus be written as

$$P(Q|obs) = \frac{P(Q, obs)}{P(obs)} = \frac{P(\varphi(Q) \wedge \varphi(obs))}{P(\varphi(obs))},$$

where $\varphi(Q) \wedge \varphi(obs)$ represents the PDAG obtained from connecting $\varphi(Q)$ and $\varphi(N_{obs})$ with a ∧-node. Note that this new ∧-node is not necessarily decomposable, i.e. the entire structure is no longer a cd-PDAG and does thus not allow probability computations. This is illustrated in Figure 7.5 for the aircraft example with $obs = \neg A$ and $Q = F$.

Chapter 7 Reliability and Diagnostic of Modular Systems

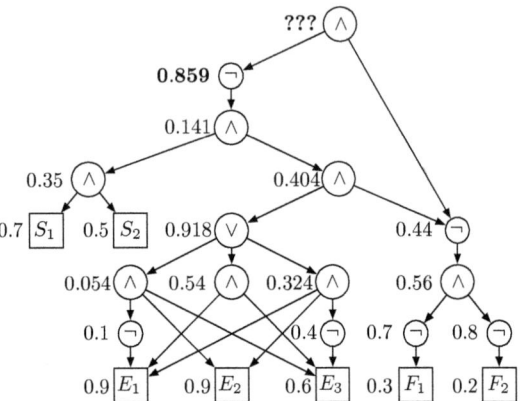

Figure 7.5: The PDAG $\varphi(\neg A) \wedge \varphi(F)$.

To make the new ∧-node decomposable, let us take a look at the organizing tree of the modular system. This reveals three possible cases:

(i) Q and N_{obs} are in distinct subtrees,

(ii) N_{obs} is a subtree of Q,

(iii) Q is a subtree of N_{obs}.

The first case implies that $\varphi(Q)$ and $\varphi(obs)$ share no common variables. This makes $\varphi(Q) \wedge \varphi(obs)$ decomposable and allows its probability to be computed by $P(\varphi(Q) \wedge \varphi(obs)) = P(\varphi(Q)) \times P(\varphi(obs))$. This implies $P(Q|obs) = P(\varphi(Q))$, which indicates that the query variable is not at all affected by the observation. For example, observing an empty fuel tank has no influence on steering. The second and the third case is more challenging, since $\varphi(Q) \wedge \varphi(obs)$ is not decomposable.

In the second case, we may generate the cd-PDAG $\varphi(N_{obs}) \wedge \varphi(Q)|\varphi(N_{obs})$ where and compute its probability to obtain the required numerator. Note that $\varphi(Q)|\varphi(N_{obs})$ is the graph obtained from $\varphi(Q)$ by replacing $\varphi(N_{obs})$ with a ⊤-terminal. The third case is analogue, except that Q and N_{obs} change their roles. An example of the third case is shown in Figure 7.6 with $obs = \neg A$ and $Q = F$ (as before). In comparison with the PDAG of Figure 7.5, the new cd-PDAG $\varphi(F) \wedge \varphi(\neg A)|\varphi(F)$ contains three new nodes, for which new probabilities need to

7.3 Recapitulation: Modular Systems

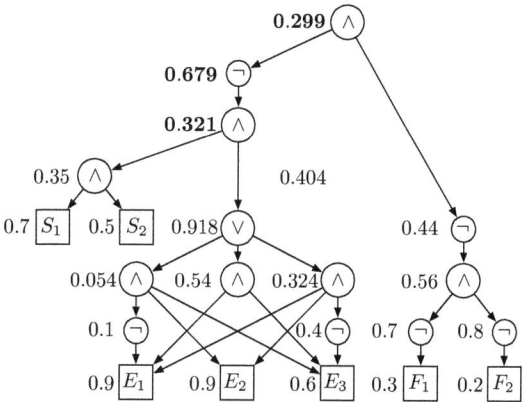

Figure 7.6: The resulting cd-PDAG $\varphi(F) \wedge \varphi(\neg A)|\varphi(F)$.

be computed (indicated in bold). Finally, we get F's conditional probability given $\neg A$ by

$$P(F|\neg A) = \frac{P(\varphi(F) \wedge \varphi(\neg A)|\varphi(F))}{P(\varphi(\neg A))} = \frac{0.299}{0.859} = 0.348.$$

In the same way, it is possible to compute the conditional probabilities of all modules and components of the system. The ones with the highest values are then the most probable diagnoses. The case of multiple observations works similarly, although a more general form of conditioning is required. In any case, conditioning is always an efficient operation.

7.3 Recapitulation: Modular Systems

In this chaper, we have seen that the reliability and diagnosis of modular systems are closely related. One could say that reliability is the special case of diagnosis without observations. cd-PDAGs turn out to be an adequate computational technique for both, since decomposability and determinism guarantee that the computation of probabilities is polynomial with respect to the size of the cd-PDAG. Furthermore, observations can be handled easily, according to the structure of the organizing tree. This structure is responsible for the fact that cd-PDAG is the language to choose, although cd-PDAG is not even a candidate for representing the more general cases of Bayesian networks or semiring valuations (with Boolean variables only).

Chapter 8

Further Applications

This chapter covers two further applications. The first one is *(probabilistic) model verification*, consider Wachter and Haenni [2006b], Darwiche and Huang [2002], Blum et al. [1980]. The second one is *compiling solution configurations in semiring valuation systems* according to Pouly et al. [2007]. Note that semiring valuation algebras (see Chapter 5) already cover a large number of applications.

8.1 (Probabilistic) Model Verification

Wachter and Haenni [2006b] continue the work of Blum et al. [1980] and Darwiche and Huang [2002] discussing the probabilistic equivalence test. In the work at hand, the probabilistic equivalence test is already introduced as the query PEQ.

Without loss of generality, we restrict our attention to the field $\mathbb{F}_p = \{0, \ldots, p-1\}$ of integers, where p is a prime number. This allows us to define hash codes in terms of arithmetic operations within $\mathbb{F}_p$, where all additions, subtractions, and multiplications are performed modulo p. For a Boolean function f the query PEQ is defined via a hash code $H_\mathbf{h}$ as follows.

Definition 31. Let $\mathbf{V} = \{V_1, \ldots, V_r\}$ be a set of r Boolean variables and let $\mathbf{h} = (h_1, \ldots, h_r) \in \mathbb{F}_p^r$ be a r-dimensional vector of integers in $\mathbb{F}_p$ where p is a prime number.

- The hash code of a variable $V_i \in \mathbf{V}$ is the corresponding coordinate of $\mathbf{h}$:

$$H_\mathbf{h}(V_i) = h_i.$$

Chapter 8 Further Applications

- The hash code of a complete assignment $\mathbf{v} = (v_1, \ldots, v_r) \in \mathbb{B}^r$ is the following product:

$$H_\mathbf{h}(\mathbf{v}) = \prod_{i=1}^{r} \begin{cases} H_\mathbf{h}(V_i), & \text{if } v_i = 1, \\ 1 - H_\mathbf{h}(V_i), & \text{if } v_i = 0. \end{cases}$$

- The hash code of a Boolean function f is the sum of hash codes of its models:

$$H_\mathbf{h}(f) = \sum_{\mathbf{v} \in [\![f]\!]} H_\mathbf{h}(\mathbf{v}).$$

This definition implies that $H_\mathbf{h}(f) = 1$ if $[\![f]\!] = \mathbb{B}^r$, $H_\mathbf{h}(f) = 0$ if $[\![f]\!] = \emptyset$, and $H_\mathbf{h}(1-f) = 1 - H_\mathbf{h}(f)$. For Boolean functions, the query PEQ is based on the following theorem.

Theorem 5. *If f and g are two distinct Boolean functions, then there are at least $(p-1)^r$ vectors $\mathbf{h} \in \mathbb{F}_p^r$ such that $H_\mathbf{h}(f) \neq H_\mathbf{h}(g)$.*

This theorem holds for arbitrary fields $\mathbb{F}_p$, as proven by Blum et al. [1980] and Darwiche and Huang [2002]. To handle multi-state variables and, hence, Boolean-valued functions, both the definition and the theorem have to be reconsidered.

Definition 32. Let $\mathbf{V} = \{V_1, \ldots, V_r\}$ be a set of r multi-state variables with $\Omega_{V_i} = \{v_{i,1}, \ldots, v_{i,s_i}\}$. For a prime number p and

$$\mathbf{h} = (h_{1,1}, \ldots, h_{1,s_1}, \ldots, h_{r,1}, \ldots, h_{r,s_r}) \in \mathbb{F}_p^{s_1 + \cdots + s_r}$$

such that $\sum_{j=1}^{s_i} h_{i,j} \equiv 1 \pmod{p}$ for $1 \leq i \leq r$, we define

- the hash code of the assignment $V_i = v_{i,j}$ by

$$H_\mathbf{h}(v_{i,j}) = h_{i,j},$$

- the hash code of the complete assignment $\mathbf{v} = (v_{1,j_1}, \ldots, v_{r,j_r}) \in \Omega_\mathbf{V}$ by

$$H_\mathbf{h}(\mathbf{v}) = \prod_{i=1}^{r} h_{i,j_i}, \text{ and}$$

8.1 (Probabilistic) Model Verification

- the hash code of a Boolean-valued function f by

$$H_{\mathbf{h}}(f) = \sum_{\mathbf{v} \in [\![f]\!]} H_{\mathbf{h}}(\mathbf{v}).$$

This definition implies that $H_{\mathbf{h}}(f) = 1$ if $[\![f]\!] = \Omega_V$, $H_{\mathbf{h}}(f) = 0$ if $[\![f]\!] = \emptyset$, and $H_{\mathbf{h}}(1-f) = 1 - H_{\mathbf{h}}(f)$. For Boolean-valued functions, the query PEQ is based on the following theorem.

Theorem 6. *If f and g are two distinct Boolean-valued functions, then there are at least $\prod_{i=1}^{r}(p^{s_i-1} - p^{s_i-2})$ vectors $\mathbf{h} \in \mathbb{F}_p^{s_1+\cdots+s_r}$ such that $H_{\mathbf{h}}(f) \neq H_{\mathbf{h}}(g)$.*

The proof of Theorem 6 is included in the appendix. This proof is also applicable to Theorem 5 which is a special case of Theorem 6.

For two non-equivalent Boolean-valued functions f and g, we call $\mathbf{h} \in \mathbb{F}_p^{s_1} \times \cdots \times \mathbb{F}_p^{s_r}$ with $H_{\mathbf{h}}(f) \neq H_{\mathbf{h}}(g)$ a *witness* for the distinctness of f and g. Otherwise, $\mathbf{h}$ is called a *liar*, as it is common in the literature on probabilistic algorithms. As a consequence of Theorem 6, we have at least $\prod_{i=1}^{r}(p^{s_i-1} - p^{s_i-2})$ witnesses and at most $\prod_{i=1}^{r}p^{s_i-1} - \prod_{i=1}^{r}(p^{s_i-1} - p^{s_i-2})$ liars, since there are only $\prod_{i=1}^{r}p^{s_i-1}$ solutions for the r equations $\sum_{i=1}^{s_i} h_{i,j} = 1$ with $1 \leq i \leq r$. Therefore, two Boolean-valued functions with identical hash codes appear to be equivalent with a failure probability

$$\pi \leq \frac{\prod_{i=1}^{r}p^{s_i-1} - \prod_{i=1}^{r}(p^{s_i-1} - p^{s_i-2})}{\prod_{i=1}^{r}p^{s_i-1}} = 1 - \frac{(p-1)^r}{p^r} \leq \frac{r}{p}, \text{ for } p \geq r.$$

To make π smaller than $\frac{1}{2}$, it is necessary to choose $p \geq 2r$. This is the usual minimal requirement, which guarantees that the total failure probability of a repeated test quickly converges towards 0. Another strategy is to choose p sufficiently large from the beginning, which guarantees a low failure probability after a single test.

According to this result, the algorithms provided by Wachter and Haenni [2006b] are easily adapted. For this, we have to replace

$$\mathbf{h} \leftarrow \text{ randomly selected from } \{0, \ldots, p-1\}^r$$

Chapter 8 Further Applications

by

$$\mathbf{h} = (h_{1,1}, \ldots, h_{1,s_1}, h_{2,1}, \ldots, h_{r-1,s_{r-1}}, h_{r,1} \ldots, h_{r,s_r})$$
$$\leftarrow \text{ randomly selected from } \{0, \ldots, p-1\}^{s_1 + \cdots + s_r}$$
$$\text{such that } \sum_{i=1}^{s_j} h_{j,i} = 1 \text{ for } j \in \{1, \ldots, r\}.$$

Up to now, the computation of the hash code is based on the function itself and its models. In the following, it is shifted towards the representation of a function.

Definition 33. Let $V = \{V_1, \ldots, V_r\}$ be a set of r multi-state variables and $\mathbf{h} = (h_{1,1}, \ldots, h_{1,s_1}, \ldots, h_{r,1}, \ldots, h_{r,s_r}) \in \mathbb{F}_p^{s_1 + \cdots + s_r}$ a vector of integers in $\mathbb{F}_p$ with $\sum_{i=1}^{s_i} h_{i,j} = 1$ for $1 \leq i \leq r$. The hash code $H_\mathbf{h}(\varphi)$ of φ is recursively defined by:

- $H_\mathbf{h}(\varphi) = \prod_i H_\mathbf{h}(\beta_i)$, if φ is a $\wedge$-node with children β_i;
- $H_\mathbf{h}(\varphi) = \sum_i H_\mathbf{h}(\beta_i)$, if φ is a $\vee$-node with children β_i;
- $H_\mathbf{h}(\varphi) = 1 - H_\mathbf{h}(\beta)$, if φ is a $\neg$-node with child β;
- $H_\mathbf{h}(\varphi) = 1$, if φ is a $\top$-terminal;
- $H_\mathbf{h}(\varphi) = 0$, if φ is a $\bot$-terminal; and
- $H_\mathbf{h}(\varphi) = \sum_{\substack{j \in \{1, \ldots, s_i\} \\ v_{i,j} \in \Omega}} h_{i,j}$, if φ is a (V_j, Ω)-terminal.

The following theorem associates both ways of computing hash codes.

Theorem 7. For all $\varphi \in$ cd-MDAG, we have $H_\mathbf{h}(f_\varphi) = H_\mathbf{h}(\varphi)$, where f_φ is the Boolean-valued function represented by φ.

Again, the proof of this theorem is included in the appendix.

Recapitulation

The language cd-MDAG already supports a number of useful queries in polynomial time. The most important ones are satisfiability, validity, clause entailment, term implication, model counting, and probability computation. While sentence entailment is known to be infeasible in the language cd-MDAG, it is still unknown if there is a polynomial equivalence test or not.

The probabilistic equivalence tests are an alternative to the missing exact equivalence test. We have shown that for an adequate choice of parameters, the failure probabilities of these tests converge quickly towards 0 if the test is repeated several times. As long as the existence of an exact test is still an open question, we propose to use these probabilistic tests instead. This seems to be an interesting alternative to the techniques used in hardware design, which are mostly based on the language OBDD and its derivatives. The advantage of using the language cd-MDAG instead of OBDD is its improved succinctness.

8.2 Solution Configurations in Semiring Valuation Algebras

When looking for the extremal value of a semiring valuation, we are sometimes not interested in the concrete value but in the assignments leading to this value. Such an assignment is called a *solution configuration*. While it is easy to obtain the solution configurations of a single valuation, it is more complicated for a joint valuation (see Section 5.2). Determining the solution configurations of a joint valuation is covered by Pouly et al. [2007] where a solution configuration is defined as follows.

Definition 34. For a semiring valuation φ based on a totally ordered idempotent semiring, $\mathbf{x} \in \Omega_{d(\varphi)}$ is a *solution configuration* if $\varphi(\mathbf{x}) = \varphi^{-d(\varphi)}(\diamond)$.

For example, consider the valuation φ based on the semiring $(\mathbb{N}, \max, \times)$ given in Figure 8.1. Obviously, there are three assignments $\mathbf{x} \in \Omega_{A,B,C}$ with

$$\varphi(\mathbf{x}) = \varphi^{-\{A,B,C\}}(\diamond) = 12,$$

namely $\mathbf{x}_1 = (0, 0, 1)$, $\mathbf{x}_2 = (0, 0, 2)$ and $\mathbf{x}_3 = (0, 1, 0)$.

This section is dedicated to the task of identifying solution configurations of some joint valuation $\varphi = \varphi_1 \otimes \cdots \otimes \varphi_n$. For this purpose, Shenoy [1996] proposed an extension of the fusion algorithm which allows to identify single solution configurations. Whenever a variable

Chapter 8 Further Applications

A	B	C	φ
0	0	0	5
0	0	1	12
0	0	2	12
0	1	0	12
0	1	1	3
0	1	2	12
1	0	0	3
1	0	1	9
1	0	2	5
1	1	0	5
1	1	1	7
1	1	2	3

$\rightarrow$

A	B	φ^{-C}
0	0	12
0	1	12
1	0	9
1	1	7

$\rightarrow$

A	$\varphi^{-\{B,C\}}$
0	12
1	9

$\rightarrow$

$\varphi^{-\{A,B,C\}}$
12

Figure 8.1: The valuation φ based on the variables A, B, and C with $\Omega_A = \Omega_B = \{0, 1\}$ and $\Omega_C = \{0, 1, 2\}$.

8.2 Solution Configurations in Semiring Valuation Algebras

is eliminated during the fusion process, this algorithm stores the frame value of the eliminated variable that leads to the maximum value. In this way, solution configurations are obtained at the end of fusion by combining the retained frame values, and from this perspective, the extended fusion algorithm corresponds to *non-serial dynamic programming*. A generalization of this algorithm to valuation algebras induced by idempotent semirings can be found in Pouly and Kohlas [2007]. Pouly et al. [2007] embark on another strategy. Instead of storing partial solution configurations (or frame values) explicitly, the solutions configurations of a valuation ψ are represented in an implicit way by constructing a Boolean function whose set of models corresponds to the solution configurations. In short, the solution configurations are compiled into a Boolean function. This is also possible with Boolean-valued functions. For example, the solution configurations of φ from above may be represented by $(A, \{0\}) \wedge (((B, \{0\}) \wedge (C, \{1, 2\})) \vee ((B, \{1\}) \wedge (C, \{0\})))$.

For valuations based on Boolean variables, Pouly et al. [2007] introduce *memorizing semiring valuations*. Memorizing semiring valuations consists of two values, a semiring value and a Boolean function representing the solution configuration. The following definition extends this definition by replacing the Boolean functions with Boolean-valued functions. The Boolean-valued function is used during the fusion process to memorize the frame values of eliminated variables that are part of the solution configurations.

Definition 35. Let A be the set of values of a totally ordered idempotent commutative semiring $(A, +, \times)$, let $\mathbf{V} = \{V_1, \ldots, V_r\}$ be a set of (multi-state) variables with $\Omega_{V_i} = \{1, \ldots, s_i\}$, and let F be the set of Boolean-valued functions over the variables $\mathbf{V}$. Then, a *memorizing semiring valuation* φ is a function

$$\varphi : \Omega_{\mathbf{V}} \to A \times F$$

from the set of assignments $\Omega_{\mathbf{V}}$ to the Cartesian product of A and F.

For $\mathbf{v} \in \Omega_{\mathbf{V}}$, $\varphi_A(\mathbf{x})$ corresponds to the semiring value a and $\varphi_F(\mathbf{x})$ corresponds to the Boolean-valued function f in $\varphi(\mathbf{x}) = (a, f)$. The following definitions of operations for memorizing semiring valuations reflects the memorizing. Again, $\Phi = \bigcup_{\mathbf{W} \subseteq \mathbf{V}} \Phi_{\mathbf{W}}$ denotes the set of all possible valuations over $\mathbf{V}$.

- *Labeling*: $\Phi \to \mathcal{P}(\mathbf{V})$, $\varphi \mapsto d(\varphi) = \mathbf{W}$, if $\varphi \in \Phi_{\mathbf{W}}$;
- *Combination*: $\Phi \times \Phi \to \Phi$, $(\varphi, \psi) \mapsto \varphi \otimes \psi$ where $\varphi \otimes \psi(\mathbf{v}) =$

$$\left(\varphi_A \left(\mathbf{v}^{\downarrow d(\varphi)} \right) \times \psi_A \left(\mathbf{v}^{\downarrow d(\psi)} \right), \varphi_F \left(\mathbf{v}^{\downarrow d(\varphi)} \right) \wedge \psi_F \left(\mathbf{v}^{\downarrow d(\psi)} \right) \right)$$

Chapter 8 Further Applications

for $\mathbf{v} \in \Omega_{d(\varphi) \cup d(\psi)}$;

- *Variable elimination*: $\Phi \times \mathbf{V} \to \Phi$, $(\varphi, V) \mapsto \varphi^{-V}$ with

$$\varphi^{-V}(\mathbf{u}) = \left(\varphi_A^{-V}(\mathbf{u}), \varphi_F^{-V}(\mathbf{u})\right) \text{ for } \mathbf{u} \in \Omega_{d(\varphi) \setminus \{V\}}.$$

For V with $\Omega_V = \{1, \ldots, s\}$, φ_A^{-V} and φ_F^{-V} are defined as follows:

$$\varphi_A^{-V}(\mathbf{u}) = \varphi_A(\mathbf{u}, 1) + \cdots + \varphi_A(\mathbf{u}, s) = \sum_{i=1}^{s} \varphi_A(\mathbf{u}, i) \text{ and}$$

$$\varphi_F^{-V}(\mathbf{u}) = \bigvee_{i=1}^{s} \left(f_{V,\{i\}}(\mathbf{u}, i) \wedge \varphi_F(\mathbf{u}, i) \wedge \lambda_i(\mathbf{u})\right) \text{ where}$$

$$\lambda_i(\mathbf{u}) = \begin{cases} f_\top(\mathbf{u}, i), & \text{if } \varphi_A(\mathbf{u}, i) = \varphi_A^{-V}(\mathbf{u}), \\ f_\bot(\mathbf{u}, i), & \text{otherwise}. \end{cases}$$

This is analog to the definition by Pouly et al. [2007] for Boolean functions and leads to the following.

Theorem 8. *A system of memorizing semiring valuations with labeling, combination and marginalization as defined above, satisfies the axioms of a valuation algebra.*

The proof of this theorem is given by Pouly and Kohlas [2007] for Boolean functions. Fortunately, the proof for Boolean-valued functions differs only in the number of states of a variable. Thus, for a given factorization $\varphi = \varphi_1 \otimes \cdots \otimes \varphi_n$ of semiring valuations over a totally ordered idempotent semiring $\mathcal{A}$, we embed the factors φ_i into a set of memorizing semiring valuations as follows: For $i = 1, \ldots, n$ we define

$$\widehat{\varphi_i} : \mathbf{x} \in \Omega_{d(\varphi_i)} \mapsto (\varphi_i(\mathbf{x}), f_\top).$$

After this initialization step, we execute the fusion algorithm and eliminate all variables. We obtain

$$\widehat{\varphi}^{-\mathbf{V}}(\diamond) = (\widehat{\varphi_1} \otimes \cdots \otimes \widehat{\varphi_n})^{-\mathbf{V}}(\diamond).$$

Clearly, the semiring component $\widehat{\varphi}_A^{\downarrow \emptyset}(\diamond)$ contains again the maximum value of φ over all its configurations, i.e.

$$\widehat{\varphi}_A^{-\mathbf{V}}(\diamond) = \varphi^{-\mathbf{V}}(\diamond).$$

Let us now focus on the Boolean-valued function $\widehat{\varphi}_F^{-\mathbf{V}}(\diamond)$ that has been built simultaneously. The following theorem confirms what we have foreshadowed all along, namely that the set

8.2 Solution Configurations in Semiring Valuation Algebras

of models of this function corresponds exactly to the solution configurations we are looking for.

Theorem 9. *For* $\mathbf{x} \in \Omega_{\mathbf{V}}$ *and* $d(\varphi) = \mathbf{V}$ *we have*

$$\left(\widehat{\varphi}_F^{-\mathbf{V}}(\diamond)\right)(\mathbf{x}) = 1 \text{ if and only if } \varphi(\mathbf{x}) = \varphi^{-\mathbf{V}}(\diamond).$$

Thus, every solution configuration of φ evaluates the constructed Boolean-valued function to 1 and is therefore a model. Conversely, every model is also a solution configuration of φ. The proof of this result is given by Pouly and Kohlas [2007] for Boolean functions. It is easily adapted to Boolean-valued ones.

For Boolean functions, Pouly et al. [2007] show that this kind of combination and variable elimination can be used to construct a PDAG representing $\widehat{\varphi}_F^{-\mathbf{V}}(\diamond)$. Furthermore, this PDAG is decomposable and deterministic, and it contains only simple-negations. Hence, the PDAG is a d-DNNF. For Boolean-valued functions, we get a decomposable, deterministic, and negation-free MDAG, i.e. a cdn-MDAG.

It is worth mentioning that during the fusion process, cdn-MDAGs are built from connecting existing cdn-MDAGs by either a conjunction or a disjunction node. However, we know that the cdn-MDAG does not support these operations in polytime. This means concretely that it is in general not possible to reconstruct a cdn-MDAG structure from the conjunction or disjunction of two cdn-MDAGs in polynomial time. Fortunately, this does not hold for the case at hand. Since these constructions are performed as valuation algebra operations, we directly obtain the cdn-properties whenever we join two existing cdn-MDAGs by the rules specified for memorizing semiring valuations. I.e. conjunctions are already decomposable and disjunctions are already deterministic.

Recapitulation

With the (extended) fusion algorithm, we are in possession of an efficient tool to compute solution configurations of optimization problems that are given as factorizations of semiring valuations. However, the requirements of diagnostics are rarely limited to the identification of solution configurations, i.e. we often want to perform some further evaluations of these solution configurations without their explicit enumeration. Therefore, we proposes to compile

Chapter 8 Further Applications

the solution configuration set into a Boolean function and by use of current knowledge compilation techniques. By doing so, we obtain a very compact, graphical representation of the solution configuration set that allows to carry out efficiently a large collection of new queries, including the enumeration of solution configurations. Additionally, this compilation process does not forfeit efficiency because it is based on the same local computation scheme.

Part III

Implementation

Chapter 9

Framework

The major goal of the implementation is to provide a framework for knowledge compilation. The idea is to have a common implementation coping different languages, and, hence, allowing a user to switch easily between these languages. Additionally, it should be possible to add further languages. Because of that we choose an object oriented implementation written in Java (1.5). The printed source code is conform to this version of Java but for the sake of simplicity and clarity dispensable details are set aside. We use UML 2.0 diagrams for illustration, but again, these diagrams are cut down to the important aspects (see Appendix B for a basic introduction). Several *design patterns* are used throughout the whole implementation. Consider Gamma et al. [1994] for details on these patterns.

The framework itself is implemented within the package kc (for **k**nowledge **c**ompilation). The content of kc is shown in Figure 9.1 which also serves as an overview of the framework. The package model contains the *model* of the framework, i.e. it provides the required data structure. The packages query and transformation contain the implementations of the different queries and transformations. In this way, we are able to use one implementation of a query or transformation within several languages. Implementations of the of the different languages are contained in language. The implementation of a language takes care that the data structure satisfies the corresponding requirements. For example, the implementation of cdn-MDAG ensures that each ∧-node is decomposable, that each ∨-node is deterministic, and that either not a single ¬-node occurs or the child of each occurring ¬-node is a terminal. The package interpreter contains implementations for obtaining a representation in a language from an representation in another language. Finally, auxiliary contains the supporting (sub-)packages, classes and interfaces. In the following, we introduce these packages shortly.

Chapter 9 Framework

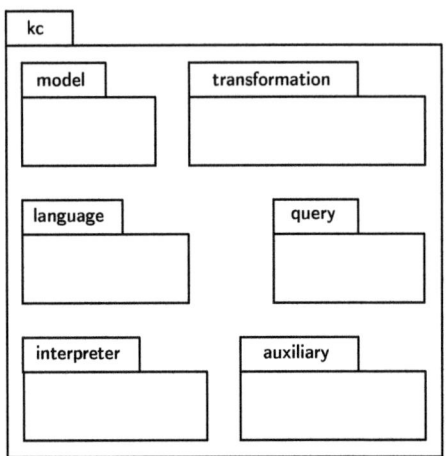

Figure 9.1: The UML diagram of the package kc.

9.1 The model Package

As mentioned before the package model covers the data structure of the framework. It consists of the one class, four interfaces, and the package node which contains fifteen classes. Figure 9.2. Note that abstract classes (and later on abstract methods) are written in italic, e.g. the class Node.

Obviously, Variable models variables, both Boolean and multi-state ones. Its details are shown in Figure B.2 within the appendix. Listing 9.1 shows how to create a Boolean-variable with name 'X' and two alternatives for creating a multi-state variable with name 'Y' and frame $\Omega_Y = \{y_0, y_1, y_2\}$.

The four interfaces represent different kinds of semirings. The interface Semiring includes two methods representing the binary operations of a semiring. In addition, there are three further interfaces. TotallyOrdered adds a total order to Semiring. Complemented adds a method that returns the complement of a value with respect to another one. Finally, Probability provides two useful methods for probability computation to TotallyOrdered. For details consider Figure B.4. These four interfaces are used according to the *adapter* design pattern for the generic implementation of several complex queries. I.e. these complex queries are able to handle a certain type of values as soon as a corresponding instance of

9.1 The model Package

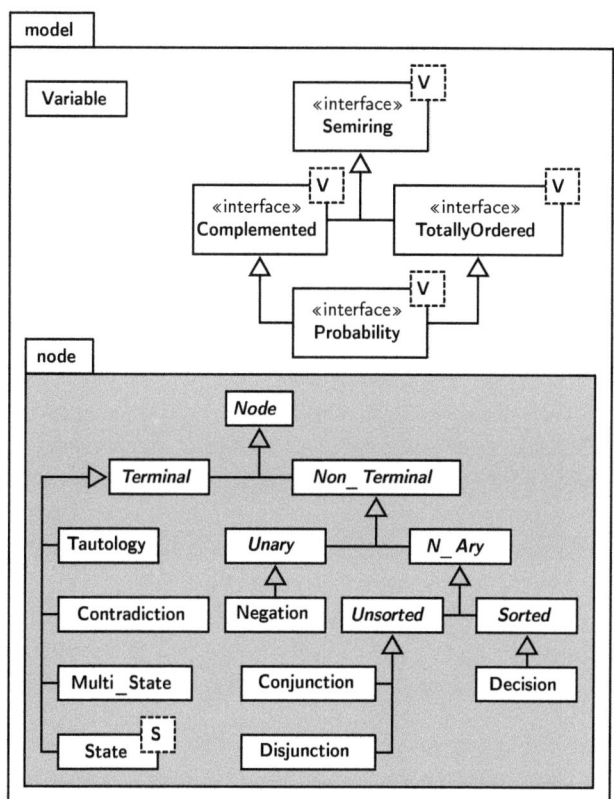

Figure 9.2: The UML diagram of the package model.

```
// Boolean variable
Variable x = Variable.boolean_variable("X");

// multi-state variable
Variable y1 = Variable.multi_state_variable("Y",
                            "y_0", "y_1", "y_2");

// alternative
String[] frame = new String[]{"y_0", "y_1", "y_2"};
Variable y2 = Variable.multi_state_variable("Y", frame);
```

Listing 9.1: Obtaining instances of Variable.

Chapter 9 Framework

semiring is available.

The package node treats the representation of nodes. Figure B.3 shows the details of the class Node. The generalizations of Node reflect the definition of the different kinds of nodes. Due to the definition of PDAG and MDAG, a node is either a terminal or a non-terminal, which is reflected by the corresponding abstract classes. For terminals, there are three different kinds of labels, namely $\top$, $\bot$, and a variable together with a subset of its frame. These labels lead to the classes Tautology, Contradiction, and Multi_State. In addition, we also included a fourth kind of terminal to be able to represent the different terminals within a multi-terminal decision diagram. The corresponding class is the generic class State.

Within the non-terminals, we distinguish between the ones with exactly one child and the ones with possibly more than one child. The abstract classes Unary and N_Ary represent this distinction. The class Negation covers the sole kind of non-terminals with exactly one child, the one labeled with $\neg$. For the non-terminals with an arbitrary number of children, we distinguish between unsorted and sorted children. The abstract classes Unsorted and Sorted mirror this dependence. The classes Conjunction and Disjunction are sub-classes of Unsorted, since they do not depend on the order of the children, whereas Decision is a sub-class of Sorted, since itdepends on the order of the children. Conjunction represents a non-terminal labeled with $\wedge$, Disjunction represents a non-terminal labeled with $\vee$, and, finally, Decision represents a non-terminal labeled with a variable.

On the way down from the abstract class Node to the non-abstract classes we adapt the methods and fields to match the current class. For example consider the method equalChildren(nodes: Node...): **boolean**. It's purpose is to return **true** if the parameter nodes is equal to the children of the current node. Within Node, the method is defined to return **false**. This is correct for terminal and non-terminals labeled with $\neg$. However, we change the behavior of the method as soon as a node may have children. In N_Ary, we add a field children of type Node[]. However, the method equalChildren is not overwritten yet. This is done within the abstract classes Sorted and Unsorted, since the order of the children may or must not be important for the implementation.

The two different accepts methods are of utmost importance, since the implementation of queries and transformations as well as interpreters for other languages are based on them. Their definition follows the *visitor* design pattern. According to Gamma et al. [1994], this pattern makes adding new operations easy, which is exactly what is needed. Furthermore, it gathers related operations and separates unrelated ones. The two methods reflect this fact via the additional parameter condition within ConditionalVisitor. Later on, we discuss the two classes of visitors.

9.2 The language Package

This package contains the implementations of the different languages. It contains two abstract classes. The first one is Language and provides some basic methods and fields for the implementation of MDAG and its sublanguages. The other abstract class is MT_Language and provides some basic methods and fields for the implementation of MTMDD and its sublanguages. Each languages is a generalization of the abstract class Language which provides a basic implementation of the common methods. In the following, Language is discussed intensively due to its importance for MDAG and its sublanguages. Language contains some field and methods besides the methods implementing queries and transformations. At first, we take at look at these fields and general methods. Afterwards, we consider the methods corresponding to queries and transformations.

9.2.1 Fields and general Methods

In the following, we consider the field and methods shown in Figure 9.3. The fields of Language include the public constants CONTRADICTION and TAUTOLOGY which represent the $\bot$-terminal and the $\top$-terminal. Both constants are declared **static final**. Besides these two, there are three more fields:

- variables stores the constructed variables.
- nodes stores the constructed nodes.
- terminals stores the constructed terminals of each variable.

Among the general methods are five static ones. The private method bitssOK tests if an array of arrays of Booleans is not **null** and does not contain any **null**. In addition, it also tests if all arrays of Boolean have the same length. This is very important for the method combine which combines the arrays of arrays and returns a new array of Booleans. If neutral is **true** this new array corresponds to the conjunction of the values stored in the specified arrays. Otherwise the the new array corresponds to the disjunction of the values stored in the specified arrays.

Chapter 9 Framework

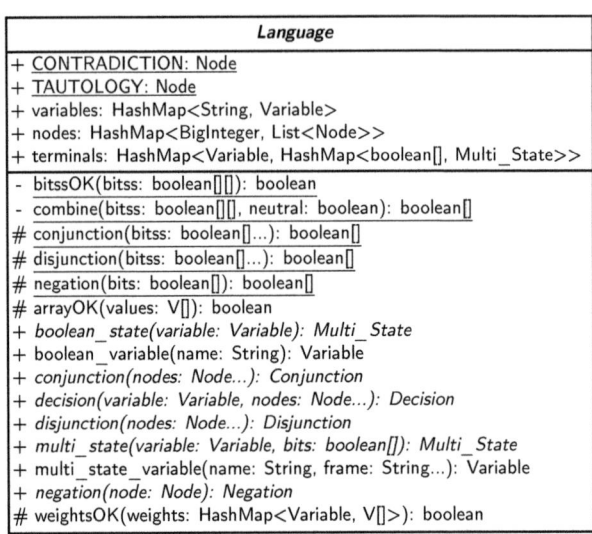

Figure 9.3: A part of the UML diagram of the abstract class `Language` which shows the field and the general methods.

These two methods are used within the protected methods `conjunction` and `disjunction` to obtain an array of Booleans corresponding to the conjunction or disjunction of arrays of Boolean. In case that `bitssOK` returns **false**, these two methods return **null**. The last static method is `negation` which returns a new array of Booleans corresponding to the negation of its parameter.

The eight public methods consist of two ones concerning variables and six abstract ones concerning nodes. The two methods `boolean_variable` and `multi_state_variable` return a variable for the specified parameters or **null** if something is not correct. At first, both methods check if `variables` already contains an entry for the specified name. If there is no entry, a new variable is constructed. In case that the new variable is not equal to **null**, it is also added to `variables` before it is returned. In case, that `variables` already contains a variable for the specified name, the specified frame and the frame of the variable are compared. If the frames are equal, the stored variable is returned, otherwise **null** is returned. The six abstract methods concern the construction of nodes. It is important that their realization works similar to `boolean_variable` and `multi_state_variable`. Of course, the realizations have to use `nodes` instead of `variables`. In addition, the methods `boolean_state` and `multi_state` have

9.2 The `language` Package

```
+ areComplementary(a: Node, b: Node): boolean
+ areEquivalent(a: Node, b: Node): boolean
+ areProbabilisticComplementary(a: Node, b: Node, failure: double): boolean
+ areProbabilisticEquivalent(a: Node, b: Node, failure: double): boolean
+ entailsClause(node: Node, literals: Multi_State...): boolean
+ entailsSentence(a: Node, b: Node): boolean
+ impliedByTerm(node: Node, literals: Multi_State...): boolean
+ isConsistent(node: Node): boolean
+ isInconsistent(node: Node): boolean
+ isInconsistentConjunction(a: Node, b: Node): boolean
+ isNotValid(node: Node): boolean
+ isValid(node: Node): boolean
+ isValidDisjunction(a: Node, b: Node): boolean
```

Figure 9.4: A part of the UML diagram of the abstract class `Language` which shows the methods corresponding to predicates.

to proceed similar with `terminals`. The fields `nodes` and `terminals` are very important for structural reductions which lead to canonicity in case of G-FMDD and π-OMDD.

The two protected methods are used to test if the parameters satisfy the requirements. `arrayOK` returns **true** if the parameter `values` is not **null** and does not contain **null**. `weightsOK` returns **true** if the parameter `weights` is not **null** and it does not contain an entry where either the key is **null** or the length of the value does not fit the length of the frame of the corresponding variable. These methods are useful when realizing the abstract methods from above and below.

9.2.2 Methods for Queries and Transformations

The parts of the UML diagram of `Language` containing the methods concerning predicates, complex queries, and transformations are displayed in the Figures 9.4, 9.5, and 9.6 respectively. Note that the methods of some complex queries contain a kind of semiring. This semiring includes the required semiring operations for the different methods and is very important for the generic implementation. The idea behind these semirings is the *adapter* design pattern Gamma et al. [1994]. I.e. these generic methods are able to work with a certain type if a matching semiring is provided.

As soon as a language supports a query in polytime, it should be implemented accordingly. Otherwise, the call of a method corresponding to a not supported query should result in an error. For the methods corresponding to transformations, we follow a different strategy,

+ *argmax(node:* Node, *weights:* HashMap<Variable, V[]>,
  semiring: TotallyOrdered<? extends V>): Node
+ *countCounterModels(node:* Node): BigInteger
+ *countModels(node:* Node): BigInteger
+ *countWeightedCounterModels(node:* Node, *weights:* HashMap<Variable, V[]>,
  semiring: Complemented<? extends V>): V
+ *countWeightedModels(node:* Node, *weights:* HashMap<Variable, V[]>,
  semiring: Complemented<? extends V>): V
+ *enumerateCounterModels(node:* Node): List<List<Node>>
+ *enumerateModels(node:* Node): List<List<Node>>
+ *maximalCardinality(node:* Node): BigInteger
+ *maximum(node:* Node, *weights:* HashMap<Variable, V[]>,
  semiring: TotallyOrdered<? extends V>): V
+ *minimalCardinality(node:* Node): BigInteger
+ *probability(node:* Node, *probabilities:* HashMap<Variable, V[]>,
  semiring: Probability<? extends V>): V
+ *selectCounterModel(node:* Node): List<Node>
+ *selectModel(node:* Node): List<Node>

Figure 9.5: A part of the UML diagram of the abstract class Language which shows the methods corresponding to complex queries.

```
+ and(a: Node, b: Node): Node
+ and(nodes: Node...): Node
+ existentialDeterministicForget(node: Node, variable: Variable): Node
+ existentialDeterministicForget(node: Node, variables: Variable...): Node
+ existentialForget(node: Node, variable: Variable): Node
+ existentialForget(node: Node, variables: Variable...): Node
+ not(node: Node): Node
+ or(a: Node, b: Node): Node
+ or(nodes: Node...): Node
+ termCondition(node: Node, literals: Multi_State...): Node
+ generalTermCondition(node: Node, literals: Multi_State...): Node
+ deterministicGeneralTermCondition(node: Node, literals: Multi_State...):
                                                                       Node
+ universalDecomposableForget(node: Node, variable: Variable): Node
+ universalDecomposableForget(node: Node, variables: Variable...): Node
+ universalForget(node: Node, variable: Variable): Node
+ universalForget(node: Node, variables: Variable...): Node
```

Figure 9.6: A part of the UML diagram of the abstract class Language which shows the methods corresponding to transformations.

since we provide an implementation of each transformation no matter if the transformation is supported by the current language or not. These two strategies reflect the two phases of knowledge compilation. During the off-line reasoning phase the knowledge base is constructed which requires the transformations. The idea is to put the time-killing operations in this phase. This argues for the implementation of all transformations for each language. The on-line reasoning phase consists of answering queries based on the knowledge base. Since the queries shall be answered fast, it makes sense to implement only the supported queries of a language.

9.3 The Remaining Packages

The packages query, transformation, interpreter, and auxiliary are the remaining ones. The content of the first three packages is obvious: the classes implementing the different queries and transformations and interpreters between languages. Some of these classes may be used by the implementation of several languages. For example, as soon as a language supports a query, the class implementing the query may be used within the implementation of the language and its sublanguages. In the following chapter, we take a look at a sample of the queries.

Chapter 9 Framework

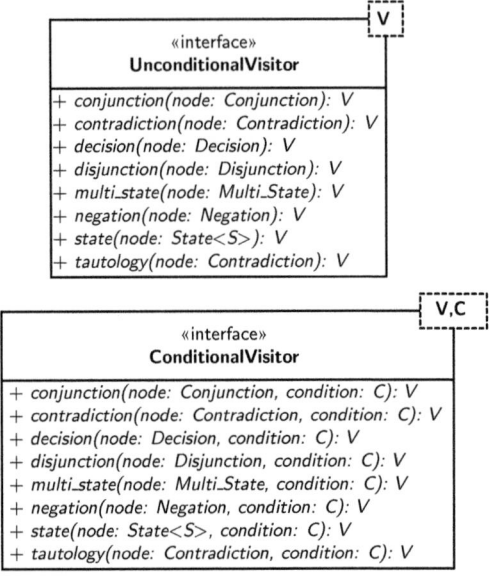

Figure 9.7: The interfaces `UnconditionalVisitor` and `ConditionalVisitor`.

Each interpreter is an implementation of the interface `interpreter` as shown in Figure B.1. The diversity of queries and transformations (see Figures 9.4, 9.5, and 9.6) makes it very hard to provide a similar interface for queries and transformations. In our case, this is rather an advantage than a disadvantage. To understand this, it is important to know each query, each transformation, and each interpreter implements one of the two visitor interfaces contained in the package `auxiliary`. In case of an interpreter, the method `interpret` makes preparations, calls the methods of visitor, and takes care of the result. In case of queries and transformations, we also employ such an administrative method. Due to the different parameters of the corresponding methods, we refrain form implementing an interface containing all these various methods.

As mentioned above, the package `auxiliary` contains two interfaces used within the packages `query`, `transformation`, and `interpreter`. The interfaces are `UnconditionalVisitor` and `ConditionalVisitor`. Their UML diagram is shown in Figure 9.7. The difference between the two interfaces is the additional parameter `condition: C` within each method. Both interfaces contain one method for each (non-abstract) generalization of `Node`. Within these generalizations, the two methods

```
<V,C> V accepts(ConditionalVisitor<V,C> visitor, C condition)
```
and ``` <V> V accepts(UnconditionalVisitor<V> visitor)```

call the method of the parameter `visitor` corresponding to the current class, e.g. the class `Negation` employs `visitor.negation(`**this**`, condition)` and `visitor.negation(`**this**`)`. The following chapter includes some realizations of the two visitor interfaces.

9.4 Recapitulation: Framework

The framework introduced in this chapter provides an implementation of the common features of the different languages based on various generic interfaces and abstract classes. The design patterns visitor and adapter incorporated within the framework which makes it even more adaptable. This allows us to implement different languages by reusing existing code and adding new code whenever necessary.

Chapter 10

Algorithms

In this chapter, we discuss some exemplary algorithms. As mentioned before the implementation of most of the queries relies on one of the two visitor interfaces.

10.1 Inconsistency and Consistency

The implementation of these two queries extends the class `HashingUV`. `HashingUV` is a generic abstract class belonging to the package `kc.auxiliary`, and it implements the interface `UnconditionalVisitor`. In short, the class contains a field `HashMap<Node, V> map` and ensures via the method `visit` that the result of visiting a node is stored in `map` and reused if the node is visited again. For better understanding, take a look at the implementation of `visit` as pictured in Listing 10.1.

```
protected W visit(Node node) {
  W result = map.get(node);
  if(result == null) {
    result = node.accepts(this);
    map.put(node, result);
  }
  return result;
}
```

Listing 10.1: The implementation of the method `visit` within `HashingUV`.

Chapter 10 Algorithms

Now, let us turn the attention to the implementation of the queries. We start with the implementation of the test of inconsistency and *consistency*. In short, a formula, node and so on is *consistent* if it is not *inconsistent*. Darwiche [2001a] provides an algorithm which computes if the Boolean function represented by a DNNF is consistent or not. The algorithm below is the adaption of this algorithm to multi-state variables. Instead of a DNNF representation, we assume a cn-MDAG representation. The treatment of instances of Negation and State within the implementation InConsistency reflects this assumption. First of all, InConsistency extends the HashingUV. I.e. the method visit takes care of hashing and reusing hashed results. Hence, we only have to consider the methods corresponding to the visitor interface.

The methods contradiction always returns **false**, whereas the methods multi_state and tautology always return **true**. Furthermore, the methods state throws an exception, more exactly an UnsupportedOperationException. The implementation of the remaining methods is given in Listing 10.2. The method negation makes clear that we assume a representation with at most simple-negations, i.e. only terminals may be negated.

As mentioned before, the requirements for this algorithm decomposability and simple-negations (if any). Hence, we may use this algorithm for all sublanguages of cn-MDAG which includes all languages supporting IN except cd-MDAG. Sometimes, it is useful to implement an algorithm fitted towards some of these sublanguages. The implementation of the different languages should access this class via the two methods consistent and inconsistent.

10.2 (Counter) Model Selection and Enumeration

As the heading suggests, the algorithms for these four queries are closely related. Darwiche and Marquis [2002] provide an algorithm for enumerating the models of a DNNF based on inconsistency and term conditioning. In the following, we adapt this algorithm to the corresponding multi-state language cn-MDAG. In addition, we also highlight the differences between the different queries.

Let L be a language that supports the query inconsistency IN and the transformation term conditioning TC. For $\varphi \in$ L, we obtain the models of φ as follows. First, if φ is inconsistent ($\varphi \equiv \bot$) then it does not have any models. Otherwise, construct a tree representation of the models of φ for an ordering $V_1, \ldots, V_r$ of $vars(\varphi)$. We start with a tree T consisting of a

10.2 (Counter) Model Selection and Enumeration

```
public Boolean conjunction(Conjunction node) {
  Node[] children = node.getChildren();
  for(Node child : children)
    if(! visit(child)) return false;
  return true;
}

public Boolean decision(Decision node) {
  Node[] children = node.getChildren();
  for(Node child : children)
    if(visit(child)) return true;
  return false;
}

public Boolean disjunction(Disjunction node) {
  Node[] children = node.getChildren();
  for(Node child : children)
    if(visit(child)) return true;
  return false;
}

public Boolean negation(Negation node) {
  Node child = node.getChild();
  if(child instanceof Contradiction)   return true;
  else if(child instanceof Multi_State) return true;
  else if(child instanceof Tautology)  return false;
  else throw new UnsupportedOperationException(
       "Inconsistency and consistency of Negation only
        defined for Contradiction, Mutli_State,
        and Tautolgy!");
}
```

Listing 10.2: The implementation of several methods of UnconditionalVisitor within the class InConsistency.

Chapter 10 Algorithms

single node, the root of T. For $i = 1$ to r, repeat the following for each leaf node α in T with $\Omega_{V_i} = v_1, \ldots, v_{s_i}$:

> For $j = 1$ to s_i, if $\varphi_j = \varphi | (\alpha \wedge (V_i = v_j))$ is consistent (i.e. $\varphi_{i,j} \not\equiv \bot$), add $(V_i = v_j)$ as a child to α.

According to Darwiche and Marquis [2002], the key points of this algorithm are:

- Each consistency test can be performed in polytime in the size of φ, since L supports both IN and TC.

- For each i and each leaf node α at least one φ_j is consistent.

- The number of tests performed is polynomial in the number of leaf nodes in the final tree and the number of variables in φ. Note that we assume that the size of the frames of the variables is bounded.

As mentioned this algorithm is closely related to counter model enumeration. For counter model enumeration, simply swap the query inconsistency IN with the validity VA. This means to replace "inconsistent" with "valid" and "consistent" with "not valid". To obtain a single model or counter model, simply reset j to 1 and raise i by one as soon as φ_j is consistent and not valid respectively. In both cases, we obtain a tree consisting of a single path. For bounded frames, the time is polynomial in the size of φ which includes the number of variables.

Due to the relationship between model and counter model enumeration and between model and counter model selection, we use two abstract classes. One of them concerns the enumeration while the other one concerns the selection. Both classes provide the corresponding algorithm up to testing if the conditions to continue are satisfied or not. This is represented by the following (**protected abstract**) method:

```
boolean testCondition(Node node, Language language);
```

As long as a node is consistent, we have to continue. Hence, for model enumeration and model selection, the method is implemented as:

```
boolean testCondition(Node node, Language language) {
    return language.isConsistent(node);
}
```

10.3 (Counter) Model Counting and related Queries

For counter models, we must continue as long as a node is not valid. Thus, the implementation for counter model enumeration and counter model selection is:

```
boolean testCondition(Node node, Language language) {
    return ! language.isValid(node);
}
```

Within the implementation, the tree representing models and counter models consists of decision nodes which are build without applying the structural reduction rules. For model and counter model selection, we work with a list of nodes instead of tree. Additionally, it is possible to store and reuse intermediate results. Due to the dependence on the order of the variables, these results may only be used within one call. Hence, the all intermediate results are removed before the final result is returned.

10.3 (Counter) Model Counting and related Queries

The premises for the following algorithm are decomposability and determinism. On one side, decomposability ensures that all conjunctions are consistent since their children don't share variable. On the other side, determinism ensures that each model is considered at most once. Similar to the implementation of the queries consistency and inconsistency, this set of queries is also implemented via a hashing visitor. For model and counter model counting it's HashingUV. For the remaining queries, it is a hashing version of ConditionalVisitor where the condition consists of two fields: the weights and the semiring. In this case, the results are hashed according to the condition and the current node. For model and counter model counting, Listing 10.3 shows the source code of the implementation of the some methods corresponding to the visitor interface. The missing methods, contradiction and tautology, simply return BigInteger.ONE and BigInteger.ZERO respectively. The method countPossibleAssignments counts the possible assignments, i.e. it multiplies the size of the frames of the variables included in its parameter.

For the probabilistic queries PEQ and PCP, we may use a very similar implementation based on BigInteger but implementing the other vistor interface ConditionalHashing. The condition is the selected prime number and we ensure that all operations are performed modulo this prime number. The method countPossibleAssignments is simply replaced by BigInteger.One. The next query is the computation of probabilities PR for which the condition consists of the

```
public BigInteger conjunction(Conjunction node) {
  BigInteger result = BigInteger.ONE;
  for(Node child : node.getChildren())
    result = result.multiply(visit(child));
  return result;
}
public BigInteger decision(Decision node) {
  BigInteger result = BigInteger.ZERO;
  for(Node child : node.getChildren())
    result = result.add(visit(child));
  return result;
}
public BigInteger disjunction(Disjunction node) {
  BigInteger result = BigInteger.ZERO;
  for(Node child : node.getChildren())
    result = result.add(visit(child));
  return result;
}
public BigInteger multi_state(Multi_State node) {
  BigInteger result = BigInteger.ZERO;
  for(boolean bit : node.getBits())
    if(bit) result = result.add(BigInteger.ONE);
  return result;
}
public BigInteger negation(Negation node) {
  Node child = node.getChild();
  return countPossibleAssignments(child)
    .subtract(visit(child));
}
public <S> BigInteger state(State<S> node) {
  throw new UnsupportedOperationException(
    "Models and counter models not defined for State.");
}
```

Listing 10.3: The implementation of several methods of UnconditionalVisitor within the class Counter.

probability distribution of each variable and the corresponding semiring. This semiring has two identity elements (0 and 1), one for the addition and one for the multiplication. In addition, the semiring provides the complement of each value. Besides the methods `decision`, `multi_state`, and `negation`, we only have to change from `BigInteger` to the corresponding semiring value. The method `negation` is changed to return the complement of the value of its child with respect to 1. And the methods `decision` and `multi_state` have to ensure that the values from of the corresponding probability distribution are incorporated. For the two remaining queries, the change is slightly more complex, since the involved semiring doesn't have to have the two identity elements. The direct consequence of this is that the methods `contradiction` and `tautology` become unsupported operations. This has direct consequences for `decision`. The remaining methods are also influenced by the missing identity elements. Overall, the adaption is straight forward, so there is no need to show the source code here.

10.4 Minmal Cardinality, Maximum, and Arguments of Maximum

Darwiche [2001a] introduces an algorithms for the computation of the minimal cardinality of a Boolean function f. Additionally, he also provides an algorithm that returns the Boolean function representing the models of f with the minimal cardinality. In the following, we consider both algorithms for Boolean-valued functions. Since a multi-state variable may have more than two states, we have to specify a weight for each state. In addition to the weights, a semiring is required. This semiring needs to be totally ordered and non-negative. Of its two operations only multiplication is used, since the comparison of two semiring values is supposed to be the addition. However, the comparison is handled via a separate method. For example, the minimal cardinality algorithm relies on non-negative integers where the semiring multiplication corresponds to the common addition. Although, the semiring addition corresponds to the minimization, this is handled via the method `compare` instead. The distinction is not necessary from a mathematical point of view, but it is very useful for the implementation. By changing the method `compare`, we switch easily between computing the minimum or maximum.

According to Darwiche [2001a], the premises of the algorithm are decomposability and simple-negations (if any). The last premise points up that minimization or maximization

Chapter 10 Algorithms

does not act jointly with negations (except simple-negations). Due to complexity, we only take a look at a first implementation of the method `decision`. The source code is shown in Listing 10.4. The implementation of `decision` also includes some basic hints of the implementation of the remaining methods. Note that the methods `contradiction`, `state`, and `tautology` are unsupported operations.

As before the condition contains a semiring (here a totally ordered one) and the weights of the states of the variables. At first, we provide access to the semiring and the weights corresponding to the variable of this node. This is followed by the access to the children of the current node. After this, a few values are initialized. In the **while**-loop, the weight consistent child is determined, i.e. a instances of `Contradiction` are omitted. If the first consistent child is an instance of `Tautology`, we use simply the weight of the corresponding state of the variable, otherwise we multiply the weight with the result of visiting the child. Note that instances of `State` are also omitted since this algorithm is not directed towards multi-terminal decision diagrams. After having determined the first weight, the remaining weights are computed analog and compared with the actual extreme value stored in result.

A important part is the call of the method `comparison`. When determining an extreme value, it is implemented as follows:

```
private V comparison(V a, V b,
  TotallyOrdered<V> semiring) {
    if(semiring.compare(a, b) < 0)
      return b;
    else
      return a;
}
```

For determining the models or arguments yielding the extremal value, it is implementation varies corresponding to the current method form which is it called. In case of `decision`, it is implemented as shown in Listing 10.5. Of course, `decision` would return a instance of `Node` instead of an instance of v. This is easily adapted to the other methods.

As mentioned before, Listing 10.4 corresponds only to a first implementation. The result might be faulty under certain circumstances. Consider again the method `decision`. To compensate the possible error, determine the variables occurring in the current node and within its children. Afterwards, determine the extremal weight for each variable. When considering a child, make sure to include the weights of the variables not included within the

10.4 Minmal Cardinality, Maximum, and Arguments of Maximum

```
public V decision(Decision node, Condition condition) {
  TotallyOrdered<V> semiring = condition.semiring;
  V[] weights = condition.weights.get(node.getVariable());
  Node[] children = node.getChildren();
  V result = null;
  Node current = null;
  int index = 0;
  while(result == null && index < children.length) {
    current = children[index];
    if(current instanceof Contradiction
       || current instanceof State<?>);
    else if(current instanceof Tautology)
        result = weights[index];
    else
        result = semiring.multiply(
            visit(current, condition), weights[index]);
    index++;
  }
  for(; index < children.length; index++) {
    current = children[index];
      if(current instanceof Contradiction
         || current instanceof State<?>);
      else if(current instanceof Tautology)
        result = comparison(result, weights[index],
            semiring);
      else
        result = comparison(result,
            semiring.multiply(visit(current, condition),
            weights[index]), semiring);
  }
  return result;
}
```

Listing 10.4: The implementation of the method `decision` within the implementation of maximum (and minimum respectively).

Chapter 10 Algorithms

```
private V comparison(V a, V b, TotallyOrdered<V> semiring,
 Node current, Node[] nodes, int index) {
  int comparison = semiring.compare(a, b);
  if(comparison < 0) {
    for(int i = 0; i < index; i++)
      nodes[i] = Language.CONTRADICTION;
    nodes[index]= current;
    return b;
  } else {
    if(comparison == 0)
      nodes[index] = current;
    else
      nodes[index] = Language.CONTRADICTION;
    return a;
  }
}
```

Listing 10.5: The implementation of the method comparison for decision nodes.

child. In case of the arguments of the maximum, we have to ensure that the corresponding assignment of the variable is include. This concerns the methods decision and disjunction. To avoid a rerun of computing the minimal weight for each variable, we simply add this information to the condition.

The arising question is which circumstances would lead to a faulty result. Fortunately its answer is pretty simple. We might obtain a faulty result as soon as a variable does not have a weight that is neutral with respect to the semiring operation multiplication of the semiring. In Darwiche's algorithm for minimal cardinality each variable has a state with a neutral weight. For the corresponding models, Darwiche imply the use of smooth DNNF. In general, we may avoid this as described above.

10.5 Existential Forgetting and Term Conditioning

To round off the discussion on algorithms, we finally consider two transformations, more exactly existential forgetting and term conditioning.

Existential forgetting is based on the projection algorithm provided by Darwiche [2001a]. Listing 10.6 shows some of the implementation of some of methods defined by the interface

10.5 Existential Forgetting and Term Conditioning

```
public Node conjunction(Conjunction node,
  Condition condition) {
  return condition.language.and(visit(node.getChildren(),
    condition));
}
public Node decision(Decision node, Condition condition) {
  Variable variable = node.getVariable();
  Node[] children = visit(node.getChildren(), condition);
  if(condition.variables.containsKey(variable))
    return condition.language.or(children);
  else
    return condition.language.decision(variable,
      children);
}
public Node disjunction(Disjunction node,
  Condition condition) {
  return condition.language.or(visit(node.getChildren(),
    condition));
}
public Node multi_state(Multi_State node,
  Condition condition) {
  Variable variable = node.getVariable();
  if(condition.variables.containsKey(variable))
    return Language.TAUTOLOGY;
  else
    return node;
}
public Node negation(Negation node, Condition condition) {
  return condition.language.not(visit(node.getChild(),
    condition));
}
```

Listing 10.6: The implementation of some methods defined by the interface ConditionalHashing within the class for existential forgetting.

Chapter 10 Algorithms

ConditionalHashing. The missing methods simply return their parameter node similar to the method multi_state if the variable is not contained. The method decision points up the difficulty of the algorithm for decision diagrams. Hence, this algorithm is only useful for cn-MDAG, MDNF, and MMODS. But therefore, it leads to an algorithm for forgetting deterministic variables for the languages cdn-MDAG and d-MDNF. All we have to care about are the two calls condition.language.or(...). Since the variables are deterministic, determinism does not have to be ensured. Obviously, the class Condition consists of two fields, one for the language and one for the variables. For constant access, the last one is a hash map. The implementation of general term conditioning follows a similar idea. In this case, the key of the hash map is the variable and the value is an array of Booleans. I.e. each entry in the hash map represents a single multi-state terminal.

Now, let us have a look at a part of the source code of term conditioning as displayed in Listing 10.7. Again, the methods contradiction, state, and tautology are once more omitted, since they simply return their parameter node. In contrast to the implementation of existential forgetting the remaining methods don't use the methods corresponding to the transformations but the node creating methods which only perform structural reductions.

10.6 Recapitulation: Algorithms

This chapter covers the algorithms of several queries and transformations. The remaining queries and transformations are discussed within the appendix. At first, some queries implement either ConditionalVisitor or UnconditionalVisitor which shows the importance of these interfaces and the benefits of the visitor design pattern. Another important realization is the dependence of some queries on a (commutative) semiring. The study of this relationship between queries and semirings might lead to further interesting results.

10.6 Recapitulation: Algorithms

```
public Node conjunction(Conjunction node,
  Condition condition) {
  return condition.language.conjunction(
      visit(node.getChildren(), condition));
}
public Node decision(Decision node, Condition condition) {
  Variable variable = node.getVariable();
  Node[] children = node.getChildren();
  Integer index = condition.variables.get(variable);
  if(index != null)
    return visit(children[index.intValue()],
        condition);
  else
    return condition.language.decision(variable,
        visit(children, condition));
}
public Node disjunction(Disjunction node,
  Condition condition) {
  return condition.language.disjunction(
    visit(node.getChildren(), condition));
}
public Node multi_state(Multi_State node,
  Condition condition) {
  Integer index = condition.variables.get(
    node.getVariable());
  if(index != null)
    if(node.getBits()[index.intValue()])
      return Language.TAUTOLOGY;
    else
      return Language.CONTRADICTION;
  else return node;
}
public Node negation(Negation node, Condition condition) {
  return condition.language.negation(
      visit(node.getChild(), condition));
}
```

Listing 10.7: The implementation of some methods defined by the interface ConditionalHashing within the class for term conditioning.

Part IV

Conclusion

Chapter 11

Summary

The previous chapters cover the important area of knowledge compilation, some of its applications and the implementation (in Java 1.5) of a framework for knowledge compilation. We started with the existing knowledge compilation map and defined new languages by dropping the common property of the NNF and its sublanguages. This property was identified as simple-negation and led to a better understanding of the representation of Boolean functions. Among the new languages the two most important ones are PDAG, the common roof of the considered languages, and cd-PDAG, supporting even more queries than DNNF. After the introduction of the new language and the rollback of the languages included in the map of Darwiche and Marquis [2002], we started to extend the map. At first, all languages were compared according to the size of the representation of Boolean functions. For this, we reused and extended the previous results. However, there are still some languages where the result is partial if there is any at all. Afterwards, the focus changed to the queries supported by the different languages. This analysis started with the definition of various queries including new ones. Based on the definition, some correlations between the queries were pointed out. These correlations proved to be very useful for the analysis. Another very useful factor is the inheritance of supported queries, i.e. if a language supports a query, all its sublanguage also support that query. Finally, we finished the discussion of the knowledge compilation map for Boolean functions by studying different transformations. In contrast to queries which provide information about a Boolean function without altering it, the purpose of transformation is to obtain an the alteration of Boolean functions involved. Again, we started with the definition of the transformations. In this step, some new transformations were added. The analysis ended with an overview showing which transformations are supported by a language. Up to this point, the knowledge compilation map concerned only Boolean functions. To increase the range of the map, we discussed Boolean-valued

Chapter 11 Summary

functions, in addition to two generalizations of them. Luckily, it is possible to reduce the two generalizations to Boolean-valued functions or tuples thereof. This led to a new knowledge compilation map for Boolean-valued functions. Compared with the map for Boolean functions, it contains two additional queries (general term conditioning and its deterministic version), and it distinguishes between variables with two states and variables with three or more states for the queries concerning forgetting variables.

Following the installation of the knowledge compilation map, we considered some application areas. The first area were semiring valuation algebras, a special case of valuation algebras. Semiring valuation algebras are highly generic and cover many other application areas. Inspired by improvements in the area of Bayesian networks, we discussed these improvements in the context of semiring valuation algebras. This discussion led to four possible candidates for representing semiring valuations. Three of them are included in the knowledge compilation map, namely MDNF, G-FMDD, and π-OMDD. The last one, π-OMTMDD is closely related to π-OMDD. Hence, we were able to reuse some of the results. Choosing to represent the knowledge within one of these four languages, may lead to a speedup of the algorithms used in the area of semiring valuation algebras. After this very general application area, we considered an application in the area of Bayesian networks. Like Darwiche, we decided to represent the network by a logical formula. However, we followed a different approach. The question was which language should be used to represent the formula (which corresponds to a Boolean-valued function). For this purpose, we identified the required queries and transformations. Among the possible candidates, cdn-MDAG turned out to be the most succinct one. This fits with the results of Darwiche since cdn-MDAG is the Boolean-valued version of d-DNNF. We could improve this even further by applying the results from semiring valuation algebras. The third application area, a special case of Bayesian networks, covers reliability and diagnostics of modular systems. Here, we followed the same idea as for Bayesian network. Interestingly, the simplicity of modular systems (compared with Bayesian networks) led to another set of required queries and transformations. Most notably, the transformation NOT was required. In the end, it turned out that cd-MDAG is the most succinct language which satisfied the requirements. We closed the reflection of application areas with two applications corresponding to queries. At first, we took a look at testing the equivalence in a probabilistic way. Afterwards, we considered an alternative approach to representing the models yielding the maximal (or minimal) weight.

In the end, we discussed the ideas behind the basic implementation of the knowledge compilation map. The framework was separated into six packages. The name of the package summarized content of the packages. The package model contained the classes and interfaces for the representation of nodes, variables and semiring. Note that the interface for semiring served as an adapter. The languages itself were contained in the package language. Each language was supposed to extend the abstract class Language. Two important interfaces were included in the package auxiliary, namely: ConditionalVisitor and UnconditionalVisitor. Both followed the visitor design pattern and added flexibility to the implementation of nodes.

Chapter 12

Open Problems

During the course of the thesis, we addressed several problems. Some of these problems were solved and some not. In addition, we also raised new problems. In the following, we review some of the open problems.

Languages: Only some languages are considered in the map at hand. Adding more languages is important to keep the map up to date. Besides several languages in the area of decision diagrams, it is also possible to obtain new (complete) languages via a closure of existing (incomplete) ones, e.g. the disjunctive closure of conjunctions of *horn clauses* or the conjunctive closure of disjunctions of *horn terms*.

Succinctness: Besides the open problems in the context of succinctness relations between languages within this map, each new language adds more problems to this topic. Although obvious relations between the languages are very helpful to reduce the number of problems, they are not sufficient to answer all problems.

Queries: For some languages, there are still some queries left to prove if they are supported by the language. Adding a new language also requires several proofs. However, we might use sublanguage relationships to derive the result. I.e. the queries supported by a language L are also supported by the sublanguages of L. The analysis of the relation between semirings and queries might lead to new queries and should deepen the understanding of the requirements of queries.

Transformations: For some languages, there are still some transformations left to prove if they are supported by the language. Adding a new language also requires several proofs.

Chapter 12 Open Problems

Boolean-valued functions: Besides the open problems inherited from the knowledge compilation map for Boolean functions, there are also new problems regarding queries and transformations. Another open problem is the comparison of the different approaches for representing generalizations of Boolean-valued functions.

It is also necessary to identify new application areas. Although semiring valuation algebras already cover a big number of applications, there are still applications that are not covered. Of course, the implementation also needs to be kept up to date matching new languages, queries, and transformations and results within these contexts.

Appendix

Appendix A

Proofs

As the heading suggests this chapter contains the proofs of the various propositions and theorems. The following sections group various proofs together.

A.1 Succinctness

Proof of Proposition 1.1.
We start proving the succinctness within the first group and use these transformations to show the results for the two remaining groups. For the first group, it is sufficient to show that PDAG can be transformed in polynomial size into the each other language, since all other languages (even BED) are sublanguages of PDAG.

Let $\varphi \in$ PDAG be an arbitrary PDAG. Then, we obtain the corresponding $\varphi_c \in$ c-PDAG be replacing each $\wedge$-node of φ as shown in Figure A.1(a). This transformation requires at most $s + 1$ additional edges for a $\wedge$-node with s children. In the end, we obtain φ_c, which does not contain any $\wedge$-node, with $|\varphi_c| \leq 3|\varphi|$. The transformation from φ to $\varphi_d \in$ d-PDAG is analog to the previous one except that each $\vee$-node is replaced instead of each $\wedge$-node as shown in Figure A.1(b). This time, the transformations provides φ_d, which does not contain any $\vee$-node, with $|\varphi_d| \leq 3|\varphi|$. Transforming φ into $\varphi_n \in$ NNF is done by moving the negation nodes down to the leaves as shown in Figure A.1(c). Hence, we obtain φ_n, which contains $\neg$-nodes only in proximity of leaves, with $|\varphi_n| \leq 2|\varphi|$. Note that in all these transformations consecutive $\neg$-nodes are removed by the corresponding structural reduction rule. For the last transformation, we need to ensure that all $\wedge$- or $\vee$-nodes have only two children. A $\wedge$-/$\vee$-node ψ with $s > 2$ children is handled as follows: First, split the children into $\lceil \frac{s}{2} \rceil$ pairs.

Appendix A Proofs

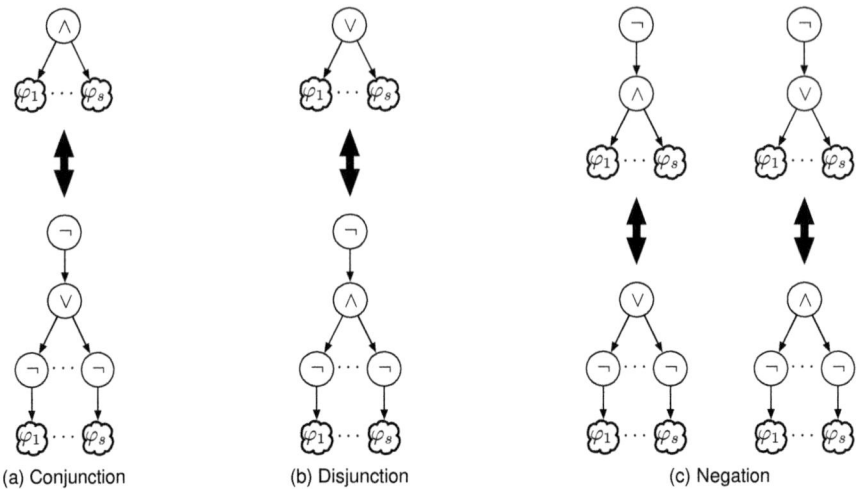

Figure A.1: A graphical representation of the De Morgan's laws.

For each pair, add an ∧-/∨-node with the pair as children. Consider the new ∧-/∨-nodes as children and repeat until only one node remains. This transformation requires $r = \lceil \log s \rceil$ repetitions and at most $2^r - 1 < 2s$ new ∧-/∨-nodes. Hence, we obtain $\varphi_b \in$ BED with $|\varphi_b| \leq 4|\varphi|$.

Since f-NNF is a sublanguage of f-PDAG and cd-PDAG is a sublanguage of CD-PDAG, it is sufficient to consider the transformations form f-PDAG to f-NNF and from CD-PDAG to cd-PDAG. The transformation from f-PDAG to f-NNF is the same as the one from PDAG to NNF, since the height is not affected by moving the ¬-nodes down to the leaves. The transformation from CD-PDAG to cd-PDAG is built from two of the previous transformations. First, all deterministic ∧-nodes are replaced as in the transformation from PDAG to c-PDAG. Then, all decomposable ∨-nodes are replaced as in the transformation from PDAG to d-PDAG. In the end, we obtain $\varphi_{cd} \in$ cd-PDAG from $\varphi_{CD} \in$ CD-PDAG with $|\varphi_{cd}| \leq 3|\varphi_{CD}|$. □

Proof of Proposition 1.2.
Since AND/OR is a super-language of OBDD, it is sufficient to show that there is a polynomial transformation from AND/OR to OBDD. Let $\varphi \in$ AND/OR be an arbitrary AND/OR graph with pseudo tree T. From T, we obtain a variable order π_T by a deep-first walkthrough. The label of each node is appended to π_T as soon as the node is visited. The requirements

A.1 Succinctness

of the pseudo tree ensure that each variable occurs only once in a label of a node. The deep-first walkthrough ensures that all labels of a branch are added before the next branch is handled. Now, we recursively transform (bottom-up) each $\wedge$-node ω into an equivalent $\omega' \in \pi_T$-OBDD. Due to the construction of π_T, there is a unique order of the children ω_i of ω, such that for two children $\omega_{i_1}, \omega_{i_2}$ with $\omega_{i_1} < \omega_{i_2}$, we have $V_{i_1} < V_{i_2}$ according to π_T for each variable $V_{i_1} \in vars(\omega_{i_1})$ and for each variable $V_{i_2} \in vars(\omega_{i_2})$. Let $\omega_1 < \ldots < \omega_s$ be this order of children. Now, we obtain ω' equivalent to ω by taking the edges of ω_i leading to the $\top$-terminal and redirecting them to the root of ω_{i+1} for $1 \leq i < s$. Since this transformation does not add edges but removes the edges of the $\wedge$-node, we end up with $\varphi' \in \pi_T$-OBDD equivalent to $\varphi \in$ AND/OR and $|\varphi'| \leq |\varphi|$. □

Proof of Proposition 1.3.
Due to the transitivity of $\preceq$, we have the following three (general) scenarios between the three languages L_1, L_2, and L_3.

(G1) $L_1 \preceq L_2$ and $L_2 \preceq L_3$ implies $L_1 \preceq L_3$ (transitivity).

(G2) $L_1 \preceq L_2$ and $L_1 \not\preceq L_3$ implies $L_2 \not\preceq L_3$.

(G3) $L_1 \not\preceq L_3$ and $L_2 \preceq L_3$ implies $L_1 \not\preceq L_2$.

These three scenarios turn out to be very useful in the following. Since PDAG and NNF as well as f-PDAG and f-NNF are equally succinct, we are able to reuse most of the results of Darwiche and Marquis [2002]. Note that they denote π-OBDD by OBDD$_<$. Table A.1 repeats the results of Proposition 1.3 together with some additional information. Each $\preceq$ without index is due to sublanguage relationships. For all other relations, the index revers to the corresponding proof in this dissertation which relies on Darwiche and Marquis [2002].

(a) Darwiche and Marquis [2002] show in Table 9 that DNF $\not\preceq$ PI and CNF $\not\preceq$ IP which slightly generalizes the results DNF $\not\preceq$ CNF and CNF $\not\preceq$ DNF by Gogic et al. [1995]. In addition, they show IP $\not\preceq$ DNF and PI $\not\preceq$ CNF. Due to (G2), this includes L $\not\preceq$ PI and L $\not\preceq$ CNF for L $\in$ {IP, d-DNF, MODS} as well as PI $\not\preceq$ IP and PI $\not\preceq$ DNF. Whereas (G1) yields MODS $\not\preceq$ DNF. Finally, (G3) leads to $L_1 \not\preceq L_2$ for $\in_1$ {CNF, IP, PI, MODS} and $L_2 \in$ {PDAG, DNNF} as well as L $\not\preceq$ PDAG for L $\in$ {DNF, IP, d-DNF, MODS, PI}.

(b) In Table 10, Darwiche and Marquis [2002] show that CNF $\not\preceq$ π-OBDD and DNF $\not\preceq$ π-OBDD.

159

Appendix A Proofs

Table A.1: Succinctness relationships of the considered languages. * means that the result holds unless the polynomial hierarchy collapses.

A.1 Succinctness

Due to (G2) and (G3), we obtain $L_1 \not\preceq L_2$ for

$$L_1 \in \{\text{DNF}, \text{CNF}, \text{d-DNF}, \text{IP}, \text{PI}, \text{MODS}\} \text{ and}$$
$$L_2 \in \{\text{PDAG}, \text{cd-PDAG}, \text{DNNF}, \text{d-DNNF}, \text{FBDD}, \text{OBDD}, \pi\text{-OBDD}\}.$$

Note that, we obtain $L_1 \not\preceq G$-FBDD for some graph orders G.

(c) Table 11 of Darwiche and Marquis [2002] contains the results FBDD $\not\preceq$ d-DNNF, OBDD $\not\preceq$ FBDD and π-OBDD $\not\preceq$ OBDD. According to (G2) and (G3), this implies $L_1 \not\preceq L_2$ for

$$L_1 \in \{\text{FBDD}, G\text{-FBDD}, \text{OBDD}, \pi\text{-OBDD}\} \text{ and}$$
$$L_2 \in \{\text{PDAG}, \text{cd-PDAG}, \text{DNNF}, \text{d-DNNF}\},$$

as well as π-OBDD $\not\preceq$ FBDD. From π-OBDD $\not\preceq$ OBDD, we get π_1-OBDD $\not\preceq$ π_2-OBDD for some variable orders π_1, π_2. Analog, π-OBDD $\not\preceq$ OBDD we have G-FBDD $\not\preceq$ FBDD. This implies G_1-FBDD $\not\preceq$ G_2-FBDD for some graph orders G_1, G_2 as well as G-FBDD $\not\preceq$ L and L $\not\preceq$ G-FBDD for L $\in \{\text{OBDD}, \pi\text{-OBDD}\}$ depending on the graph order G and the variable order π.

(d) Darwiche and Marquis [2002] proof in Table 12, that DNNF $\not\preceq$ CNF unless the polynomial hierarchy PH collapses. This is based on DNNF supporting the query clause entailment (CE) which is not supported by CNF. Because of this fact, the argumentation is also applicable to d-DNNF and cd-PDAG instead of DNNF. Due to (G3), these results also hold for PDAG instead of CNF.

(e) FBDD $\not\preceq$ IP and FBDD $\not\preceq$ PI is shown in [Darwiche and Marquis, 2002, Table13]. The scenarios (G2) and (G3) lead to $L_1 \not\preceq L_2$ for

$$L_1 \in \{\text{FBDD}, G\text{-FBDD}, \text{OBDD}, \pi\text{-OBDD}\} \text{ and}$$
$$L_2 \in \{\text{PDAG}, \text{DNNF}, \text{DNF}, \text{CNF}, \text{IP}, \text{PI}\}.$$

(f) In Table 14, Darwiche and Marquis [2002] proof d-DNNF $\not\preceq$ DNF unless the polynomial hierarchy PH collapses. The argumentation is based on the fact that d-DNNF $\preceq$ DNF would lead to the collapse of PH. The proof of cd-PDAG $\not\preceq$ DNF is analog. Furthermore, (G3) leads to d-DNNF $\not\preceq$ DNNF and cd-PDAG $\not\preceq$ DNNF.

(g) According to [Darwiche and Marquis, 2002, Table 15], L $\preceq$ MODS holds for L $\in \{\text{IP}, \text{CNF}, \pi\text{-OBDD}, \text{OBDD}, \text{FBDD}\}$ as well as MODS $\not\preceq$ IP. For MODS $\not\preceq$ d-DNF consider

Appendix A Proofs

$V_1 \vee (\neg V_1 \wedge V_2 \wedge \cdots \wedge V_r)$ which has 2^{r-1} models and a d-DNF representation linear in r. For G-FBDD, we get G-FBDD $\preceq$ MODS analog to π-OBDD $\preceq$ MODS except that the decision tree respects the graph ordering G instead of the total ordering π. □

A.2 Queries

Proof of Propositions 1.4 and 1.5.
See Lemma A.3, Lemma A.4, and Lemma A.7 of Darwiche and Marquis [2002] and consider the algorithms presented in Section 10.2.

□

Proof of Proposition 1.6.
See Darwiche [2001a] and consider the algorithms presented in Section 10.4. □

Proof of Proposition 1.7.
Due to the existence of a transformation form PDAG to NNF and f-PDAG to f-NNF in time polynomial in the size of the representation, we are able to reuse the results of Darwiche and Marquis [2002]. Note that Darwiche and Marquis denote π-OBDD by OBDD$_<$. Inconsistency IN as the negation of consistency CO and term conditioning by CD instead of TC. Table A.2 repeats the results of Proposition 1.7 together with some additional information. The index revers to the corresponding proof in this dissertation which depends heavily on the implications of queries as shown in Figure 3.2 and the corresponding parts of Darwiche and Marquis [2002]. These implications are used in two ways: e.g. if Q_1 implies Q_2 then on one side

- proofing that Q_1 is supported, also proves that Q_2 is supported; while on the other side
- proofing that Q_2 is not supported, also proves that Q_1 is not supported.

(*a*) We group the result of [Darwiche and Marquis, 2002, Tables 16 and 17], since all languages support the transformation TC. IN is not supported by PDAG, f-PDAG, and CNF, while VA is not supported by PDAG, f-PDAG, DNNF and DNF. Due to the correlations between the different queries, IN and VA are implied by each of the queries SE, EQ, CP,

A.2 Queries

Queries	IN CE MS ME	VA IM $\overline{\text{MS}}$ $\overline{\text{ME}}$	CT WCT PR PEQ PCP	EQ	CP	SE	SI	SV	CA MAX ARG
PDAG	$\circ_a$	$\circ_a$	$\circ_a$	$\circ_a$	$\circ_a$	$\circ_a$	$\circ_a$	$\circ_a$	$\circ_a$
f-PDAG	$\circ_a$	$\circ_a$	$\circ_a$	$\circ_a$	$\circ_a$	$\circ_a$	$\circ_a$	$\circ_a$	$\circ_a$
cd-PDAG	$\checkmark_b$	$\checkmark_b$	$\checkmark_b$	?	?	$\circ_c$	$\circ_c$	$\circ_c$	?
d-NNF	$\circ_d$	$\circ_d$	$\circ_d$	$\circ_d$	$\circ_d$	$\circ_c$	$\circ_c$	$\circ_c$	$\circ_d$
DNNF	$\checkmark_b$	$\circ_a$	$\circ_a$	$\circ_a$	$\circ_a$	$\circ_a$	$\circ_a$	$\circ_a$	$\checkmark_b$
d-DNNF	$\checkmark_b$	$\checkmark_b$	$\checkmark_b$	?	?	$\circ_c$	$\circ_c$	$\circ_c$	$\checkmark_b$
BDD	$\circ_d$	$\circ_d$	$\circ_d$	$\circ_d$	$\circ_d$	$\circ_c$	$\circ_c$	$\circ_c$	$\circ_d$
FBDD	$\checkmark_b$	$\checkmark_b$	$\checkmark_b$	?	?	$\circ_c$	$\circ_c$	$\circ_c$	$\checkmark_b$
G-FBDD	$\checkmark_b$	$\checkmark_b$	$\checkmark_b$	$\checkmark_c$	$\checkmark_c$	$\checkmark_c$	$\checkmark_c$	$\checkmark_c$	$\checkmark_b$
OBDD	$\checkmark_b$	$\checkmark_b$	$\checkmark_b$	$\checkmark_c$	$\checkmark_c$	$\circ_c$	$\circ_c$	$\circ_c$	$\checkmark_b$
π-OBDD	$\checkmark_b$	$\checkmark_b$	$\checkmark_b$	$\checkmark_c$	$\checkmark_c$	$\checkmark_c$	$\checkmark_c$	$\checkmark_c$	$\checkmark_b$
DNF	$\checkmark_b$	$\circ_a$	$\circ_a$	$\circ_a$	$\circ_a$	$\circ_a$	$\checkmark_f$	$\circ_a$	$\checkmark_b$
CNF	$\circ_a$	$\checkmark_b$	$\circ_a$	$\circ_a$	$\circ_a$	$\circ_a$	$\circ_a$	$\checkmark_f$	$\circ_a$
d-DNF	$\checkmark_b$	$\checkmark_b$	$\checkmark_b$	?	?	?	$\checkmark_f$	?	$\checkmark_b$
IP	$\checkmark_b$	$\checkmark_e$	$\circ_e$	$\checkmark_e$	?	$\checkmark_e$	$\checkmark_f$	?	$\checkmark_b$
PI	$\checkmark_e$	$\checkmark_b$	$\circ_e$	$\checkmark_e$	?	$\checkmark_e$	?	$\checkmark_f$	?
MODS	$\checkmark_b$	$\checkmark_b$	$\checkmark_b$	$\checkmark_c$	$\checkmark_c$	$\checkmark_c$	$\checkmark_c$	$\checkmark_c$	$\checkmark_b$

Table A.2: Subsets of PDAG and their supported queries. The symbol $\checkmark$ means "supports", $\circ$ means "does not support unless P = NP", and ? means "unknown".

Appendix A Proofs

and CT. In addition, IN is implied by each of the queries SI, CE, CA/MAX, and MS, wheile VA is implied by each of the queries SV, IM and $\overline{\text{MS}}$.

(b) On one side, the algorithm described Section 10.1 computes the inconsistency or consistency of $\varphi \in$ DNNF in time polynomial in the size of φ. Since DNNF also supports the transformation, the queries CE, MS and ME (see Section 10.2), and CA, MAX and ARGMAX (see Section 10.4) are also supported. This holds not only for DNNF but for its all sublanguages. The remaining algorithm (Section 10.3) proofs that model counting is supported by cd-PDAG. This implies several other queries. And, of course, the result holds also for the sublanguages of cd-PDAG. On the other side, it is known that IM and VA are supported by CNF and its sublanguage PI.

(c) Gergov and Meinel [1994], Bryant [1992] show that π-OBDD supports the EQ. Since π-OBDD also supports the query IN and the transformations TC, AND_2, and NOT, it also supports the queries CP, SE, SI, and SV. The same holds for G-FBDD. On one side, Meinel and Theobald [1998] proof in Theorem 8.11 that OBDD supports EQ, since OBDD supports the transformation NOT, it also supports the CP. On the other side, Meinel and Theobald [1998] proof in Lemma 8.14 that SE is not supported. Here the support of NOT implies that SI and SV are not supported. Since the queries SE, SI and SV are not supported by OBDD, they are not supported by the super-languages of OBDD, i.e. FBDD, BDD, d-DNNF, DNNF, d-NNF, cd-PDAG, and PDAG do not support these three queries. MODS supports EQ, CP, SE, SI, and SV, since π-OBDD $\preceq$ MODS.

(d) According to Lemma A.8 of Darwiche and Marquis [2002], every $\varphi \in$ DNF $\cup$ CNF can be turned into an equivalent $\varphi' \in$ BDD in time polynomial in the size of φ. Hence, if a query is not supported by DNF or CNF, then it is not supported by BDD and its super-languages (amongst others d-NNF).

(e) By definition PI supports CE and IP supports. According to [Darwiche and Marquis, 2002, Table 24] the fact PI $\subseteq$ CNF and IP $\subseteq$ DNF implies that PI and IP support SE. Again, supporting SE implies the support EQ. However, the queries CT, WCT, PEQ, PCP, and PR are not supported according to the results of Roth [1996], Marquis [2000] and the argumentation in [Darwiche and Marquis, 2002, Table 24].

(f) Since $\varphi \models \neg\psi \equiv \varphi \wedge \psi \models \bot$ and $\neg\varphi \models \psi \equiv \top \models \varphi \vee \psi$, the query SI is supported if IN and the transformation AND_2 are supported, while the query SV is supported if VA and the transformation OR_2 are supported. In case of $\varphi, \psi \in$ d-DNF, we treat φ and ψ as DNFs to answer SI. □

A.3 Transformations

Proof of Proposition 1.8.

- TC: Consider [Darwiche and Marquis, 2002, CD in Proof of Proposition 5.1] where CD denotes TC. cd-PDAG and d-DNF support TC, since TC preserves decomposability, determinism, simple-negation, and flatness.

  For $\varphi \in$ G-FBDD, the requirements $vars(\varphi|\psi) \cap vars(\varphi) = \emptyset$ and both input and output belonging to the same language clash. Consider the graph-order G as shown in Figure 2.10e and φ as shown in Figure 2.10b. Then, the root of $\varphi|V_1$ is labeled with V_3 but this is not enough to determine the actual position in G. Due to this fact, the output $\varphi|\psi$ belongs to $G|\psi$-FBDD. Since both G and φ are special cases of FBDD where term conditioning is allowed, we refer to the corresponding entries there. The same holds for $FO_\exists$, $FO_\exists^d$, $FO_\forall$, and $FO_\forall^c$.

- $FO_\exists$: Consider [Darwiche and Marquis, 2002, FO in Proof of Proposition 5.1] where $FO_\exists$ is denoted by **FO**. cd-PDAG does not support $FO_\exists$, since it does not support $SFO_\exists$.

- $FO_\exists^d$: First, if a language supports $FO_\exists$ then it supports also $FO_\exists^d$. d-DNNF and d-DNF support $FO_\exists^d$ due to the definition of deterministic variables.

- $SFO_\exists$: Consider [Darwiche and Marquis, 2002, SFO in Proof of Proposition 5.1] where $SFO_\exists$ is denoted by **SFO**. cd-PDAG does not support $SFO_\exists$ for the same reason as d-DNNF. Note that each $\varphi \in$ f-PDAG has an equivalent $\varphi' \in$ DNF or an equivalent $\varphi'' \in$ CNF where the size of φ' or φ'' is polynomial in the size of φ. Since both DNF and CNF support $SFO_\exists$, it is also supported by f-PDAG.

- $SFO_\exists^d$: First, if a language supports $SFO_\exists$ then it supports also $SFO_\exists^d$. cd-PDAG, d-DNNF, and d-DNF support $SFO_\exists^d$ due to the definition of deterministic variables.

- $SFO_\forall$: A language supporting and in addition to TC also supports $SFO_\forall$. For OBDD, it follows from the fact that only one $\varphi \in$ OBDD is considered and π-OBDD supports $SFO_\forall$. Again, each $\varphi \in$ f-PDAG has an equivalent $\varphi' \in$ DNF or an equivalent $\varphi'' \in$ CNF where the size of φ' or φ'' is polynomial in the size of φ. Since both DNF and CNF support $SFO_\forall$, it is also supported by f-PDAG.

Appendix A Proofs

- SFO$_\forall^c$: First, if a language supports SFO$_\forall$ then it supports also SFO$_\forall^c$. cd-PDAG, DNNF, d-DNNF, and FBDD support SFO$_\forall^c$ due to the definition of decomposable variables.

- AND, AND$_2$, OR, OR$_2$, NOT: Consider [Darwiche and Marquis, 2002, $\wedge$C, $\wedge$BC, $\vee$C, $\vee$BC, and $\neg$C in Proof of Proposition 5.1] where $\wedge$C denotes AND, $\wedge$BC denotes AND$_2$, $\vee$C denotes OR, $\vee$BC denotes OR$_2$, and $\neg$C denotes NOT. For cd-PDAG, the argumentation of OBDD (and, hence, d-DNNF) also holds for the transformations AND, AND$_2$, OR, and OR$_2$, while the transformation NOT is supported by definition. G-FBDD can not support more queries than π-OBDD, since each ordering π corresponds to a certain graph ordering G_π, i.e. AND and OR are not supported by G-FBDD. On the other side, both AND$_2$ and OR$_2$ are supported, since the apply algorithm Bryant [1986] may be used. Finally, NOT are supported by G-FBDD, since it is sufficient to switch the $\top$- and the $\bot$-terminal. $\square$

A.4 MDAG

Proof of Proposition 1.9.
Each part of this proof is based on the fact that each $\varphi_M \in$ MDAG based on Boolean variables can be translated into $\varphi_P \in$ PDAG in time polynomial in $|\varphi_M|$ and the size of φ_P is polynomial in the size of φ_M. For all $V \in \mathbf{V}$, replace a terminal labeled with $(V, \{1\})$ by a V-terminal and a terminal labeled with $(V, \{0\})$ by a $\neg$-node with the child V-terminal, or vice versa to switch from PDAG to MDAG. I.e. Boolean functions can be represented by both PDAG and MDAG and the size of the different representations is similar.

Let L$_M$ and L$'_M$ be two sublanguages of MDAG and let L$_P$ and L$'_P$ be the corresponding Boolean counter-parts with L$_P \npreceq$ L$'_P$. Now, we assume L$_M \preceq$ L$'_M$. In particular, we can translate each representation $\varphi \in$ L$_M$ of a Boolean function into an equivalent representation $\varphi' \in$ L$'_M$ of this function where the size of φ' is polynomial in the size of φ. I.e. L$_P \preceq$ L$'_P$ which contradicts our precondition. The argumentation for the results on queries and transformations is analog.
$\square$

Proof of Proposition 1.10.
Consider Table A.1. Due to Proposition 1.9, each P$_1 \npreceq$ P$_2$ and each P$_1 \npreceq^*$ P$_2$ relation between two PDAG sublanguages P$_1$, P$_2$ is passed on to their corresponding MDAG sublanguages M$_1$, M$_2$. Furthermore, a sublanguage relationship between P$_1$ and P$_2$, indicated by $\preceq$ without an index, naturally leads to a sublanguage relationships between M$_1$ and M$_2$. Thus, we only have

to analyze the relations where the corresponding entry is $\preceq_g$. First, we construct a decision tree corresponding to π or G. With a similar argumentation as in Proof of Proposition 1.3 we get: $\text{L} \preceq \text{MMODS}$ for $\text{L} \in \{\text{FMDD}, G\text{-FMDD}, \text{OMDD}, \pi\text{-OMDD}, \text{MCNF}\}$. □

Proof of Proposition 1.11.
Again, we only have to approve only $\sqrt{}$ entries of Table 3.4 because of Proposition 1.9. This covers all results with index a and d. Fortunately, the algorithms presented in Chapter 10 base on MDAG. Hence, the index b holds. For index c the argumentation stays the same, just the number of branches changes. Of the remaining indices, e would have to be proved if we include the multi-state versions of IP and PI, Finally, the argumentation of f is independent of the context. □

Proof of Proposition 1.12.
Once more due to Proposition 1.9, only $\sqrt{}$ entries of Table 3.6 have to be considered. As before, TC preserves the given properties (due to the restriction on one state per variable). The algorithm in Chapter 10 proofs that cn-MDAG, MDNF, and MMODS support FO. cdn-MDAG and d-MDNF support $\text{FO}_\exists^d$ due to the definition. Of course, supporting $\text{FO}_\exists$ implies supporting $\text{FO}_\exists^d$, $\text{SFO}_\exists$ and $\text{SFO}_\exists^d$, while supporting $\text{FO}_\exists^d$ or $\text{SFO}_\exists$ implies $\text{SFO}_\exists^d$ only. For Boolean variables, the argumentation of a language L supporting $\text{SFO}_\exists$, $\text{SFO}_\exists^d$, $\text{SFO}_\forall$, and $\text{SFO}_\forall^c$ follows the argumentation of its Boolean counterpart. This argumentation is also used for variables with more than two states, when considering the languages MDAG, dn-MDAG, and MDD (both support OR as well as AND). $\text{SFO}_\exists^d$ is supported by cd-MDAG by definition. FMDD, OMDD, and π-OMDD can not support $\text{SFO}_\exists$, otherwise it would clash with the fact that these languages do not support OR. The same argument is also valid for $\text{SFO}_\forall$. MDAG, dn-MDAG, MDD, and MCNF support $\text{SFO}_\forall$ since each of these for langauges supports both TC and AND. The remaining supported transformations follow analog to the corresponding Boolean case. □

A.5 Bayesian Networks

Proof of Theorem 3.
Obviously, Lemma 3 and Lemma 4 of Wachter and Haenni [2006c] also hold for Boolean-valued functions instead of Boolean functions, and this theorem is a consequence of them.
□

Appendix A Proofs

Proof of Theorem 4.
As suggested in Proof of Theorem 5 of Wachter and Haenni [2006c], we start with a leaf X of the Bayesian network. Since both Lemma 6 and Theorem 1 of Wachter and Haenni [2006c] also hold for Boolean-valued functions, they ensure that X is deterministic w.r.t ψ_Δ. Due to the fact that Boolean-valued functions are a kind of semiring valuation algebra, eliminating X from ψ_Δ does only affect ψ_X (axiom (v)). This is repeated for the remaining variables of the BN, but X does no longer count as a child. According to axiom (iv), the order of the elimination is arbitrary. □

A.6 (Probabilistic) Model Verification

Proof of Theorems 5 and 6.
Proof by induction on r. For $r=0$, there are only two functions, namely $f_\top$ and $f_\bot$ with $H(f_\top) = 1$ and $H(f_\bot) = 0$ which is analog to the Boolean case.

Assume the theorem is true for $r - 1$ variables. Let f, g be the Boolean-valued functions represented by
$$\varphi = ((V_r = v_{r,1}) \wedge \varphi_1) \vee \cdots \vee ((V_r = v_{r,s_r}) \wedge \varphi_{s_r})$$
and
$$\psi = ((V_r = v_{r,1}) \wedge \psi_1) \vee \cdots \vee ((V_r = v_{r,s_r}) \wedge \psi_{s_r}),$$
where φ_i, ψ_i represent the Boolean-valued functions f_i, g_i over the variables V_i with $1 \le i \le r - 1$. Now, if $f \not\equiv g$ then there is at least one $k \in \{1, \ldots, s_r\}$ with $\varphi_k \not\equiv \psi_k$, i.e. $f_k \not\equiv g_k$. Due to the assumption that the theorem holds for $r - 1$ variables there are at least $\prod_{j=1}^{r-1}(p^{s_j-1} - p^{s_j-2})$ vectors $\mathbf{h}' = (h_{1,1}, \ldots, h_{1,s_1}, h_{2,1} \ldots, h_{r-2,s_{r-2}}, h_{r-1,1}, \ldots, h_{r-1,s_{r-1}}) \in \mathbb{F}_p^{s_1+\cdots+s_{r-1}}$ such that $H_{\mathbf{h}'}(f_k) \ne H_{\mathbf{h}'}(g_k)$. For $\mathbf{h}$ where the values $h_{r,\ell}, 1 \le \ell \le s_r$ are not fixed yet, we have

$$H_{\mathbf{h}}(f) = H_{\mathbf{h}}(g)$$
$$\Leftrightarrow \sum_{j=1}^{s_r} h_{r,j} H_{\mathbf{h}'}(f_j) = \sum_{j=1}^{s_r} h_{r,j} H_{\mathbf{h}'}(g_j)$$
$$\Leftrightarrow \sum_{j=1}^{s_r} h_{r,j}(H_{\mathbf{h}'}(f_j) - H_{\mathbf{h}'}(g_j)) = 0.$$

A.6 (Probabilistic) Model Verification

This equation and $\sum_{j=1}^{s_r} h_{r,j} = 1$ build a system of two linear equations involving s_r variables. Since $H_{\mathbf{h}'}(f_k) \neq H_{\mathbf{h}'}(g_k)$, the system has at most p^{s_r-2} solutions. Hence, there are at least $(p^{s_r-1} - p^{s_r-2})$ solutions with $H_{\mathbf{h}}(f) \neq H_{\mathbf{h}}(g)$ for each vector $\mathbf{h}'$ with $H_{\mathbf{h}'}(f_k) \neq H_{\mathbf{h}'}(g_k)$. □

Proof of Theorem 7.
Proof by induction on the maximal number of edges from the node φ to a terminal which is called the *depth* of φ. For $depth(\varphi) = 0$, φ is a terminal. If φ is a (V_j, Ω)-terminal, we have

$$H_{\mathbf{h}}(\varphi) = \sum_{\substack{i \in \{1,\ldots,s_j\} \\ v_{j,i} \in \Omega}} h_{j,i} = H_{\mathbf{h}}(f_\varphi).$$

If φ is a $\top$-terminal or a $\bot$-terminal, the definition exploits the corresponding facts about valid or inconsistent Boolean-valued function, respectively.

For $depth(\varphi) = j$ we have to consider three kinds of nodes. First, if φ is a $\neg$-node with child α, we have $f_\varphi = 1 - f_\alpha$ and $H_{\mathbf{h}}(\alpha) = H_{\mathbf{h}}(f_\alpha)$, since $depth(\alpha) < j$. So $H_{\mathbf{h}}(\varphi) = 1 - H_{\mathbf{h}}(\alpha)$ exploits the the fact $H_{\mathbf{h}}(f_\varphi) = H_{\mathbf{h}}(1 - f_\alpha) = 1 - H_{\mathbf{h}}(f_\alpha)$, from which we conclude $H_{\mathbf{h}}(f_\varphi) = H_{\mathbf{h}}(\varphi)$.

Without loss of generality, we assume for the two other node types that the children of φ are α_1 and α_2. Since $depth(\alpha_i) < j$, we also have $H_{\mathbf{h}}(\alpha_i) = H_{\mathbf{h}}(f_{\alpha_i})$.

If φ is a $\vee$-node, we know that it is deterministic, i.e. α_1 and α_2 have no common element in the corresponding satisfying sets. This leads to $H_{\mathbf{h}}(\varphi) = H_{\mathbf{h}}(\alpha_1) + H_{\mathbf{h}}(\alpha_2) = H_{\mathbf{h}}(f_{\alpha_1}) + H_{\mathbf{h}}(f_{\alpha_2}) = H_{\mathbf{h}}(f_\varphi)$.

If φ is a $\wedge$-node, we know that it is decomposable, i.e. each variable in $vars(\varphi)$ occurs either in α_1 or in α_2. This implies $S_\varphi = S_{\alpha_1}|_{\mathbf{V}_1} \times S_{\alpha_2}|_{\mathbf{V}_2}$, where $\mathbf{V}_i = vars(\alpha_i)$. This leads to $S_{f_\varphi} = S_{f_{\alpha_1}}|_{\mathbf{V}_1} \times S_{f_{\alpha_2}}|_{\mathbf{V}_2}$. With $H_{\mathbf{h}}(f_{\alpha_i}) = H_{\mathbf{h}}(f_{\alpha_i}|_{\mathbf{V}_i})$, we get

$$H_{\mathbf{h}}(\varphi) = H_{\mathbf{h}}(\alpha_1) \cdot H_{\mathbf{h}}(\alpha_2) = H_{\mathbf{h}}(f_{\alpha_1}) \cdot H_{\mathbf{h}}(f_{\alpha_2}) = H_{\mathbf{h}}(f_\varphi).$$

□

Appendix B

Detailed UML Diagrams of selected Classes and Interfaces

We start with a very short introduction to UML diagrams. Each diagram consists of up to three blocks, the first block contains the name of the class or interface, the second one contains its attributes, and the third block contains the methods and constructors. In the previous diagrams, we omitted the the second and the third block. If a class or interface does not contain any attributes, it is common to omit that block.

As mentioned before, the first block contains the name of the class or interface. Beyond that it also marks interfaces by adding «interface» before the name and abstract classes by writing the name in italics, e.g. *Node*.

The attribute block specifies the names of the fields followed by their type (name: String), while the method and constructor block displays the name of the methods and constructors, their parameters with the corresponding type, and the type of the return value of the method (equalChildren:nodes: Node...): **boolean**). Abstract methods are written in italics, like abstract classes (*toString(): String*). In addition, **static** methods and attributes are underlined. Finally, the accessibility of the attributes and methods is decoded by - for **private**, # for **protected**, and + for **public**.

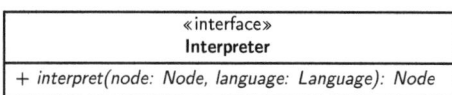

Figure B.1: The interface Interpreter.

Appendix B Detailed UML Diagrams of selected Classes and Interfaces

Variable
- BOOLEAN_FRAME: String[] = {"0", "1"}   + frame: String[]   - map: HashMap<String, Integer>   + name: String
+ boolean_variable(name: String): Variable   + multi_state_variable(name: String, frame: String...): Variable   - Variable(name: String, frame: String...): Variable   + equals(o: Object): boolean   + getBits(states: String...): boolean[]   + getIndex(state: String): int   + getState(index: int): String   + getStates(bits: boolean[]): ArrayList<String>   + hashCode(): int   + toString(): String

Figure B.2: The class Variable.

Node
+ boolean_state(variable: Variable): Multi_State   + conjunction(nodes: Node...): Conjunction   + contradiction(): Contradiction   + decision(variable: Variable, nodes: Node...): Decision   + disjunction(nodes: Node...): Disjunction   + multi_state(variable: Variable, bits: boolean...): Multi_State   + negation(node: Node): Negation   - nodesOK(nodes: Node[]): boolean   + state(state: S): State<S>   + tautology(): Node   # Node(): Node   + accepts(visitor: ConditionalVisitor<V,C>, condition: C): V   + accepts(visitor: UnconditionalVisitor<V>): V   + equalChildren(nodes: Node...): boolean   + equals(o: Object): boolean   + getBits(): boolean[]   + getChild(): Node   + getChildren(): Node[]   + getVariable(): Variable   + toString(): String

Figure B.3: The class Node.

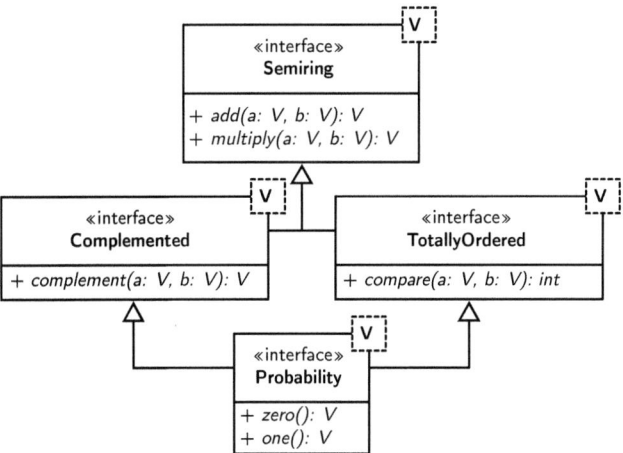

Figure B.4: The interfaces Semiring, Complemented, TotallyOrdered, and Probability.

Bibliography

S. B. Akers.
Binary decision diagrams.
IEEE Transactions on Computers, 27(6):509—516, 1978.

H. R. Andersen and H. Hulgaard.
Boolean expression diagrams.
In G. Winskel, editor, *LICS'97, 12th Annual IEEE Symposim on Logic in Computer Science*, pages 88–98, Warsaw, Poland, 1997. IEEE Computer Society.

D. Bellot and P. Bessière.
Approximate discrete probability distribution representation using a multi-resolution binary tree.
In *ICTAI'03, 15th IEEE International Conference on Tools with Artificial Intelligence*, pages 498–503, Sacramento, USA, 2003.

M. Blum, A. K. Chandra, and M. N. Wegman.
Equivalence of free boolean graphs can be decided probabilistically in polynomial time.
Information Processing Letters, 10(2):80–82, 1980.

G. Boole.
The Laws of Thought.
Walton and Maberley, London, 1854.

C. Boutilier, N. Friedman, M. Goldszmidt, and D. Koller.
Context-specific independence in Bayesian networks.
In E. Horvitz and F. Jensen, editors, *UAI'96, 12th Conference on Uncertainty in Artificial Inteligence*, pages 115–123, Portland, USA, 1996.

R. E. Bryant.
Graph-based algorithms for Boolean function manipulation.
IEEE Transactions on Computers, 35(8):677–691, 1986.

Bibliography

R. E. Bryant.
Symbolic Boolean manipulation with ordered binary decision diagrams.
ACM Computing Surveys, 24(3):293–318, 1992.

M. Cadoli and F. Donini.
A survey on knowledge compilation.
AI Communications, 10(3–4):137–150, 1997.

A. Cano, S. Moral, and A. Salmeron.
Penniless propagation in join trees.
International Journal of Intelligent Systems, 15(11):1027–1059, 2000.

M. Chavira and A. Darwiche.
Compiling Bayesian networks using variable elimination.
In *IJCAI'07, 20th International Joint Conference on Artificial Intelligence*, pages 2443–2449, Hyderabad, India, 2007.

A. Darwiche.
Decomposable negation normal form.
Journal of the ACM, 48(4):608–647, 2001a.

A. Darwiche.
On the tractable of counting theory models and its application to belief revision and truth maintenance.
Journal of Applied Non-Classical Logics, 11(1-2):11–34, 2001b.

A. Darwiche.
Compiling knowledge into decomposable negation normal form.
In *IJCAI'99, 16th International Joint Conference on Artificial Intelligence*, pages 284–289, Stockholm, Sweden, 1999.

A. Darwiche and J. Huang.
Testing equivalence probabilistically.
Technical Report D–123, Computer Science Department, UCLA, Los Angeles, USA, 2002.

A. Darwiche and P. Marquis.
A knowledge compilation map.
Journal of Artificial Intelligence Research, 17:229–264, 2002.

Bibliography

R. Davis, H. E. Shrobe, and P. Szolovits.
What is a knowledge representation?
AI Magazine, 14(1):17–33, 1993.

R. Dechter.
Bucket elimination: a unifying framework for reasoning.
Artificial Intelligence, 113(1–2):41–85, 1999.

R. Dechter and R. Mateescu.
AND/OR search spaces for graphical models.
Artificial Intelligence, 171(2–3):73–106, 2007.

H. Fargier and P. Marquis.
Extending the knowledge compliation map: Closure principles.
In *ECAI'08: 18th European Conference on Artificial Intelligence*, Patras, Greece, 2008.

G. Fischer.
Lineare Algebra.
Vieweg, 11th edition, 1997.

D. Galles and J. Pearl.
Axioms of causal relevance.
Artificial Intelligence, 97(1–2):9–43, 1997.

E. Gamma, R. Helm, R. Johnson, and J. Vlissides.
Design Patterns – Elements of Reusable Object-Oriented Software.
Addison-Wesley, 1994.

D. Geiger and D. Heckerman.
Advances in probabilistic reasoning.
In *UAI'91, 6th Annual Conference on Uncertainty in Artificial Intelligence*, pages 118–126, Los Angeles, USA, 1991.

J. Gergov and C. Meinel.
Efficient analysis and manipulation of OBBDs can be extended to FBDDs.
IEEE Transactionc on Computers, 43(10):1197–1209, 1994.

G. Gogic, H. Kautz, H. Papadimitriou, and B. Selman.
The comparative linguistics of knowledge representation.

Bibliography

In *IJCAI'95, 14th International Joint Conference on Artificial Intelligence*, pages 862–869, Montreal, Canada, 1995.

J. L. Gross and J. Yellen.
Handbook of Graph Theory.
CRC Press, 2003.

R. Haenni.
Towards a unifying theory of logical and probabilistic reasoning.
In F. B. Cozman, R. Nau, and T. Seidenfeld, editors, *ISIPTA'05, 4th International Symposium on Imprecise Probabilities and Their Applications*, pages 193–202, Pittsburgh, USA, 2005.

R. Haenni and N. Lehmann.
Belief function propagation based on Shenoy's fusion algorithm.
In *IPMU'00, 8th International Conference on Information Processing and Management of Uncertainty in Knowledge-Based Systems*, pages 1928–1931, Madrid, Spain, 2000.

R. Haenni, J. Kohlas, and N. Lehmann.
Probabilistic argumentation systems.
In D. M. Gabbay and P. Smets, editors, *Handbook of Defeasible Reasoning and Uncertainty Management Systems*, volume 5: Algorithms for Uncertainty and Defeasible Reasoning, pages 221–288. Kluwer Academic Publishers, Dordrecht, Netherlands, 2000.

H. Hulgaard, P. F. Williams, and H. R. Andersen.
Equivalence checking of combinational circuits using Boolean expression diagrams.
IEEE Transactions on Computer-Aided Design of Integrated Circuits and Systems, 18(7): 903–917, 1999.

J. Jain, J. Bitner, D. S. Fussell, and J. A. Abraham.
Probabilistic design verification.
In *ICCAD'91, 9th International Conference on Computer-Aided Design*, pages 468–471, Santa Clara, USA, 1991.

J. Kohlas.
Information Algebras: Generic Stuctures for Inference.
Springer, London, 2003.

J. Kohlas.

Valuation algebras induced by semirings.
Technical Report 04–03, Department of Informatics, University of Fribourg, Switzerland, 2004.

J. Kohlas.
Zuverlässigkeit und Verfügbarkeit.
Teubner, 1987.

J. Kohlas and N. Wilson.
Exact and approximate local computation in semiring induced valuation algebras.
Technical Report 06–06, Department of Informatics, University of Fribourg, Switzerland, 2006.

P. Marquis.
Consequence finding algorithms.
In D. M. Gabbay and P. Smets, editors, *Handbook of Defeasible Reasoning and Uncertainty Management Systems*, volume 5: Algorithms for Uncertain and Defeasible Reasoning, pages 41–145. Kluwer Academic Publishers, Dordrecht, Netherlands, 2000.

C. Meinel and T. Theobald.
Algorithms and Data Structures in VLSI Design: OBDD Foundations and Applications.
Springer, 1998.

J. Pearl.
Probabilistic Reasoning in Intelligent Systems.
Morgan Kaufmann, San Mateo, USA, 1988.

K. Pipatsrisawat and A. Darwiche.
New compilation languages based on structured decomposability.
In *AAAI'08, 23rd AAAI Conference on Artificial Intelligence*, Chicago, USA, 2008.
To appear.

D. Poole and N. L. Zhang.
Exploiting contextual independence in probabilistic inference.
Journal of Artificial Intelligence Research, 18:263–313, 2003.

M. Pouly and J. Kohlas.
Local computation & dynamic programming.
Technical Report 07-02, Department of Informatics, University of Fribourg, Switzerland, 2007.

Bibliography

M. Pouly, R. Haenni, and M. Wachter.
Compiling solution configurations in semiring valuation systems.
In A. Gelbukh and A. F. Kuri Morales, editors, *MICAI'07, 6th Mexican International Conference on Artificial Intelligence*, LNAI 4827, pages 248–259, Aguascalientes, Mexico, 2007.

S. Rai, M. Veeraraghavan, and K. S. Trivedi.
A survey on efficient computation of reliability using disjoint products approach.
Networks, 25(3):147–163, 1995.

A. Rauzy, E. Châtelet, Y. Dutuit, and C. Bérenguer.
A practical comparison of methods to assess sum-of-products.
Reliability Engineering and System Safety, 79(1):33–42, 2003.

D. Roth.
On the hardness of approximate reasoning.
Artificial Intelligence, 82(1-2):273–302, 1996.

S. Russell and P. Norvig.
Artificial Intelligence: A Modern Approach.
Prentice Hall, 2nd edition, 2003.

C. Schneuwly, M. Pouly, and J. Kohlas.
Local computation in covering join trees.
Technical Report 04–16, Department of Informatics, University of Fribourg, Switzerland, 2004.

P. P. Shenoy.
Valuation-based systems: A framework for managing uncertainty in expert systems.
In L. A. Zadeh and J. Kacprzyk, editors, *Fuzzy Logic for the Management of Uncertainty*, pages 83–104. John Wiley and Sons, New York, USA, 1992.

P. P. Shenoy.
Binary join trees.
In E. Horvitz and F. V. Jensen, editors, *UAI'96, 12th Conference on Uncertainty in Artificial Inteligence*, pages 492–499, Portland, USA, 1996.

P. P. Shenoy and G. Shafer.
Axioms for probability and belief-function propagation.

Bibliography

In R. D. Shachter, T. S. Levitt, J. F. Lemmer, and L. N. Kanal, editors, *UAI'88, 4th Conference on Uncertainty in Artificial Intelligence*, pages 169–198, Minneapolis, USA, 1988.

P. P. Shenoy and G. Shafer.
Axioms for probability and belief function propagation.
In G. Shafer and J. Pearl, editors, *Readings in Uncertain Reasoning*, pages 575–610. Morgan Kaufmann, San Mateo, USA, 1990.

J. E. Smith, S. Holtzman, and J. E. Matheson.
Structuring conditional relationships in influence diagrams.
Operations Research, 41(2):280–297, 1993.

T. S. Verma and J. Pearl.
An algorithm for deciding if a set of observed independencies has a causal explanation.
In D. Dubois and M. P. Wellman, editors, *UAI'92, 8th Conference on Uncertainty in Artificial Intelligence*, pages 323–330, Stanford, USA, 1992.

M. Wachter and R. Haenni.
Propositional DAGs: a new graph-based language for representing Boolean functions.
In P. Doherty, J. Mylopoulos, and C. Welty, editors, *KR'06, 10th International Conference on Principles of Knowledge Representation and Reasoning*, pages 277–285, Lake District, U.K., 2006a. AAAI Press.

M. Wachter and R. Haenni.
Probabilistic equivalence checking with propositional DAGs.
Technical Report iam-06-001, University of Bern, Switzerland, 2006b.

M. Wachter and R. Haenni.
Logical compilation of Bayesian networks.
Technical Report iam-06-006, University of Bern, Switzerland, 2006c.

M. Wachter and R. Haenni.
Multi-state directed acyclic graphs.
In Z. Kobti and D. Wu, editors, *CanAI'07, 20th Canadian Conference on Artificial Intelligence*, LNAI 4509, pages 464–475, Montréal, Canada, 2007a.

M. Wachter and R. Haenni.
Logical compilation of Bayesian networks with discrete variables.

Bibliography

In K. Mellouli, editor, *ECSQARU'07, 9th European Conference on Symbolic and Quantitative Approaches to Reasoning under Uncertainty*, LNAI 4724, pages 536–547, Hammamet, Tunisia, 2007b.

M. Wachter, R. Haenni, and J. Jonczy.
Reliability and diagnostics of modular systems: a new probabilistic approach.
In C. A. González, T. Escobet, and B. Pulido, editors, *DX'06, 17th International Workshop on Principles of Diagnosis*, pages 273–280, Peñaranda de Duero, Spain, 2006.

M. Wachter, R. Haenni, and M. Pouly.
Optimizing inference in Bayesian networks and semiring valuation algebras.
In A. Gelbukh and A. F. Kuri Morales, editors, *MICAI'07, 6th Mexican International Conference on Artificial Intelligence*, LNAI 4827, pages 236–247, Aguascalientes, Mexico, 2007.

I. Wegener.
Branching Programs and Binary Decision Diagrams – Theory and Applications.
Number 56 in Monographs on Discrete Mathematics and Applications. SIAM, 2000.

S. K. Wong and C. Butz.
Contextual weak independence in Bayesian networks.
In K. B. Laskey and H. Prade, editors, *UAI'99, 15th Conference on Uncertainty in Artificial Intelligence*, pages 670–679, Stockholm, Sweden, 1999.

N. L. Zhang and D. Poole.
Exploiting causal independence in Bayesian network inference.
Journal of Artificial Intelligence Research, 5:301–328, 1996.

Die VDM Verlagsservicegesellschaft sucht für wissenschaftliche Verlage abgeschlossene und herausragende

Dissertationen, Habilitationen, Diplomarbeiten, Master Theses, Magisterarbeiten usw.

für die kostenlose Publikation als Fachbuch.

Sie verfügen über eine Arbeit, die hohen inhaltlichen und formalen Ansprüchen genügt, und haben Interesse an einer honorarvergüteten Publikation?

Dann senden Sie bitte erste Informationen über sich und Ihre Arbeit per Email an *info@vdm-vsg.de*.

Sie erhalten kurzfristig unser Feedback!

VDM Verlagsservicegesellschaft mbH
Dudweiler Landstr. 99   Telefon   +49 681 3720 174
D - 66123 Saarbrücken   Fax   +49 681 3720 1749
www.vdm-vsg.de

Die VDM Verlagsservicegesellschaft mbH vertritt

Printed by Books on Demand GmbH, Norderstedt / Germany